6/23/08

To Brad

With all good wishes

Advance praise for

Party of Defeat

"*Party of Defeat* is a well-documented and disturbing account of the unprecedented attacks by leaders of the Democratic Party on a war they supported and then turned their backs on. In a democracy, criticism of war policy is legitimate and necessary. But deliberate undermining of a war policy, as the authors argue, is another matter entirely. Every American concerned about the future of their country in the war on terror should consider the arguments in this book."

18 MEMBERS OF CONGRESS

(Senators Jim Bunning, Tom Coburn, James Inhofe, Jon Kyl, Jeff Sessions, and former Senator Rick Santorum; Representatives Ginny Brown-waite, Howard Coble, David Dreier, Peter Hoekstra, Peter King, Howard "Buck" McKeon, Mike Pence, Ed Royce, Jim Saxton, John Shadegg, Lamar Smith, Mark Souder, Tom Tancredo; committees represented: Intelligence, Foreign Affairs, International Relations, Homeland Security, Judiciary)

"Candid. Brilliant. Forceful. Brave.
Do not miss under any circumstances."

R. JAMES WOOLSEY, FORMER DIRECTOR, CIA

"*Party of Defeat* is an eye-opening account of one of the greatest political betrayals in American history: the unprecedented attack by leaders of an opposition party on a war they authorized and on America's commander-in-chief while America's troops were still in harm's way."

SEAN HANNITY, FOX NEWS CHANNEL ANCHOR

"David Horowitz and Ben Johnson have written a timely and important analysis of the American political debate over the war on terror."

AMBASSADOR JOHN BOLTON

"This book is a must read for every American who cares about the security of the United States."

REP. GINNY BROWN-WAITE

"Brilliant, factual and historic, David Horowitz and Ben Johnson have documented how and why the Democratic leadership split the nation in the global war on terror. It will be judged as the seminal book on an unprecedented attack against America's president and military in combat. Every American must read this book."

LIEUTENANT GENERAL THOMAS MCINERNEY, USAF (RET.)

"Having been one of David Horowitz's more severe critics as a young officer in the foxholes of Vietnam, I can say with some authority that he is now bringing a message of national importance to the American people."

MAJOR GENERAL JAMES E. LIVINGSTON, USMC (RET.)
RECIPIENT OF THE MEDAL OF HONOR

"David Horowitz and Ben Johnson explain in detail the unprecedented attacks on a sitting President and expose the lack of understanding at the highest levels about the nature of our enemy. This book must be read by all Americans."

MAJOR GENERAL PAUL VALLELY, USA (RET.)

"In concise and riveting fashion, David Horowitz and Ben Johnson have laid out a bill of particulars against an anti-war Left whose efforts to undermine the terror war are little short of treasonous. It offers a stark reminder of the folly of fighting a war on two fronts: one on the streets and battle fields of Iraq, the other here at home against ourselves."

JOEL SURNOW, CREATOR OF *24*

PARTY OF DEFEAT

PARTY OF DEFEAT

How Democrats and Radicals
Undermined America's War on Terror
Before and After 9-11

DAVID HOROWITZ
& BEN JOHNSON

SPENCE PUBLISHING COMPANY • DALLAS
2008

Published in the United States by
Spence Publishing Company
111 Cole Street
Dallas, Texas 75207

Library of Congress Control Number: 2007943528
ISBN 978-1-890626-74-7

Printed in the United States of America

Contents

Acknowledgment   viii

Timeline   ix

Introduction: A House Divided   3

PART I
THE WAR AGAINST AMERICA AND THE WEST

1   *The Path to 9-11*   21

2   *The Response to 9-11*   51

PART II
THE WAR IN IRAQ

3   *Why America Went to War*   63

4   *The War Against the War*   94

Conclusion   153

Notes   165

Index   189

Acknowledgement

The authors wish to thank Elizabeth Ruiz for tracking down facts and sources.

Timeline

September 1978—The Islamic Revolution begins in the city of Iranian city of Qom.

December 1978—President Jimmy Carter states America will not get "directly involved" to support the Shah of Iran, an American ally.

January 16, 1979—The Shah leaves, never to return. The new revolutionary leader Ayatollah Khomeni denounces America as the "Great Satan."

November 4, 1979—Iranian "students" take sixty-six hostages at the U.S. embassy in Tehran, holding most of them for 444 days.

—

November 1980—Ronald Reagan elected president.

January 20, 1981—Reagan inaugurated; hostages released.

October 23, 1983—Iran's newly formed terrorist organization Hezbollah kills 230 U.S. Marines in Beirut, Lebanon.

April 5, 1986—Libyan terrorists bomb a Berlin disco, killing one U.S. soldier and injuring fifty. Reagan bombs dictator Mohammar Qaddafi's home in retaliation.

—

November 1988—George H. W. Bush elected president.

August 1, 1990—Iraq invades Kuwait. President Bush responds, "This will not stand."

February 24, 1991—Bush organizes a UN coalition and launches Operation Desert Storm to reverse the aggression. Fighting lasts one hundred hours.

April 3-9, 1991—Truce agreements sealed in UN Resolutions 687 and 689, leaving Saddam Hussein in power.

—

November 1992—Bill Clinton elected president

February 26, 1993—Islamic terrorists bomb the World Trade Center.

October 3, 1993 —Islamic terrorists shoot down a U.S. helicopter over Mogadishu, Somalia, killing eighteen U.S. soldiers.

June 25, 1996—Iranian-backed terrorists bomb the Khobar Towers complex in Saudi Arabia, killing 19 U.S. servicemen and injuring 372 other people.

August 7, 1998—Al-Qaeda bombs U.S. embassies in Kenya and Tanzania, killing 224 and injuring thousands.

October 31, 1998—Clinton signs "Iraq Liberation Act" calling for regime change by force.

December 1998—Clinton fires four hundred cruise missiles into Iraq during "Operation Desert Fox."

October 12, 2000—Al-Qaeda terrorists bomb the U.S.S. Cole in the port of Aden, Yemen, killing seventeen U.S. sailors.

—

November 2000—George W. Bush elected president

September 11, 2001—Al-Qaeda attacks the Twin Towers and the Pentagon killing nearly three thousand Americans.

October 7, 2001—U.S. forces invade Afghanistan to topple the Taliban regime.

January 29, 2002 —President Bush calls Iran, Iraq, and North Korea an "Axis of Evil."

September 12, 2002 —Bush addresses UN and tells delegates the institution will become irrelevant if it allows Iraq to defy its resolutions.

September 2002—U.S. troops begin to mass on Iraq's border.

September 5 and 23—Former President Jimmy Carter and former Vice President Al Gore break precedent and attack the president's foreign policy on Iraq.

October 2002—A majority of Senate Democrats and bipartisan majorities in both houses vote to authorize the use of force against Iraq.

November 8, 2002 —UN Security Council unanimously approves Resolution 1441, an ultimatum ordering Iraq to comply with the Gulf War truce or face "serious consequences."

November 27, 2002—UN weapons inspectors return to Iraq for the first time since December 1998.

December 7, 2002—Resolution 1441 deadline expires. US and Britain declare Iraq in "material breach," and prepare for war.

January 18, 2003—Massive "anti-war" demonstrations prompt British Prime Minister Tony Blair to press for a second Security Council resolution

January 28, 2003—In his State of the Union address, Bush warns the U.S. will not allow Saddam to become an imminent threat.

February 5, 2003—Secretary of State Colin Powell presents evidence to the UN that Saddam is developing Weapons of Mass Destruction.

March 17, 2003—President Bush gives Saddam 48 hours to leave the country or face war.

March 19, 2003—War commences in Iraq.

April 9, 2003—U.S. forces liberate Baghdad.

July 2003—The Democratic National Committee launches a media campaign claiming that Bush lied about the reasons for going to war.

July 2003—Anti-war leaders Medea Benjamin and Leslie Cagan open an office in Iraq whose aim is to undermine the American "occupation."

September 18, 2003— Senator Ted Kennedy declares the war in Iraq "a fraud."

October 2, 2003—David Kay releases his report on WMD programs in Iraq.

February 8, 2004—Al Gore screams from a MoveOn.org platform that Bush "betrayed us! He betrayed America!"

April 28, 2004—60 Minutes II airs photographs of harassed detainees at Iraq's Abu Ghraib prison. The New York Times features the story on its front page for thirty-two days.

May 7, 2004—Abu Musab al-Zarqawi beheads American citizen Nicholas Berg in retaliation for Abu Ghraib.

July 9, 2004—A bipartisan Senate Intelligence Committee dismisses the claim that the president lied about Saddam's attempt to seek uranium in Niger.

September 6, 2004—Democratic presidential nominee John Kerry calls Iraq, "the wrong war in the wrong place at the wrong time."

—

November 2004—George Bush re-elected president

December 2004—Anti-war leader Medea Benjamin and Code Pink deliver $600,000 in cash and medical supplies to "the other side" in Fallujah.

January 30, 2005—A majority (58 percent) of Iraqis vote in the nation's first democratic election in half a century.

August 6, 2005—Gold Star mother Cindy Sheehan begins anti-war protest outside President Bush's ranch in Crawford, Texas.

October 25, 2005—Iraqi voters approve the drafted Iraqi constitution.

November 2, 2005—The Washington Post leaks classified information about CIA's "rendition" program.

November 17, 2005—Rep. Jack Murtha calls for withdrawal of all U.S. troops from Iraq within six months.

November 30, 2005—*Los Angeles Times* "exposes" U.S. government program to place pro-American propaganda stories in Iraqi media.

December 15, 2005—Iraqis hold third democratic election as more than 70 percent of Iraqis turn out to vote for Iraqi parliament.

December 16, 2005—The New York Times runs a front page story exposing a classified national security program to target terrorists speaking with al-Qaeda members abroad.

February 22, 2006—Terrorists bomb the Golden Dome Mosque in Samarra, Iraq, touching off intense Sunni-Shi'ite sectarian violence.

June 7, 2006—U.S. forces kill Abu Musab al-Zarqawi, the leader of Al-Qaeda in Iraq.

June 23, 2006—Three major U.S. newspapers publish classified information and reveal the existence of the government's top-secret Terrorist Finance Tracking Program.

November 2006—Democrats win majorities in both congressional houses.

December 30, 2006—Saddam Hussein hanged for crimes against the Iraqi people.

December 9, 2006—New House Speaker-elect Nancy Pelosi declares, "my highest priority, immediately, is to stop the war in Iraq."

January 10, 2007—President Bush announces a "Surge" in Iraq.

February 13, 2007—House Speaker Nancy Pelosi and Jack Murtha propose a "slow-bleed" strategy to reduce the number of troops available to fight in Iraq.

April 19, 2007—Senate Majority Leader Harry Reid declares, "The war is lost, and the Surge is not accomplishing anything."

June 13, 2007—Nancy Pelosi and Harry Reid co-sign a letter to the president stating, "the escalation has failed to produce the intended results."

June 15, 2007—The Surge reaches full numerical strength, and effectively begins operations.

August 2007—Major terrorist attacks in Iraq fall by 50 percent.

September 10, 2007 —MoveOn.org ad brands U.S. military commander in Iraq "General Betray Us."

November 7, 2007—General Petraeus announces the U.S. military has expelled al-Qaeda from Baghdad.

"The whole world is watching this war and the two adversaries: the Islamic nation, on the one hand, and the United States and its allies on the other. It is either victory and Glory or misery and humiliation."

OSAMA BIN LADEN
December 28, 2004

"In the long run, we have less to fear from foes without than from foes within; for the former will be formidable only as the latter break our strength."

THEODORE ROOSEVELT
"The Foes of Our Own Household," 1917

"To fight and conquer in all your battles is not supreme excellence; supreme excellence consists in breaking the enemy's resistance without fighting."

SUN TZU
The Art of War

PARTY OF DEFEAT

A House Divided

THE OBJECT OF WAR is to break an enemy's will and destroy his capacity to fight. Therefore, a nation divided in wartime is a nation that invites its own defeat. Yet that is precisely how Americans are facing the global war that radical Islamists have declared on them.

The enemies who confront us are religious barbarians, armed with the technologies of modern warfare but guided by morals that are medieval and grotesque. Their stated goal is the obliteration of America and the conquest of the West. They have assembled a coalition that includes sovereign states such as Iran and Syria, Muslim armies such as al-Qaeda, Hezbollah, and Hamas, and terrorist cells that are globally dispersed and beyond counting.

This jihad has access to biological, chemical, and possibly nuclear weapons. It actively threatens the regimes in Lebanon, Afghanistan, Pakistan, Somalia, Turkey, and Egypt. Among its allies are non-Muslim states such as the Communist regimes in North Korea, Venezuela, and China. Its enablers include Saudi Arabia, Russia, and the vast political networks of the international Left.[1] Its pool of sympathizers and supporters can be counted in the hundreds of millions, and its political fronts are embedded in almost every nation and every continent, including Europe and the United States.

The warriors of the jihad are promised salvation for slaughtering innocents; their highest honor is to sacrifice themselves for Allah by murdering infidels; their goal is to restore an Islamic empire that once stretched into the heart of Europe, until it was defeated in the battle of Vienna on September 11, 1683. Three hundred years later, Osama bin Laden turned this date of humiliation into a day of vengeance—and revival. Striking America's homeland on September 11, 2001, jihadists murdered thousands of unsuspecting civilians, and came within a terrorist attack or two of destabilizing the American economy and unleashing chaos.

As the victim of these unprovoked and savage attacks, and as the defender of democratic values in three world wars, America would seem a worthy cause. Instead, America is on the defensive, harshly criticized by its traditional allies and under political attack by significant elements of its own population.

In this epic conflict Americans appear more divided among themselves than they have been at any time in the century–and–a half since the Civil War. Never in those years was an American commander-in-chief the target of such extreme attacks by his own countrymen with his troops in harm's way. Never in its history has America faced an external enemy with its own leaders so at odds with each other.

Even as American soldiers have fought a fanatical enemy on the battlefields of Iraq, their president has been condemned as a deceiver who led them to war through "lies;"[2] as a destroyer of American liberties;[3] as a desecrator of the Constitution;[4] as a usurper who stole his high office;[5] as the architect of an "unnecessary war;"[6] as a "fraud;"[7] as a leader who "betrayed us;"[8] and as a president who cynically sent the flower of American youth to die in foreign lands in order to enrich himself and his friends.[9]

These reckless, corrosive charges are made not by fringe elements of the political spectrum, but by national leaders of the Democratic Party, including a former president, a former vice president and presidential candidate, and three members of the United States Senate (among them a one-time presidential candidate). These attacks occurred not after years of fighting in Iraq, when some might regard the result as a "quagmire," but during the first months of the conflict, when the fighting had barely begun. They were made not over a war that was forced on Americans, or surreptitiously launched without their consent, but a war authorized by both political parties. They were directed not merely at its conduct, but at the rationale of the war itself—in other words, at the very justice of the American cause.

Although they voted for the bill to authorize the war, leaders of the Democratic Party, such as Senator Hillary Clinton, turned around after it was in progress and claimed that it was "George Bush's war," not theirs.[10] They argued that Bush alone had decided to remove Saddam, when in fact it was a Democratic president, Bill Clinton, who made regime change the policy of the United States.[11] They argued that the war was "unnecessary" because Iraq was "no threat."[12] But who would have regarded Afghanistan as a threat before 9-11? They maintained that because the war in Iraq was a war of "choice," it was therefore immoral.[13] But every war fought by America in the twentieth century, with the exception of World War II, was also a war of choice.

Above all, they claimed the president had manipulated intelligence about Iraqi weapons of mass destruction, and thus the premise of the war. But copies of the National Intelligence Estimate on which the president's decision was based were provided to every Democratic senator who voted for or against it. The findings were confirmed by government intelligence agencies around the world, including those of France, Britain, Russia, and Jordan.[14] In other words, President Bush could not have manipulated the intelligence on which the vote was based and the war was actually authorized.

In attempting to make the war in Iraq a sinister plot of the Bush administration, Democrats claimed that it was a distraction from the war with the Islamic terrorists who had attacked America. "The issue is the war they got us into," Nancy Pelosi told 60 Minutes just before she became Speaker of the House and the second elected official in line for the presidency. "If the president wants to say the war in Iraq is part of the war on terror, he's not right."

> 60 Minutes: Do you not think that the war in Iraq now, today, is the war on terror?
>
> Pelosi: No. The war on terror is the war in Afghanistan.
>
> 60 Minutes: But you don't think that the terrorists have moved into Iraq now?
>
> Pelosi: They have. The jihadists in Iraq. But that doesn't mean we stay there. They'll stay there as long as we're there.
>
> 60 Minutes: You mean if we leave Iraq, the terrorists will leave?
>
> Pelosi: Yes.[15]

What nation can prevail in a war if half its population believes that the war is unnecessary and unjust, that its commander-in-chief is a liar, and that its own government is the aggressor? What president can mobilize his nation if his word is not trusted? And what soldier can prevail on the field of battle if half his countrymen are telling him that he shouldn't be there in the first place?

It was July 2003, only four months after American forces entered Iraq, when the Democratic Party launched its first all-out attack on the president's credibility and the morality of the war. The opening salvos were reported in a *New York Times* article: "Democratic presidential candidates offered a near-unified assault today on President Bush's credibility in his handling of the Iraq War signaling a shift in the political winds by aggressively invoking arguments most had shunned since the fall of Baghdad."[16]

While American forces battled al-Qaeda and Ba'athist insurgents in the Iraqi capital, the Democratic National Committee released a television ad that focused not on winning those battles, but on the very legitimacy of the war. The theme of the ad was "Read His Lips: President Bush Deceives the American People." The alleged deception was sixteen words that had been included in the State of the Union address he delivered on the eve of the conflict.[17]

These words summarized a British intelligence report claiming that Iraq had attempted to acquire fissionable uranium in the African state of Niger, thus indicating Saddam's (well-known) intentions to develop nuclear weapons. The report was subsequently confirmed by a bipartisan Senate committee and a British investigative commission, but not until many months had passed and the Democratic attacks had taken their toll.[18] On the surface, the attacks were directed at the president's credibility for repeating the British claim. But their clear implication was to question the decision to go to war—in other words, to cast doubt on the credibility of the American cause. If Saddam had not sought fissionable uranium in Niger, it was suggested, then the White House had lied in describing Saddam as a threat.

In the midst of a war, and in the face of a determined terrorist resistance in Iraq, Democrats had launched an attack on America's presence on the field of battle. This separated their assault from the normal criticism of war policies. Senator John Edwards, then a candidate for the Democrats' 2004 presidential nomination, had voted to authorize the war and was still claiming to support it. In an interview with the *New York Times*, he identified the significance of the Democrats' attack: "The most important attribute that any president has is his credibility—his credibility with the American people, with its allies and with the world." But even as Edwards said this, he joined the Democrats' attack, publicly insinuating that the president was a liar who had deceived the American people on the gravest issue imaginable. "When the president's own statements are called into question," Edwards explained to the reporter, "it's a very serious matter."[19]

When the nation is at war, it is graver still. To destroy the credibility of the commander-in-chief while his troops are in battle is to cripple his ability to support them and to win the war they are fighting. For this reason, throughout the history of armed conflict, a united home front has been an indispensable element of victory. For the same reason, a principal aim of psychological-warfare operations has been to target the credibility of the enemy's leaders and the morality of the enemy cause.

General Ion Mihai Pacepa was the highest-ranking intelligence official ever to defect from the Soviet bloc during the Cold War. In a commentary about the attacks on President Bush during the war in Iraq, Pacepa recalled: "Sowing the seeds of anti-Americanism by discrediting the American president was one of the main tasks of the Soviet-bloc intelligence community during the years I worked at its top levels."[20] No president can marshal his nation's resources if his people distrust him or don't believe in their own cause. To attack a president's credibility in the middle of a war, over a matter as ambiguous as a sixteen-word summary of an allied intelligence report, is an attempt to undermine the war itself.

During the Vietnam War, General Pacepa wrote, Soviet intelligence "spread vitriolic stories around the world, pretending that America's presidents sent Genghis Khan–style barbarian soldiers to Vietnam who raped at random, taped electrical wires to human genitals, cut off limbs, blew up bodies and razed entire villages. Those weren't facts. They were our tales, but . . . as Yuri Andropov, who conceived this *dezinformatsiya* war against the U.S., used to tell me, people are more willing to believe smut than holiness."[21]

Nor did this Soviet campaign to discredit the United States stop with Vietnam. As Pacepa explains: "The final goal of our anti-American offensive was to discourage the United States from protecting the world against communist terrorism and expansion. Sadly, we succeeded. After U.S. forces precipitously pulled out of Vietnam, the victorious communists massacred some two million people in Vietnam, Laos and Cambodia. Another million tried to escape, but many died in the attempt. This tragedy also created a credibility gap between America and the rest of the world, damaged the cohesion of American foreign policy, and poisoned domestic debate in the United States."[22]

It is one of the ironies of the campaign against the war in Iraq that its opponents cite the political conflict over Vietnam as a precedent for their extraordinary attacks on a war in progress. In doing so, they misconstrue the past and misunderstand its lessons. During Vietnam, the nation's political leaders, both Democrats and Republicans, were united in their support of the war effort for more than ten years. Their bipartisan unity came to an end only when both parties conceded that a victory was no longer politically possible. It was only in the presidential campaign of 1972, eleven years after the first American advisers were sent to Vietnam that Senator George McGovern ran against the war itself. By that time both parties were agreed on a policy of military withdrawal, and by that time truce negotiations with the Communists, initiated by a Republican administration, had already begun.

The conflict over war policy during the 1972 campaign was over the proper way to accomplish the withdrawal favored by both parties. It was over *how* to leave, not *whether* to leave. The McGovern Democrats favored a policy of immediate and unconditional retreat. Their campaign slogan was "Come Home, America." The Nixon Republicans wanted to negotiate a truce whose terms would preserve the non-Communist regime in South Vietnam, and deny victory to the Communist aggressors. Their slogan was "Peace with Honor."

The McGovernites did not believe American forces should have been in Vietnam in the first place. McGovern's candidacy was a

strategic campaign to block America's Cold War policy of containing Communist expansion. Unlike the Democrats of the Kennedy
and Johnson administrations, the McGovern Democrats believed
America was the problematic imperial power, not the Soviet Union.
This represented a sea change in the Democratic Party, whose leaders
had actually launched the Cold War policy of containing Soviet Communism beginning with the Truman administration in 1947. It was
the Democrats, led by John F. Kennedy, who had initiated America's
military presence in Vietnam. Until the McGovern candidacy, the
Democratic leadership, including its presidential candidate in 1968,
Hubert Humphrey, had supported the Vietnam War. It was the first
time since the Civil War that an opposition party had conducted a
national campaign to challenge the *justice* of America's war aims.

The campaigns against the wars in Iraq and Vietnam may seek
the same end—the defeat of American power—but the differences
between them are revealing. In regard to Iraq, the Democrats' attacks on the justice of the American cause came not after ten years
of stalemate, but within three months of the swiftest, most successful campaign in military history. The attacks were conducted not by
movement activists but by leaders of the Democratic Party, and they
came in the first months of a war that both parties had until then
supported, and that the previous Democratic administration had
endorsed, and that both parties had voted to authorize. The attacks
on this war have no precedent in the American past.

The effort to remove the Iraqi regime by force, which Democrats
now maintain was provocative and unnecessary, originated with a
Democratic president, Bill Clinton. Four years before Bush ordered
American troops into Iraq, Clinton asked Congress to pass an "Iraq
Liberation Act," which specifically called for regime change by force.
To emphasize the seriousness with which he regarded the threat that
Saddam posed, Clinton ordered the American military to fire more
than four hundred cruise missiles into Iraq.[23] The Iraq Liberation

Act authorized American aid for any insurgent group that was ready to overthrow the regime. It was ratified by both political parties—Democrats and Republicans—with barely a dissenting vote.

Four years later, when Bush asked Congress to authorize the use of force to accomplish the same goal, a Democratic majority in the Senate supported his request. When American forces entered Iraq on March 19, 2003, a large majority of the Democratic leadership, including the former president, his secretaries of state and defense, and his entire national security team, supported the invasion. When the Iraqi regime was overthrown three weeks later, the Democratic leadership joined in the celebration, although some dissenters, such as Representative Nancy Pelosi, were already complaining that it cost too much.[24]

Dissent is a cherished and justly protected right in a democracy. But it is also a privilege. The right to dissent exists only on condition that the government that guarantees it is able to defend itself against enemies who would destroy it. No bulwark has been more durable or more important to the stability and survival of America's democratic order than the solidarity of its leaders in wartime. A president under relentless attack from the domestic opposition has less political space for flexible response. The more severe the attacks, the more limited his room for political maneuver. If the Bush administration has been slow to admit error in the present war, or to take corrective measures on the field of battle, the unrestrained attacks on its integrity and motives have undoubtedly been a significant factor.

Should more troops have been deployed to win the war, as General Eric Shinseki advised at the outset? What Democratic leader at the time proposed legislation to provide the funding which would have made such a remedy possible? What Republican legislator, faced with attacks that brand his president a liar who tricked the nation into a needless war, would join a chorus of Democrats in attacking their president's policy on that war?

Another aspect of reckless criticism that opponents of the war are loathe to discuss is the impact of such attacks on enemy morale. If America's enemies have been encouraged by these divisions at home, this consequence cannot be simply dismissed as though it did not exist. In time of war, criticism of war policy—particularly reckless and rejectionist attacks on the nation's war aims and efforts—cannot be granted "no fault" status, as though no repercussions ensued. In a democracy, policy must always be subject to scrutiny, even in wartime, but so must criticism of that policy.

This book is about unprecedented attacks on an American president and a war in progress. It is about the impact of a divided national leadership on the prosecution of the war. It is an attempt to understand the defection of leaders from a war they supported and from a national purpose they presumably share. It is also an effort to understand the influence on the Democratic Party of a radical Left that has defected from this purpose and no longer regards itself as part of the nation. This Left sees itself instead as part of an abstract "humanity," transcending national borders and patriotic allegiances, whose interests coincide with a worldwide radical cause.

Democrats have an explanation for their defection from a war they originally supported: the president is to blame. But this is a claim that will not stand up to even the most cursory inspection. Between the invasion of Iraq in March 2003, which the Democrats supported, and their attacks on the legitimacy of the war, which began in June, three months later, no event transpired on the battlefield and no change took place in the administration's war policy that would explain their defection. What changed was the internal politics of the Democratic Party, and this was a direct result of the antiwar campaign organized by the Left.

By coincidence, the buildup to the war took place during the early stages of a presidential-primary campaign, in the winter and spring of 2003. By June, the candidacy of an obscure Vermont governor named Howard Dean, a veteran of the anti-Vietnam Left, had gathered such momentum that he appeared to have become the front-runner for the Democratic nomination.[25] It was this political fact that precipitated an about-face on the war by more prominent Democrats, such as John Kerry and John Edwards, who eventually captured the party's nominations. It was the antiwar radicals in the Dean campaign, not any events on the ground in Iraq, that produced the change in the position of leading Democrats and eventually of the Democratic Party as a whole. It was the political force of the antiwar movement, rather than any fact about the war, that explains the change.

Aware that their attacks on the home front would appear indefensible to many Americans, critics of the war have attempted to argue that it was Bush who had created the political schism. Four years into the war, *New York Times* columnist Robert Wright wrote a typical broadside titled, "An Easter Sermon," which drew an invidious comparison between Bush and Jesus Christ, and blamed the president for dividing the nation. The column focused on a statement Bush made in an address to Congress nine days after 9-11. In it he said: "Either you are with us, or you are with the terrorists."

Wright's column appeared in April 2007, even as a newly invested Democratic Congress was proposing legislation to force an American retreat in Iraq. In the column, Wright portrayed Bush as a polarizing figure who questioned his critics' loyalties. Wright cited a contrasting Gospel statement by Jesus, "Whoever is not against us is for us," as a model for what Bush should have said. Commented Wright: "Weeks after 9-11, George Bush says roughly the opposite. His famous 'You're either with us or against us' means that those who don't follow his lead will be considered enemies. The rest is history."[26]

But this is a false reading of Bush's sentence as well as of the New Testament, since Jesus also said, "He that is not with me is against me."[27] It is also a false account of the history that followed, since it was Bush's critics who made the White House and its supporters their enemies, not the other way around. Typical was an early attack by billionaire George Soros, the most influential non-elected figure in Democratic politics. Soros's assault came in the fall of 2003, five months after the Democratic leaders had launched their scorched-earth campaign over the Niger incident, and just as they were escalating their offensive.

According to Soros, Bush's statement was proof not only that he was a divisive force in domestic politics, but that he was pursuing a "supremacist ideology" reminiscent of the Nazis: "When I hear Bush say, 'You're either with us or against us,' it reminds me of the Germans," Soros said. "It conjures up memories of Nazi slogans on the walls, like *Der Feind Hört mit* ('The enemy is listening')."[28]

Such rhetoric illustrated the degree to which the political debate had already become poisonous on the Democratic side only eight months into the war. No administration official had used such language to describe Democratic leaders opposed to the conflict.[29] The statement that a wartime enemy would be listening to its adversary was in any case hardly a Nazi idea. During World War II, almost identical slogans were popular in America, such as "Loose lips sink ships." During the Cold War the code of bipartisanship was sealed in the phrase "Politics stops at the water's edge," to acknowledge the importance of political unity in wartime.

Soros's statement was an example of the very politics it pretended to decry. If pointing to the fact that wartime divisions might entail some dangers made one a Nazi, as Soros suggested, what did *that* kind of comment do to the tenor of public debate? Yet no Democrat challenged Soros when he employed such a venomous allusion.

In fact, the meaning of Bush's statement was grossly distorted by both Wright and Soros. The president's remark was made in the context of an assessment of the threat America faced after 9-11. The purpose of his speech was to outline a new American response to the global war that Muslim fanatics had declared on America and the

West. This war had come to American shores eight years earlier, in 1993, with the first attack on the World Trade Center. It had been followed by attacks on American targets in Saudi Arabia, Africa, and Yemen. But there had been no appropriate American response.

Bush's agenda was to announce such a response. Henceforth, America would answer with a war of its own: "Our response involves far more than instant retaliation and isolated strikes. Americans should not expect one battle, but a lengthy campaign, unlike any other we have ever seen. It may include dramatic strikes, visible on TV, and covert operations, secret even in success. We will starve terrorists of funding, turn them one against another, drive them from place to place, until there is no refuge or no rest."[30]

The president called the new response a "War on Terror." It was a war, he said, that was rooted in ideology: "They are the heirs of all the murderous ideologies of the 20th century. By sacrificing human life to serve their radical visions, by abandoning every value except the will to power, they follow in the path of fascism, and Nazism, and totalitarianism." He described the war as not merely with al-Qaeda, the Islamic group that had struck the Twin Towers and the Pentagon on 9-11, but with every element of the jihad: "Our war on terror begins with al-Qaeda, but it does not end there. It will not end until every terrorist group of global reach has been found, stopped and defeated."

Having laid down these guidelines, Bush was ready to draw the line that caused Wright, Soros, and the Democratic leadership such consternation. Because the United States was now ready to recognize the global nature of the threat, it was also ready to recognize the complicity of Islamic governments such as Iran, Afghanistan, Libya, Syria, and the Sudan in supporting the Islamic jihad and making possible the terrorist attacks. It was putting these regimes on notice: Sovereignty would no longer protect nation-states that aided and abetted the Islamic crusade. Governments would now be held responsible for the global terrorists within their borders.

If governments did not cooperate in the War on Terror and here the Taliban in Afghanistan was foremost in Bush's mind they would be regarded as enemies, too: "And we will pursue nations that provide aid or safe haven to terrorism. Every nation, in every region, now has a decision to make. Either you are with us, or you are with the terrorists. From this day forward, any nation that continues to harbor or support terrorism will be regarded by the United States as a hostile regime."

Either you are with us, or you are with the terrorists. This was a warning to *governments*—to the Taliban and other Islamic regimes that might provide havens and support for al-Qaeda. This is the statement that Wright and Soros, and the president's Democratic opponents, first distorted and then misrepresented as an attack on domestic critics. Bush had said nothing of the sort. It was a projection of the way his critics felt about *him*.

This new war policy of holding governments that harbored terrorists accountable was precisely what had been missing when terrorists struck the World Trade Center in 1993. After that attack, the bomb maker, an Iraqi named Abdul Rahman Yasin, was able to escape to Baghdad. The Clinton administration did not pursue Yasin to Iraq, nor did it hold the regime of Saddam Hussein accountable for providing refuge to him. If Clinton had done so, perhaps his fellow Democrats would better understand the connection between the Iraqi regime and the Islamic jihad against their country.

Instead, the Clinton White House regarded the World Trade Center bombing as a criminal act carried out by individuals unconnected to a global jihad. The identical attitude was evident when an al-Qaeda warlord in Somalia, Mohammed Farah Aideed, ambushed U.S. Army Rangers in the city of Mogadishu, also in 1993. The failure to grasp the place of these attacks in a global jihad led directly to America's vulnerability on 9-11. It is what Bush has meant on those occasions when he has accused Democrats of "forgetting the lessons of 9-11," or failing to understand them. This is the real political fault line in the disputes over the War on Terror and its battleground in Iraq.

Democrats believe that the War on Terror is a blunder committed by the Bush administration, even an *invention* of the Bush administration, rather than an actual war that has been declared on America by Osama bin Laden and the global forces of Islamofascism. This was the point of the celebrated statement candidate John Edwards made in 2007, during the presidential primary campaign: "The war on terror is a slogan designed only for politics," Edwards claimed. "It is not a strategy to make America safe. It's a bumper sticker, not a plan."[31] And further: "We need a post-Bush, post-9-11, post-Iraq military that is mission-focused on protecting Americans from 21st century threats, not misused for discredited ideological purposes. By framing this as a war, we have walked right into the trap the terrorists have set—that we are engaged in some kind of clash of civilizations and a war on Islam."[32]

The same point had been made by Soros a year earlier. In a *Wall Street Journal* article, he explained that the War on Terror was "a misleading figure of speech [which] applied literally has unleashed a real war fought on several fronts—Iraq, Gaza, Lebanon, Afghanistan, Somalia—a war that has killed thousands of innocent civilians and enraged millions around the world . . . [W]e can escape it only if we Americans repudiate the war on terror as a false metaphor."[33]

In this view, George Bush and America are responsible for the war that radical Islam has launched against us. This is not a tactical difference between opponents of the war policy in Iraq and its supporters. It is strategic, and it explains why we have turned a corner in our history for which there is no precedent, and why the divisions over the war are deeper and more troubling than any of the specific issues that confront us.

PART I

THE WAR AGAINST AMERICA
AND THE WEST

The Path to 9-11

THE ISLAMIC WAR AGAINST THE WEST was begun more than two decades before the invasion of Iraq with an American retreat. In February 1979, Ayatollah Khomeini and his radical followers overthrew the government of the shah of Iran and seized power in a nation that until then had been a staunch American ally. It was the first successful Islamic revolution since the collapse of the Ottoman Empire. That had led to the end of the caliphate, which until then had been Islam's Vatican. The ayatollah's revolution was an inspiration to Osama bin Laden and other Islamic radicals who believed that a jihad—a holy war—had begun to restore the caliphate and to establish the rule of Islamic law, first in the Middle East and then throughout the world.

CARTER

The crucial events in this historic turning were focused on the United States and the humiliation of a global superpower. These were symbolized by the taking of hostages at the U.S. embassy on November 4, 1979, and the massing of a million Iranians in the streets of Teheran chanting, "Death to America." Their spiritual and temporal leader, Ayatollah Khomeini, defined the enemy in theological terms as the devil incarnate—the "Great Satan."

The seizing of an embassy was an internationally recognized act of war, but America's president, Jimmy Carter, chose not to regard it as such. For Carter, America was to blame for the attacks it suffered, because it had supported a "human-rights violator" in the person of the shah. Carter's failure to respond forcefully to the Iranian provocation proved to Islamic radicals everywhere that a group of dedicated fanatics could topple the most progressive government in the Muslim world and terrorize the most powerful nation on earth—the Great Satan itself—with impunity. This was the pivotal moment in the conflict that would come to define the post–Cold War world, and it was a moment of American impotence and defeat.

As a direct consequence of Carter's appeasement, the Islamic regime in Iran has become today "the most active state sponsor of terrorism" and a nascent nuclear power, whose military aggressions extend in a crescent from Afghanistan through Iraq and Lebanon to the Gaza Strip.[1] The current Iranian dictator, Mahmoud Ahmadinejad, made his discipleship of the ayatollah unmistakably clear when he told an "anti-Zionist" conference in early October 2005, "The accomplishment of a world without America and Israel is both possible and feasible."[2] Khomeini could not have said it better.

Ahmadinejad is a graduate of the student gangs that in 1979 captured the embassy personnel and took them hostage, and his Iran is actively engaged in killing American soldiers in Iraq and Afghanistan, and Israeli civilians in the Middle East. It has created its own terrorist army, Hezbollah, a state within the state of Lebanon, to conduct a genocidal war against Israel. It has forged alliances with Venezuela's Marxist dictator, Hugo Chávez, and with the Communist ruler of North Korea, Kim Jong Il, to broaden the "Axis of Evil." It is an inspiration and weapons supplier for terrorists from Algeria to the Philippines, and it is the center of terrorism worldwide.

None of these developments would have been possible if a Democratic president had not convinced himself that that his own country was the problem and that the appeasement of America's enemies was the path to solving global conflicts. Nor would Carter have held these views without the influence exerted on the Democratic Party by the "antiwar" movement, which had forced America's retreat in Vietnam. The change in the party's outlook had taken place during the 1972 presidential campaign, in which the Democratic candidate, George McGovern, was the standard-bearer of the anti–Vietnam War Left. McGovern had broken with the postwar foreign-policy consensus, which held that Communist aggression must be contained and that American power was a bulwark of freedom. McGovern's campaign theme was "Come Home, America," and his policy for dealing with the Communist aggression in Vietnam was one of unilateral withdrawal and retreat.

The "antiwar" Left promoted the idea of an American global retreat, not out of an aversion to war as such, but because they were themselves at war with American purposes. America, McGovern said, was responsible for "Asian children running ablaze from bombed-out schools."[3] Worse, these sadistic tactics were deployed in the service of a malignant goal. Until the McGovern campaign, American leaders, both Democrats and Republicans, were agreed on the fact that American troops were in Vietnam to prevent the Communist conquest and slaughter that eventually followed America's withdrawal. But in the eyes of the McGovernites, America was not the defender of South Vietnam's freedom; it was Vietnam's destroyer. "Let us resolve," McGovern charged his party, "that never again will we send the precious young blood of this country to die trying to prop up a corrupt military dictatorship abroad."[4] Like others who pretended to oppose the Vietnam War because the regime America supported was headed by a corrupt dictator, McGovern also opposed the war in Iraq, where American troops were sent to overthrow a corrupt dictator.

While John F. Kennedy had summoned a previous generation of Democrats to "ask not what your country can do for you— [but] what you can do for your country," the McGovern Democrats asked, "Why is our country hated?"—as though there might be a reasonable answer. Unlike President Bush, who believes that America is hated for its freedoms, the Left believes America is hated because it fits the profile the enemy has framed for it, an imperial oppressor of the weak and poor. McGovern's call for America to come home was not a plan to conserve America's strength and restore America's integrity. It was a plan to quarantine the American virus and save others from the infection.

Americans repudiated McGovern at the polls in the 1972 election, handing him one of the most humiliating electoral defeats in American history. Only Massachusetts and the District of Columbia cast its votes in his column. But the forces of the Left did not withdraw in disgrace from the battle over America's future; they merely regrouped to fight another day. Determined to force America's retreat in Indochina, the antiwar Democrats seized on a break-in at the Watergate complex to accomplish their ends. Enjoying a majority in Congress, they were able to exploit the fiasco to unseat a wartime president and cripple America's effort to prevent the Communists from conquering Cambodia and South Vietnam.[5]

Foreign-affairs expert Anthony Lake, who was soon to be Jimmy Carter's State Department policy planner, displayed the new political wisdom in a *Washington Post* column he wrote in March 1975. It was the eve of the Communist conquest of Cambodia, and in the column Lake argued for cutting off aid to the anti-Communist regime: "At Stake in Cambodia: Extending Aid Will Only Prolong the Killing."[6] In fact, the reverse was true; when American aid was cut off by the Democratic Congress, the regime fell and two million Cambodians were slaughtered by the Communists. But Lake's advice proved to be a succinct summary of the Democrats' philosophy of appeasement and the McGovern strategy of bringing America home.

In reality, American troops had been brought home two years earlier, as result of the 1973 truce in Vietnam. But this did not satisfy the Left, which wanted to see the regimes in South Vietnam and Cambodia toppled and the Communist "liberators" in power. To achieve this goal, radicals lobbied the Democratic Congress to cut off American aid. Watergate enabled them to do this.

Far from being chastened by these events, the Left was encouraged. The fevers of defeatism unleashed by the McGovern campaign flourished, and the Democrats held their 1976 convention in New York City, a center of the liberal culture. Ambassador Jeane Kirkpatrick, a Democrat who had left her party, would later call the new party leadership the " 'blame America first' crowd." Minimizing the threat of Communism, they viewed Marxist aggressions as understandable reactions to "root causes," such as American "militarism" and "imperialism," and the global market system. Instead of asking, "How does the totalitarian enemy threaten us and what can we do about it?" the Blame-America-Firsters were asking, "Why do they hate us?" and "How can we appease them and atone for our guilt?" These questions rapidly became the twin concerns of a new, "progressive" foreign-policy consensus, and the New York convention nominated Carter as its presidential candidate.

The new self-doubts Carter hoped to create replaced the confidence that had inspired American generations to victories in two world wars. They translated into policies that cut back America's military defenses, hamstrung America's intelligence agencies, and weakened the nation's resolve. All of these pathologies, which soon became familiar as "the Vietnam Syndrome," invited assaults from America's enemies, including the gathering forces of Islamic jihad.

To this Democratic Party radicalism, Carter brought an element of personal naïveté and moralizing condescension, which accelerated the process. Like others on the Left, he believed criminals could be reformed and America's enemies could be induced towards pacifist agendas. The Communist leaders were rational people who would respond to "positive inducements," if we only shed our "inordinate fear of Communism" long enough to offer them concessions.[7]

Carter's self-deprecating overtures to the Soviet Union began on his first day in office, when, without consulting his military advisers, he withdrew U.S. missiles from South Korea. Soon, he proposed removing all American troops from the Korean peninsula and slashing the defense budget by six billion dollars. The Communists responded to these gestures of military weakness with a renewed offensive, deploying their agents in Nicaragua, El Salvador, Ethiopia, and Angola. Then, even as the Islamic Revolution was seizing power in Iran, the Kremlin sent its Red Army divisions across international borders for the first time since 1945 to invade Afghanistan. A decade later, the ruins of this aggression would become a seedbed of the Islamic jihad.

Rattled by these events, Carter conceded that the Soviet aggression had caused a "dramatic change in my own opinion of what the Soviets' ultimate goals are."[8] It was a little late for such realizations, and Carter's effort at a change in course was only half-hearted. He postponed plans for further cuts in the military budget and made an unsuccessful gesture towards re-introducing the military draft, which was denounced as "evil" by the radicals to the left of him.

The world—and Afghanistan's peasants in particular—had paid a high price for Jimmy Carter's remedial education, and the American public repudiated him in the 1980 election. Eventually, the Soviet conquerors, whose scorched-earth campaign resulted in a million civilian deaths, were repelled by Muslim warriors armed by the Reagan administration. Although Carter was the executive ultimately responsible, the Left subsequently blamed Reagan when it became known that Osama bin Laden and some of his cohorts had served as volunteers with the Afghan mujahideen. Contrary to myth, however, the

U.S. did not fund bin Laden.[9] Moreover, the course Reagan pursued was the only one possible, since there was not the slightest prospect of sending American troops to Afghanistan while the Democrats controlled Congress and the Vietnam Syndrome prevailed.

If confusion, guilt, and self-doubt marked Carter's approach to America's enemies, moral superiority and self-righteousness characterized his dealings with allies, most pointedly the shah of Iran. To Carter, the shah's regime looked like the kind of dictatorship McGovern had promised that America would never again defend. In fact, although the shah was a dictator, he was also a reformer who gave Iranians far more freedom than the mullahs. He had repealed the Islamic law requiring women to wear the veil and for the first time gave them the right to acquire an education.

It was the shah's progressive acts that enraged the mullahs against him, but they did not impress Carter, who made the shah the prime target of his global crusade for "human rights." The immediate beneficiaries, of course, were the shah's anti-American and totalitarian opponents. Daniel Patrick Moynihan, a centrist Democrat, expressed his revulsion at the way Carter was "unable to distinguish between America's friends and enemies." Moynihan thought it was because Carter shared "the enemy's view of the world."[10]

As the Islamic Revolution gathered strength, Carter persuaded the shah to release its leaders from prison and encouraged him to step aside and make way for the mullahs. Before a Democratic "mini-convention," Carter publicly condemned the shah's human-rights record, speculating that the ruler might not survive the crisis and stipulating that the U.S. would not get "directly involved"—in short, tacitly inviting the clerical fascists to topple him.[11] Carter's rival for the 1980 Democratic nomination, Senator Edward Kennedy, went further, condemning the shah's government as "one of the most oppressive regimes in history"—a ludicrous claim that overlooked, among other near-to-hand examples, the murderous North Vietnamese Communists, whose victory Kennedy had facilitated, and who were busily conducting summary executions of a hundred thousand of their new subjects.[12]

As the shah became the focus of Carter's moralistic attacks, America's support was withdrawn from a regime that had been a strategic American ally fighting the Communists.[13] Carter thus undermined the ruler of the most pro-Western Muslim government in history as it confronted a rebellion led by religious fanatics, who had declared America to be the Great Satan, and who openly boasted that their goal was to drag Iran back into the eighth century, and establish a misogynistic theocracy in the process.

At the same time, Carter and the Democrats were also working to purge the U.S. intelligence apparatus, which was responsible for monitoring Iran's Islamic revolutionaries. The Democrat-led Watergate investigations had targeted the CIA, which had been drawn into the imbroglio by Nixon. As part of its assault on the American "empire," the antiwar Left portrayed the CIA as the very symbol of Washington's culpability before the world. Consequently, at the same time Carter was undermining the shah, his CIA director, Stansfield Turner, was taking an ax to intelligence assets that might otherwise have identified the threat. Turner cut 820 human-intelligence positions from the agency,[14] forcing it to rely on foreign intelligence services for analyses.

In August 1978, Carter's newly reformed CIA reported, "Iran is not in a revolutionary or even a 'pre-revolutionary' situation." The Ayatollah's revolution was launched in the city of Qom the next month. One otherwise glowing Carter biography recounts: "There was little or no informed understanding anywhere in the U.S. government about the political implications of Islamic fundamentalism. Gary Sick, who handled Iran on the National Security [Council] Staff under [Zbigniew] Brzezinski, recalled a meeting at which Vice President Mondale asked CIA director Stansfield Turner, 'What the hell is an *ayatollah* anyway?' 'I'm not sure I know,' Turner responded."[15]

As American progressives had hailed the Vietnamese Communists as liberators,[16] they now saw virtue in the monstrous forces they were helping bring to power in the Islamic Middle East. Carter's ambassador to Iran compared Ayatollah Khomeini to the Hindu pacifist Mahatma Gandhi. UN ambassador Andrew Young called the fanatic misogynist and America-hater "a 20th century saint."[17] Princeton professor Richard Falk, who later became a prominent opponent of the war in Iraq, described the ayatollah's inner circle as "uniformly composed of moderate, progressive individuals," and argued, "Iran may yet provide us with a desperately-needed model of humane government for a third-world country."[18]

In fact, the mullahs quickly made the shah's regime look like a model of humane government by contrast. Among the first two decrees of the ayatollah's revolution were the outlawing of divorce and the legalization of polygamy. In their first year in power, the "progressive" revolutionaries executed more people than had been killed in the thirty-seven years of the shah's rule. Meanwhile, Carter, whose lectures on human rights had fallen on deaf ears, continued to sell Iran military equipment as though it were still an American ally and not a nation ruled by America-hating zealots.[19]

When the revolutionaries seized sixty-six Americans from the embassy and took them hostage, the progressives who had abandoned Southeast Asians to their fate did the same for their own countrymen in Iran.[20] Carter's secretary of state, Cyrus Vance, resigned rather than *discuss* a military rescue attempt. His successor, anti–Vietnam War liberal Edmund Muskie, advised Carter, "Our people at State think that we are going to have to just sit back and let this thing work its way through Iran's political system. . . . The Iranians are going to have to ultimately see how holding the hostages is hurting their Revolution."[21] Carter did not just sit back; he caved in, paying an eight-billion-dollar ransom to the ayatollah, who quickly funneled the money to terrorists around the world, in a radical version of trickle-down economics.[22]

Carter's one-term presidency ended in a paralysis caused by his policy failures, domestic as well as foreign, including 20 percent interest rates and an embarrassing attempt to rescue the hostages with a helicopter that crashed in the desert. This did not dissuade the self-adoring president from appointing himself a global expert on government, or embarking on an unending and unprecedented post-retirement career as one of the very few American presidents to actively obstruct their successors' policies.[23]

The defeat of Carter and the election of Ronald Reagan brought a newfound clarity to U.S. foreign policy. Reagan denounced the Soviet Union as an "evil empire" destined for "the ash-heap of history." But while Reagan looked for ways to speed the end of the Soviet regime, Carter and his ally Ted Kennedy established private relations with the Kremlin dictators, which they maintained throughout the 1980s, out of concern that Reagan was an American extremist who couldn't be trusted not to endanger the peace.

In a 1982 speech before the Council on Foreign Relations, Carter accused Reagan of a "one-sided attitude of belligerence toward the Soviet Union," showing that whatever he had learned from the Soviet invasion of Afghanistan had been quickly forgotten. Soviet Ambassador Anatoly Dobrynin recounted how Carter paid him "a surprise visit" on January 30, 1984, to "voice concern at the extent of Reagan's arms buildup. He described Reagan's peace rhetoric as a pure campaign maneuver. The former president was 'utterly convinced' that there would not be a single agreement on arms control as long as Reagan remained in power."[24] If Carter was more explicit, Dobrynin did not say, but the implication was clear: the Soviets should see to it that Ronald Reagan was not re-elected.

The Soviets had cause to seek Reagan's defeat. Reagan put into action President Kennedy's pledge to "support any friend, oppose any foe, in order to assure the survival and the success of liberty," most notably against Marxists in Afghanistan, El Salvador, and Nicaragua.

This brought the Left's anti-Americanism to a boil. In Nicaragua, warned House Speaker Tip O'Neill, America had allied itself with "terrorists, marauders, and paid mercenaries." Democratic senator (and 2008 presidential candidate) Christopher Dodd insisted that "we continue to ally ourselves with repression," while Dodd himself cozied up to the Nicaraguan dictatorship. For his part, Democratic congressman Vic Fazio repeated the "blame America first" mantra: "We have unclean hands."[25]

However, Reagan was not to be dissuaded from staying his course. Less than two weeks after Libyan terrorists bombed a Berlin discotheque, killing two U.S. servicemen and a Turkish woman and injuring more than two hundred people, including fifty U.S. servicemen, Reagan ordered an aerial attack on Libya. "Despite our repeated warnings," Reagan explained, "[Libyan dictator Mohammar Qaddafi] continued his reckless policy of intimidation, his relentless pursuit of terror. He counted on America to be passive. He counted wrong. I warned that there should be no place on earth where terrorists can rest and train and practice their deadly skills. I meant it. I said that we would act with others, if possible, and alone if necessary to ensure that terrorists have no sanctuary anywhere. Tonight, we have."[26]

Jimmy Carter, who had begged Qaddafi to intervene with Ayatollah Khomeini during the Iran hostage crisis, condemned the retaliation as a "serious mistake."[27] Democratic congressman Mervyn Dymally defended Qaddafi, calling him "a victim of terrorism."[28] Senator John Kerry wrote, "It is obvious that our response was not proportional to the disco bombing and even violated the administration's own guidelines to hit clearly defined terrorist targets."[29] Kerry did not explain what he thought might be "proportional"—bombing a disco full of Libyan soldiers? But then Kerry characterized the Reagan years generally as a time of "moral darkness."[30] History vindicated Reagan's hard line: Qaddafi attempted no further terrorist acts against the United States.

In August 1990, Iraq's despot, Saddam Hussein, annexed the tiny nation of Kuwait, and President George H. W. Bush assembled a worldwide coalition to push back the aggressors. In response, Jimmy Carter conducted a one-man diplomatic mission to undermine the effort, sending a letter to UN Security Council members urging them to oppose America's war.[31] Five days before military operations were set to begin, Carter begged Syria, Saudi Arabia, and Egypt—which were all members of the coalition that Bush had assembled—to try appeasement instead: "I urge you to call publicly for a delay in the use of force while Arab leaders seek a peaceful solution to the crisis."[32] He told the American public, "The devastating consequences will be [felt] . . . for decades to come, in economic and political destabilization of the Middle East region." Senator Kennedy joined Carter's campaign to undermine public support for the war, saying it would be "brutal and ugly. The 45,000 body bags the Pentagon has sent to the region are all the evidence we need of the high price in lives and blood that we will have to pay." In fact the body bags were never used, as American casualties were minimal. Senator Kerry joined the Carter-Kennedy chorus: "If we do go to war, for years people will ask why Congress gave in. They will ask why there was such a rush to so much death and destruction when it did not have to happen."[33] In the end, only ten of the Senate's fifty-five Democrats voted to oppose Iraq's aggression and expel Saddam from Kuwait.[34]

The ground war lasted four days and ended in the crushing defeat of Saddam's Republican Guard. After it was over, President Bush said, "The specter of Vietnam has been buried forever in the desert sands of the Arabian Peninsula . . . [W]e've kicked the Vietnam Syndrome once and for all."[35] The obituary was premature. In 1992, Arkansas governor Bill Clinton defeated Bush and breathed new life into the forces of appeasement.

CLINTON

For all Jimmy Carter's faults, he made a faint-hearted attempt in his last year in office to correct his blindness towards the Soviet threat. Instead of cutting defense spending by 25 percent as he had planned, he increased it and put on ice his ambitions to expand arms-control agreements with the untrustworthy Kremlin. Clinton, too, made gestures at reversing the anti-military image his party had acquired. He deployed American forces more than any other postwar president, although he sent them almost exclusively on humanitarian missions. Moreover, the sheer number of these missions—more deployments in the eight years of the Clinton administration than in the forty-five years of the Cold War with the Soviet Union—had the effect of sapping military morale and contributing to the low opinion military personnel held towards their commander-in-chief.[36]

During the Clinton administration, the Islamic jihad against the West became a gathering storm. It included unprecedented attacks on American soil and American military assets overseas in 1993, 1996, 1998, and 2000. But Clinton refused to acknowledge the threat and did virtually nothing in response. Instead Clinton and his national-security advisers pretended that these attacks were criminal activities by individuals and isolated groups, which should be treated as law-enforcement matters.

Like Carter, Clinton wasted no time in telegraphing American vulnerability to America's adversaries. On February 26, 1993—barely a month into Clinton's first term—terrorists detonated a fifteen-hundred-pound bomb in the back of a rented Ryder truck, which they had parked in the underground garage of Tower One of the World Trade Center. The explosion ripped a hole into the structure six stories deep, killing six people and wounding more than a thousand.

The mastermind of this attack, an al-Qaeda operative named Ramzi Yousef, planned the detonation so that it would release cyanide gas into the building's ventilation shafts and elevators. He later confessed that he hoped to cause Tower One to collapse onto Tower Two, killing a quarter of a million people.[37] Although he did not achieve his barbaric ambitions, he had successfully perpetrated the first major terrorist attack on American soil and the largest terrorist attack anywhere, ever. In response, President Clinton warned Americans against "overreaction." He never visited the site. The bomb maker, Abdul Rahman Yasin, an Iraqi national, fled to his home country, where he was given refuge, without any American protest to the Iraqi government.

The significance of the attack as part of a global jihad was effectively concealed from its intended target—the American people. At the same time, the Islamic terrorist movement was encouraged to think that its agents could attack Americans without serious consequences.

Eight months later, Islamic jihadists struck Americans again, in the African city of Mogadishu, where U.S. Army Rangers were providing food supplies to starving Somalis. As one of his last acts in power before Clinton's succession, President Bush had ordered U.S. troops to assist the United Nations in a limited operation to bring in food and medical supplies. Somalia was in a state of anarchy at the time, and the food earmarked for the starving inhabitants of this impoverished, black, and largely Muslim nation was being hijacked by Somali warlords, among them an al-Qaeda associate named Mohammed Aideed. Bush had dispatched twenty-one thousand troops to protect the food lines.

Five months into the new Clinton administration, all but three hundred combat troops had been withdrawn. At this point Clinton broadened the mission to "nation-building" and attempted to help the Somalis create a government. On October 3, 1993, an opportunity arose to capture a number of top aides to Mohammed Aideed. U.S. soldiers and airmen successfully completed the mission, but Aideed's forces ambushed the troops, shooting down two American

Black Hawk helicopters. Surrounded by a numerically superior enemy, the American forces could not rescue the crews without tanks and armored vehicles. Commanders had requested these vehicles two weeks earlier, but they had been turned down by Clinton's defense secretary, Les Aspin, who—like Clinton and his national-security adviser, Sandy Berger—was a veteran of the anti–Vietnam War Left. Aspin rejected the request for armor because he was fearful that sending it would give the enemy the impression that America was widening the war.[38]

Sent on a mission without sufficient resources, the U.S. troops had to hold off the terrorists in a deadly firefight until properly equipped Pakistani and Malaysian troops arrived on the scene, ten hours later. When the dust cleared, eighteen American soldiers lay dead. Jubilant terrorists dragged one soldier's corpse through the streets of Mogadishu, an atrocity displayed on international television. Clinton threw in the towel and pulled out the troops. Democratic foreign-policy expert Richard Holbrooke commented wryly that this had produced a new foreign policy malady: the "Vietmalia Syndrome."[39] On this new strategy, there was concurrence between the president and his "co-president," Mrs. Clinton, who complained, "I keep telling him to pull them [the troops] out, but I have limited influence on foreign policy."[40]

Subsequently, Osama bin Laden told ABC's John Miller that the shameful episode proved Americans "can run in less than 24 hours." He explained: "[Muslim] youth were surprised at the low morale of the American soldiers and realized more than before that the American soldiers are paper tigers. After a few blows, they ran in defeat . . . T]his great defeat pleased me very much, the way it pleases all Muslims."[41] A handful of warriors for Allah had defeated the Great Satan, now the world's lone superpower.

Having pulled off two successful attacks against the Great Satan, the jihadists stepped up their activities. In early 1995, a captured

Ramzi Yousef confessed to planning Operation Bojinka, whose goal was to blow up eleven commercial airliners. The plot was to be co-ordinated with the assassination of the pope and the crashing of an airliner into CIA headquarters in Langley, Virginia. Filipino officials accidentally discovered the plan days before it was to have been carried out, when one of the terrorists inadvertently blew up his apartment while testing an explosive device. Clinton assigned Vice President Al Gore to draft guidelines to improve airline safety. But Gore's Aviation Safety and Security Commission issued no guidelines that would do anything to prevent suicide hijacking operations such as 9-11. Its final report, which appeared in February 1997, proposed that passengers designated as "suspicious" should have their checked baggage screened, but rejected more stringent measures. However, even these insufficient guidelines were never implemented. As the 9-11 Commission reported, the administration did not allow security personnel to screen potential terrorists' carry-on luggage "[p]rimarily because of concern regarding potential discrimination." Liberal concerns over "racial profiling" trumped national security. Instead, terrorists' bags were merely held off the plane until they boarded. The Gore commission did recommend that the FBI and CIA provide no-fly lists to the FAA "to improve prescreening," but the Clinton administration never compelled the agencies to do so.[42]

Meanwhile, the Islamist attacks continued. In 1996, after the exposure of the Bojinka plot, Muslim bombers killed nineteen U.S. servicemen housed in the Khobar Towers in Saudi Arabia. Clinton's response was to call for a federal investigation. Weeks later, Osama bin Laden told sympathetic journalist Robert Fisk that the bombing was "the beginning of war between Muslims and the United States."[43] The disparity between these two responses could not have identified the problem more clearly. There was a war, but only one side was fighting.

Bin Laden now issued a Muslim theological statement, or *bayan*, formally titled, "The Declaration of War." It was written to "initiate a guerrilla warfare, where the sons of the nation, and not the military forces, take part." He also made clear the extent to which Clinton's surrender in Somalia had encouraged him. "When tens of your soldiers were killed in minor battles and one American pilot was dragged in the streets of Mogadishu you left the area carrying disappointment, humiliation, defeat and your dead with you," he wrote. "Clinton appeared in front of the whole world threatening and promising revenge, but these threats were merely a preparation for withdrawal. You have been disgraced by Allah and you withdrew; the extent of your impotence and weaknesses became very clear."[44] To emphasize how clear, bin Laden told CNN journalist Peter Arnett, "If the U.S. still thinks and brags that it still has this kind of power even after all these successive defeats in Vietnam, Beirut, Aden, and Somalia, then let them go back to those who are awaiting its return."[45]

Clinton's indifference to national-security concerns was perhaps best illustrated by an event that took place in September 1996. That August, Saddam pushed north to attack the pro-Western Kurds, the most brazen violation to date of the truce he had signed to end the Gulf War. An American strike against Iraq to counter this aggression was scheduled for the night of September 13. However, President Clinton was attending the Professional Golf Association President's Cup in Virginia that day, seven time zones away. Lt. Col. Buzz Patterson, the White House military aide who carried the nuclear football for Clinton, reported, "The attack was to be launched under cover of darkness, and we were wasting valuable time. Pilots were in the cockpits waiting to launch, targets were identified, everything was in place, all they needed was the go-ahead." Three times, acting National Security Adviser Sandy Berger telephoned for authorization to launch. Patterson conveyed each message to President Clinton, and three times the president refused to take the calls, consumed with his passion for the links. Clinton told Patterson he would return the calls later, but he called so late, the pilots had had to shut down their engines and return to standby. The opportunity had passed. "At a time when America's honor and grander principles were being challenged and the world was watching our every move . . . the president was watching golf."[46]

In the summer of 1998, while the administration was paralyzed by the president's efforts to conceal his sexual affair of three years earlier with a twenty-two-year-old White House intern, al-Qaeda blew up the U.S. embassies in Kenya and Tanzania, killing 224 people and injuring thousands. As the White House scandal mushroomed, Clinton ordered his first (and only) military response to the terrorists in his eight years in office, ordering a strike on a medicine factory in the Sudan, whose government had previously provided sanctuary for the terrorist leader, and firing missiles at bin Laden's hideouts in Afghanistan. However, so as not to alarm the Pakistani government, over whose airspace the missiles would pass, Clinton informed government officials about the attack in advance. But Pakistani intelligence had created the Taliban, and someone in the Pakistani government tipped off bin Laden, who escaped. The missiles fell on empty tents. The Clinton Justice Department then handed down a federal indictment of bin Laden for conspiring to attack the United States. Bin Laden skipped his court date.

Even the criminal investigations of the Islamic attacks were conducted in a half-hearted fashion. FBI Director Louis Freeh said officials were "lukewarm" about investigating the Khobar Towers bombing, because it was suspected that Iran was behind the attack, and the president was "[e]ager to engage Iranian moderates."[47] The moderates never materialized, and Freeh had to ask former President Bush to coax the Saudis into cooperating with the investigation that Clinton had abandoned. (An indictment was not issued until 2001, under President George W. Bush.) When an American warship, the USS *Cole*, was bombed in 2000, the Clinton administration did not respond. Clinton's ambassador to Yemen aborted the FBI investigation at the scene.

Bill Clinton's response to the four terrorist bombings and the humiliating ambush in Somalia could be summarized as nothing, nothing, failure, nothing, and capitulation. Dick Morris recounted how the successes of the anti–Vietnam War movement—in which Clinton, his first secretary of defense, Les Aspin, and his second national security adviser, Sandy Berger, had all been participants—had paralyzed the president's resolve: "He had almost an allergy to using people in uniform. He was terrified of incurring casualties; the lessons of Vietnam were ingrained far too deeply in him."[48]

The prime beneficiary of the new Vietmalia Syndrome was Osama bin Laden. The CIA's agent in charge of its bin Laden task force, Michael Scheuer, has written that Clinton "had at least eight to ten chances to capture or kill Osama bin Laden in 1998 and 1999."[49] However, he canceled all these operations—whether because of his concern with criminals' rights, his covetousness of world opinion, or his perception of the United States as a warmonger.

Among Clinton's failures in dealing with the greatest threat Americans had faced since the end of the Cold War was an incident in March 1996, when Elfatih Erwa, minister of defense of the Sudan, where bin Laden then made his base, offered to extradite him to the United States. Clinton refused the offer. Although he has since disputed these facts, he spontaneously, and perhaps inadvertently, conceded their validity during a speech on February 15, 2002. "At that time, 1996," Clinton said, "[bin Laden] had committed no crime against America, so I did not bring him here because we had no basis on which to hold him."[50]

Even more puzzling in these multiple derelictions of presidential duty was an incident that occurred six months before the bombing of the U.S. embassies. At the time, Clinton was receiving intelligence briefings warning that, "Sooner or later, bin Laden will attack U.S. interests, perhaps using WMD."[51] In February 1998, the CIA made plans for an Afghan militia to capture bin Laden at his compound, Tarnak Farms, and deliver him to the United States. But in May

1998 National Security Adviser Sandy Berger and CIA chief George Tenet called off the mission for fear bin Laden might accidentally be killed, rather than captured, which would violate the rules instituted as part of the Watergate reforms. The 9-11 Commission noted, "No capture plan before 9-11 ever again attained the same level of detail and preparation."[52]

The concerns of Berger and Tenet notwithstanding, the 9-11 Commission later pointed out that Ronald Reagan had given the CIA all the authority necessary to execute missions such as this back in 1986. However, Tenet and Berger would not sanction the mission without additional guidelines from the White House, as they were "mindful of the old 'rogue elephant' charge."[53] Unease about "paramilitary covert action" had become ingrained in Washington as a result of the campaigns of the anti–Vietnam War Left and their influence in the Democratic Party.

Six months after the failed missile strikes following the embassy bombings of August 1998, another missile attack near Kandahar was vetoed by Clinton because bin Laden was traveling with several members of the United Arab Emirates' royal family. Counterterrorism chief Richard Clarke telephoned the UAE, apparently without permission, on March 7, 1999, to discuss the royals' cozy relationship with the Saudi terrorist. The result? "[L]ess than a week after Clarke's phone call the camp was hurriedly dismantled, and the site was deserted."

That May, bin Laden escaped another planned surgical strike thanks to the administration's wish not to appear "trigger-happy."[54] One officer testified, "This was in our strike zone. It was a fat pitch, a home run."[55] The 9-11 Commission summarized the intelligence community's consensus: "If this intelligence was not 'actionable,' working-level officials said at the time and today, it was hard for them to imagine how any intelligence on Bin Laden in Afghanistan would meet the standard." Yet Berger and Tenet again balked, because during the Clinton air war against Belgrade (acceptable to liberals as a humanitarian cause) the Chinese embassy had been accidentally hit by NATO bombs. Clinton officials did not want to anger "world opinion" again. Thus, America lost "the last, and most likely the best, opportunity" for killing bin Laden before 9-11.

While muffing the chances to capture bin Laden out of concern for the niceties of political correctness, the administration took every pain imaginable to protect the terrorist's dignity in the improbable event that he should ever be captured. In preparing for one of the aborted missions, agents were told to design an ergonomically correct restraining chair, built for Osama's comfort, as he was abnormally tall. The administration also instructed agents to take care that Osama's beard not be mussed.[56] Sandy Berger's description of the Clinton administration's Iraq policy could have as easily applied to its indifference to terrorist aggression in general. Responding to Saddam's provocations, he said, was "a little bit like a Whack-a-Mole game at the circus. They bop up and you whack 'em down, and if they bop up again, you bop 'em back down again."[57] This attitude left bin Laden's fanatics free to bop down the Twin Towers on 9-11.

One reason Clinton had little time for foreign enemies was that his principal targets were domestic: Branch Davidians in Waco, black-helicopter-spotting militias in Montana, and the "vast right-wing conspiracy" his wife claimed had invented his affair with Monica Lewinsky. In addition, the notion that America had foreign enemies threatened to revive the political dynamics of the Cold War, which would put the security-averse and defense-cutting Democrats at an electoral disadvantage.

From the day Clinton took office, the theme that "the Cold War is over" and Americans were due a "peace dividend" animated his cabinet appointees and other advisers. One result of their zeal was the largest declassification of military information in recorded history. Two months after Clinton's ignominious retreat from Somalia, his secretary of energy, Hazel O'Leary, announced that her department was opening the doors to let out America's nuclear secrets: "We are declassifying the largest amount of information in the history of the Department of Energy." All told, the declassification amounted to more than eleven million pages of material on America's nuclear program, including testing data, plutonium inventory, and the use of mercury at the Oak Ridge National Laboratory.[58] This disclosure was necessary, O'Leary explained, "to expose the impact of the Cold War both in terms of its environmental health and safety impacts and also impacts on . . . the psyche of the nation." The declassification was officially termed the "Openness Initiative," which O'Leary boasted was to defeat "the bomb-building culture."[59] O'Leary publicly hoped "other nuclear nations will do the same."[60] Instead, during the Clinton years China managed to steal the most advanced elements of America's nuclear-weapons program, while North Korea, Libya, and Iran launched their own initiatives for building nuclear weapons, and Islamic terrorists undoubtedly leafed through the volumes the administration had released.

To provide America and the world with its "peace dividend," the Clinton administration slashed defense spending by Jimmy Carter's target of 25 percent.[61] Vice President Gore's highly touted "Reinventing Government" effort, which was designed to show that Democrats could be fiscally responsible and cut federal waste, turned out to be an anti-military program as well. Ninety percent of the government job reductions were achieved by cutting military personnel. At the same time, Clinton froze military wages, leading to a glut of enlisted men simultaneously on call and on food stamps.[62]

Nor was the military Clinton's only target among America's frontline defense forces. A year before 9-11, FBI chief Louis Freeh requested 864 new counterterrorism agents; he got 7. Because of the Democrats' one-sided budgetary restraint, the FBI was using ten-year-old computer technology[63] on the eve of the nation's worst attack.

Left-wing senator Pat Leahy objected to provisions allowing the FBI
to read e-mail, and investigators were forbidden to use "open source"
information: that is, they could not keep a newspaper file on their
targeted suspects. This was one reason why the *Washington Post* actually scooped FBI agents during the Khobar Towers investigation.[64]

Democrats also continued the campaign they had begun in the
Watergate years to hamstring and eventually cripple the CIA. A key
figure in this effort was New Jersey Democratic senator Robert Torricelli, subsequently retired under a cloud of corruption.[65] At the
time, Torricelli was dating pro-Castro supermodel Bianca Jagger.
Their personal and ideological paths had crossed previously, during
the Reagan administration, when Jagger was the mistress of Sand-
inista secret-police chief Tomás Borge. Torricelli had himself joined
nine Democratic colleagues in writing a "Dear Comandante" letter
to Nicaraguan dictator Daniel Ortega, condemning American-led
"military hostilities on the borders of Nicaragua."[66]

Torricelli protested the CIA's affiliation with a Guatemalan colonel
named Julio Roberto Alpirez.[67] Alpirez, a CIA asset, was present at
the death of a member of a revolutionary terrorist group at war with
the Guatemalan government. The terrorist happened to be married
to an American leftist, who complained to Jagger. Torricelli wrote
Clinton about the matter and sent a copy of the letter—complete
with the undercover informant's name—to the *New York Times*, which
printed it. This was well before the *Times*'s crocodile outrage over
the outing of CIA desk officer Valerie Plame during the Iraq War. A
report issued by the House Permanent Select Committee on Intelligence concluded that the national-security leak by Torricelli and
the *Times* had "resulted in the loss of some contacts around the
world who feared their relationship with the United States would
be disclosed, as well."[68]

Torricelli knew that a press scandal had the potential to depress
the president's poll numbers, which would spur Clinton to act. This

was apparently worth the betrayal of America's intelligence secrets and agents. It was not long before Clinton's new CIA director, John Deutsch, barred the agency from recruiting informers who were "human-rights violators" or had a violent past. Clinton's first CIA director, James Woolsey, had noted the absurdity in thinking one could "recruit only nice people in order to inform on terrorist groups."[69] But the CIA had to live with the restriction, depriving itself of the human intelligence that was found to be so sorely lacking by those investigating the intelligence failures that led to 9-11.

While Torricelli tied the CIA's hands, other Senate left-wingers tried to bleed its funding. Arizona Democrat Dennis DeConcini cut funding for Arabic and Farsi translators.[70] Massachusetts Democrat John Kerry proposed cutting intelligence spending by 1.5 *billion* dollars every year from 1996 to 2001 and cutting defense spending by 6.5 billion dollars.[71] To antiwar activists like Kerry, the CIA was a Cold War relic and a threat to the civil liberties of American leftists.

The Left had been successful in the 1970s in getting the weakened, post-Watergate Ford administration to erect a "wall" preventing FBI agents from communicating with their CIA counterparts, lest they establish a fascist state in America. In July 1995, Clinton's deputy attorney general Jamie Gorelick wrote a memo that effectively raised the wall higher. Following her memo, "The information flow withered,"[72] according to *The 9-11 Commission Report*. U.S. Attorney Mary Jo White, herself a Democrat, warned that these "prohibitions are not legally required" and "will cost lives."[73] An FBI agent who was subsequently prohibited from arresting two of the 9-11 hijackers e-mailed the FBI with this comment: "Someday somebody will die—and wall or not—the public will not understand why we were not more effective and throwing every resource we had at [the terrorist threat]."[74] These words proved to be prophetic. The wall denied FBI agents the ability to search Zaccarias Moussaoui's computer twenty-six days before 9-11, although its contents would have disclosed the 9-11 plot and prevented the attacks.

Rather than wielding America's intelligence assets effectively in the war against terror, Clinton used them to gratify the Democrats' diversity fetish. At his direction, CIA director Deutsch gave promotions based on race, sex, and ethnicity, and actively recruited gays.[75] While filling these multicultural quotas, Deutsch failed to make up the deficit created by the fact that not one analyst spoke Pashto, the language of Afghanistan. Consequently, the CIA outsourced its translation of al-Qaeda transmissions to Pakistani intelligence, whose agents regularly passed on the information to al-Qaeda agents.[76]

The same blind spots and misplaced priorities obstructed the government's intelligence-gathering efforts in Iran and other Middle Eastern bases of terrorism. "Not a single Iran-desk chief during the eight years I worked on Iran could speak or read Persian," wrote a former CIA official. "Not a single Near East Division chief knew Arabic, Persian or Turkish, and only one could get along even in French."[77] Clinton canceled two investigations into Islamic "charities" that funded terrorism, out of fear, in the words of *Newsweek*, that they "might rile religious sensitivities."[78] But sensitivities riled cut only one way. The leadership of al-Qaeda does not "look like America"; it looks like Saudi Arabia or the Muslim *umma*, and the Democrats' obsessions with American malfeasance and Muslim sensibilities allowed a force of ruthless fanatics to have their day.

At crucial turns in his administration, Bill Clinton seemed focused on the wrong enemy. In 1998, he dispatched UN ambassador Bill Richardson to Afghanistan to impose an arms embargo on the friendly forces of the Northern Alliance, the effect of which was to help the Taliban.[79] A few weeks after the Khobar Towers bombing, he declined to capture Osama bin Laden's mentor—the man who killed 241 American servicemen in Beirut in 1983—but he instructed Secret Service agents to interrogate Glenn and Patricia Mendoza for twelve hours after they told him "you suck" at a campaign appearance.[80] He waived sanctions against every foreign company that helped Iran build its nuclear capacity.[81] As al-Qaeda cells in the United States plotted

9-11, under intermittent federal surveillance, he put the full force of the U.S. government into sending the Cuban refugee youngster Elian Gonzalez back to the police state he had escaped.

When Clinton did focus on the enemy, his attention was often intermittent or distracted. He sporadically bombed Iraq for its "decade of defiance" of UN resolutions and the terms of the 1991 truce, but he took no effective action to force Iraq to comply. Iraq's defiance included the expulsion of UN inspectors from its territory, after which Clinton signed the Iraq Liberation Act, calling for the forcible removal of Saddam. But he paralyzed his ability to support this policy by lying to his wife, his cabinet, and the American people about his affair with Monica Lewinsky, and he paralyzed his government for the next year and a half. Then he embarked on an air war in the Balkans to support an al-Qaeda affiliate, the Kosovo Liberation Army, in its war against Orthodox Christian (but also Communist) Serbia, even allowing the KLA to receive military support from Iran.[82]

Even the final hours of Clinton's presidency benefited terrorists, along with his wife's political ambitions. In his last chaotic moments in power, he issued pardons for several left-wing terrorists who had not been properly vetted by the Justice Department.[83] Not coincidentally, many of the pardoned had constituencies in the state of New York, where Clinton's wife, Hillary, was seeking a Senate seat. Clinton warmed his pardon pen as Hillary's campaign was getting underway by wiping the slate clean for sixteen members of a Puerto Rican terrorist organization called "the Armed Forces of National Liberation" (FALN). The FALN had killed six people in 130 bombings between 1974 and 1983. The pardoned had all been convicted of sedition. However, New York Democratic congressman José Serrano, a longtime Castro supporter, petitioned for their release as "political prisoners."[84] Clinton granted this petition (with its absurd premise), and Serrano—along with a large contingent of the state's Puerto Rican voters—supported Hillary in the 2000 election.

Clinton also assented to the pardon requests of one of his outspoken defenders during the impeachment. New York congressman Jerrold Nadler petitioned for the release of Linda Evans and Susan Rosenberg, two convicted sixties terrorists who had been members of the Weather Underground. Rosenberg had been one of the getaway drivers in a 1981 Brink's robbery in Nyack, New York, where her comrades murdered a Brink's guard and two policemen, leaving nine children fatherless. Police arrested Rosenberg in November 1984 and found, in a rented storage unit, hundreds of pounds of explosives, firearms, and terrorist manuals. As law enforcement carted her off to prison, she defiantly proclaimed herself a "guerrilla."

The following May, police arrested Evans, who was later convicted of acquiring weapons, fake IDs, and safe houses, as well as conducting terrorist campaigns. Among her intended bombing targets were the U.S. Capitol, the FBI building, the National War College, the Navy Yard computer center, Israeli Aircraft Industries, and the New York Patrolmen's Benevolent Association. Like Rosenberg, she remained unrepentant, and following her pardon she resumed her revolutionary activities.[85] In a perverse demonstration of equality before the law, Clinton also pardoned former CIA director John Deutsch for mishandling classified national-security information.

Clinton had been touted as a leader who would end decades of liberal "softness" on national-security issues. He failed to halt, let alone reverse the trend, because the forces moving the Democratic Party leftward were deeper and broader than one clever politician might counter. During his administration, the analytical and operations branches of the CIA were cut by 30 percent. As part of the Clinton "peace dividend" following the Cold War, the agency drastically reduced its recruitment of new case officers, offered incentive pay to existing ones to retire early, and closed bases, including the station in Hamburg, where Mohammed Atta's cell planned 9-11. By the mid-1990s, there were only three CIA officers inside the largest Muslim country in the world, Indonesia, and there were no agents inside the regime in Iraq.[86]

In the words of one veteran reporter, "overall, the Clinton administration appeared to regard the CIA as a Cold War relic."[87] This was confirmed by its CIA director, George Tenet, who in his memoir recalled that when he was hired for the position, "I found it odd that there was no job interview . . . no one asked me what I would do with the intelligence community should I get the job."[88] Tenet summed up the Clinton record on intelligence in these sobering words: "The fact is by the mid-to-late 1990s American intelligence was in Chapter 11 [i.e., bankrupt], and neither Congress nor the executive branch did much about it."[89]

During his tenure as commander-in-chief, Clinton showed the jihadists that violence against the United States would go unpunished. If the terrorism was conducted against an allied power such as Israel, it might result in lavish nights in the White House for its chief instigator, as happened with Yasser Arafat. The hope was that red-carpet treatment would induce him to reform. At the same time, Clinton continued the Left's three-decades-long assault on America's intelligence agencies. He raised the wall between the FBI and the CIA higher than ever before, which fatally obstructed the efforts to capture the 9-11 plotters. He ignored vital intelligence that did make its way to him, passing up opportunities to kill Osama bin Laden on many occasions. He allowed WMD technology to be passed to terror-friendly regimes around the world, in particular the Chinese and the North Koreans.[90] He failed to implement meaningful airline safety measures that would have prevented 9-11, even though he had been warned that bin Laden was determined to hijack airplanes and use them as weapons. As commander-in-chief he was generally AWOL on the battlefront with the global Islamic jihad, and at the end of his tenure, America could not have been more vulnerable to the jihadists.

The one weakness Bill Clinton could not inflict on America's preparedness, his vice president did. Following George Bush's razor-thin victory in Florida in the 2000 election, Al Gore broke with tradition and refused to concede defeat, challenging the outcome instead. In the process, he divided the country even more bitterly than it had been divided before.

His was not the only national election to fall within a margin so narrow that a reversal seemed within reach. In the 1960 campaign, John F. Kennedy won by a handful of popular votes—and some of those votes were doubtful.[91] But the Left's constant foil, Richard Nixon, refused to challenge the result, because he understood the perils of a succession crisis in a dangerous world.

Modern communications allowed the entire nation to scrutinize the 2000 Florida recounts and the court battles that accompanied them, making Gore's challenge unprecedented in its ability to cast corrosive doubts on the legitimacy of an American election. Those doubts also served to undermine the authority of the man who became commander-in-chief. As the demagogic Jesse Jackson declared after descending on Florida to mobilize his troops: "We will delegitimize Bush, discredit him, do whatever it takes but never accept him."[92]

Although every independent recount since the election has confirmed Bush's victory, the Left has never conceded the result, or given up the belief that Bush stole his high office.[93] No one was in a better position to understand that America was under attack from Islamic terrorists than Al Gore, yet his focus remained entirely on himself. His unconquerable vanity delayed the new administration in carrying out the transition and putting its cabinet and staff in place for nearly two months, while the post-election conflict played out. The delay proved critical. Once Bush was able to put his team in place, he ordered what Clinton and Gore had failed to request in the previous eight years: a comprehensive anti-terrorism policy "to eliminate al-Qaeda." Because of the two-month delay, the plan did not arrive on Bush's desk until September 10, 2001, and it was unread when the World Trade Center and the Pentagon were attacked the following morning.[94]

The Response to 9-11

O N SEPTEMBER 11, Bill Clinton called for national unity in response to the attack: "The most important thing is we all have to be strong, calm, good Americans and rally behind the president and support the actions he will doubtlessly take in the days ahead . . . Nobody should be questioning any decisions [Bush] makes. We ought to be hanging in there, giving his national security team the time it takes."[1] That morning, virtually every political leader told the press that partisan clashes were a passion of the past.

During the 2000 campaign, Bush had presented himself as "a uniter, not a divider," a title he had earned as governor of Texas by nurturing relations with the state's Democratic leadership. His overtures were returned when the powerful Democratic lieutenant governor, Bob Bullock, endorsed Bush for re-election as governor in 1998, even though he was godfather to a child of the Democratic nominee.[2] Bush carried this bipartisan tone to Washington, despite the acrimony generated by Gore's bitter and unprecedented bid to overturn the Florida result and Inauguration Day demonstrations where protesters chanted, "Hail to the Thief."

Despite these divisive political currents, Bush's first major initiative was an outreach to his Democratic detractors. The No Child Left Behind Act—the largest federal education bill in American history—was an implementation of his campaign theme of "compassionate conservatism." It was a dramatic break with Republicans' long-standing aversion to big government programs, and the White House invited Senator Edward Kennedy, leader of the Democratic Party's left wing, to craft the legislation. Bush also renamed FBI headquarters the Robert F. Kennedy Building, a gesture unmistakably designed to fulfill Bush's election promise to "change the tone in Washington."[3]

The conciliatory gestures did not end with the Kennedys. Bush cultivated various interests he had in common with Louisiana Democrat John Breaux, his would-be point man in the Senate on entitlement reform, and with Georgia Democrat Zell Miller on the issue of tax cuts. He appointed Democrat and former Clinton cabinet member Norman Mineta to be his new secretary of transportation, a post that would have heightened significance after the attacks of 9-11.

Bush adopted the same approach to foreign-policy issues. Most consequentially, he retained Clinton CIA director George Tenet as chief intelligence official and put the lid on any investigations of the Clinton administration's numerous scandals. This was no small concession to bipartisanship. The scandals included the eleventh-hour presidential pardons of terrorists, the theft of American nuclear secrets that found their way to Communist China, and the campaign-finance scandals involving illegal transfers of cash from Chinese nationals and government entities to the Clinton-Gore machine.[4]

Most importantly, in the attempt to forge a bipartisan front in the War on Terror, the Bush White House embargoed any congressional inquiry into the security failures of the Clinton-

Gore administration and the policies of congressional Democrats that had exposed the nation to the attacks of 9-11. For example, in 1987 the Democratic Congress passed the Frank amendment to the Immigration and Nationality Act. "Under [Barney] Frank's amendment," wrote investigative reporter Gerald Posner, "a visa could only be denied if the government could prove that the applicant had committed an act of terrorism. Rendered toothless by the Frank amendment, the Reagan administration had virtually no way to block entry visas even when there was information linking the individuals to terrorist groups."[5]

The day after the 9-11 attacks, Bush convened a bipartisan meeting of congressional leaders at the White House. "This is a different type of war than our nation has ever fought," the president told them. "This is more than a particular group. It is a frame of mind that threatens freedom—they hate Christianity, they hate Judaism, they hate everyone who doesn't think like them."[6] When he finished, Senator Robert Byrd, who was to become one of the earliest and most hyperbolic opponents of the war in Iraq, said: "I congratulate you on your leadership in this very difficult, unique situation. There is still an army who believe in this country, who believe in the Divine guidance that has always led our nation, Mr. President. Mighty forces will come to your aid."[7]

House Minority Leader Dick Gephardt, who would become one of the few Democrats to remain a consistent supporter of the president's war policy, conceded that the Democratic Congress had underfunded counterterrorist intelligence. "We didn't take it seriously enough," he said.[8] Continuing his statesman-like posture in public, Gephardt told ABC's *Good Morning America* that Red-Blue divisions were a thing of the past. "There is absolutely no light or air between Democrats and Republicans, between Congress and the president," he said. "We will stand with the president to get this done and to take whatever action he deems and our defense people deem to do."[9] Freshman New York senator Hillary Clinton publicly called on the president "Not only to seek out and exact punishment on the perpetrators, but to make very clear that not only those who harbor terrorists, but those who in any way aid or comfort them whatsoever will face the wrath of our country."[10] In a once evenly and bitterly divided nation, the president now enjoyed an 85 percent approval rating.[11]

But removed from public view, fissures were already developing that would lead to what amounted to a political earthquake as the long war the president was predicting set in. In that White House meeting on September 12, Senate Majority Leader Tom Daschle took exception to the president's use of the term "war" to describe the 9-11 attacks and America's response: "*War* is a very powerful word. This war is so vastly different. Take care in your rhetorical calculations."[12] Two days later, Daschle responded to the president's request for war funds by setting down another marker: "We are concerned that we [Congress] be recognized as the coequal branches. We set both defense and foreign policy."[13]

On the Democratic back benches, there were other grumblings that seemed out of tune with the post-9-11 mood. The president had not flown directly back to the White House from Florida on the day of the attacks, having been warned by intelligence that Air Force One might be a target. On September 13, Democratic congressman Martin Meehan volunteered to the *Boston Globe*: "I don't buy the notion Air Force One was a target. That's just PR. That's just spin." On a CNN broadcast, Democratic strategist Paul Begala picked up Meehan's partisan cue: "He didn't come home for ten hours, ten hours when all the planes were accounted for, and he gave us some cock-and-bull story about Air Force One being under attack."[14]

Further to the left, the radical "antiwar" movement was already stirring. On September 14, just after the memorial service for the victims of 9-11 in the National Cathedral, Berkeley Democrat Barbara

Lee went to the House floor to speak against the war. Once a political operative for the Black Panther Party and chief of staff for pro-Castro congressman Ron Dellums, Lee cast the lone vote against authorizing a military response to the 9-11 attack. In charges that would eventually be taken up by the Democratic leadership, Lee claimed that the president wanted to "embark on an open-ended war with neither an exit strategy nor a focused target."[15] She later told an interviewer: "I think we disenfranchised the American people when we took their representatives out of the decision-making on whether to go to war."[16]

In the political trenches of the Left, the assault on America for having *provoked* the attacks had already begun. After grousing that "something just doesn't add up" and hinting at conspiratorial machinations behind the events, Michael Moore blamed terrorism on poor airline wages, on America, and on Bush: "In just 8 months, Bush gets the whole world back to hating us again. He withdraws from the Kyoto agreement, walks us out of the Durban conference on racism, insists on restarting the arms race—you name it, and Baby Bush has blown it all. . . . Many families have been devastated tonight. This just is not right. They did not deserve to die. If someone did this to get back at Bush, then they did so by killing thousands of people who DID NOT VOTE for him! Boston, New York, DC, and the planes' destination of California—these were places that voted AGAINST Bush! . . . Let's mourn, let's grieve, and when it's appropriate let's examine our contribution to the unsafe world we live in."[17]

At the time, Moore, Lee, and the radicals they spoke for seemed isolated at the margins of American politics. But in less than three years the Democratic Party would be in open revolt over the president's war policy, and singing a similar tune. Al Gore, Tom Daschle, and other Democratic leaders would be flocking to the opening of Moore's film *Fahrenheit 9-11*, whose wild accusations made Moore's initial comments seem moderate by comparison. A month after that, in July 2004, Moore would be Jimmy Carter's honored guest, watching the Democratic National Convention from the former president's box.

Meanwhile, Bush continued his efforts to forge a new bipartisanship behind the war. He began hosting breakfasts with congressional leaders of both parties: Senate Majority Leader Daschle, Minority Leader Trent Lott, Speaker of the House Dennis Hastert, and House Minority Leader Gephardt. In October 2001, the United States launched Operation Enduring Freedom, whose goal was to destroy al-Qaeda in its Afghanistan base. The breakfast meetings kept the congressional leaders informed about the operation's progress. But Bush, in his hopes for a united front, underestimated the depth of the Democrats' defection, which had shaped their foreign-policy attitudes since the Vietnam War.

In December, American forces toppled the Taliban in Afghanistan, ending that country's role as a safe harbor for al-Qaeda. The following month, Daschle's aides began leaking negative reports on the White House breakfasts to the *New York Times*. According to the leaks, the commander-in-chief was "disengaged" and "uninformed." Bush's response to this sniping was to ignore it and hope that bipartisanship would prevail. White House speechwriter David Frum recalled: "The purpose of the breakfast meetings was to draw the leaders of Congress closer to Bush. Did Daschle fear being pulled *too* close? Was he looking for some way to break Bush's embrace? Did he hope by offending Bush to be disinvited from the breakfasts, and thus (in his own mind, at least) be relieved from any duty to support the president in time of war? A friend of mine put this last question to Daschle directly—and the only reply the majority leader made was an enigmatic smile."[18]

Whatever the Senate majority leader's intent, the White House breakfasts lost their steam. Frum reports: "The five men met at the end of February—then not again until the middle of April and hardly at all after that."[19] At the same time, Daschle began ratcheting up the Democrats' attacks on the president's economic policies, a strategy designed to exploit the fact that the September events had thrown the economy into recession, and to enhance the Democrats' chances of retaking the House in the November elections. Once again Bush sought to remain above the fray.

His 2002 State of the Union address focused heavily on the war, announcing the strategy that would become known as "pre-emption" and identifying the immediate threat: "I will not wait on events, while dangers gather. I will not stand by, as peril draws closer and closer. The United States of America will not permit the world's most dangerous regimes to threaten us with the world's most destructive weapons."[20] Such states could channel these weapons to terrorists or provide them with a safe harbor, as Afghanistan had done. Bush named the threatening nations—Iran, Iraq, and North Korea—and called them the "Axis of Evil."

Following the president's address, although other Democrats complained about the president's choice of words, Al Gore, in his first foreign-policy speech since the 2000 campaign, gave firm support to the position Bush had taken. Gore told the influential Council on Foreign Relations: "Since the State of the Union there has been much discussion of whether Iraq, Iran, and North Korea truly constitute an 'Axis of Evil.' As far as I'm concerned, there really is something to be said for occasionally putting diplomacy aside and laying one's cards on the table. There is value in calling evil by its name. One should never underestimate the power of bold words coming from a president of the United States."[21] In words that he himself would boldly contradict within the next eight months, Gore went on to say that Saddam Hussein's Iraq posed "a virulent threat in a class by itself" and that toppling him by force should be an available option. "As far as I am concerned, a final reckoning with that government should be on the table," he said. "We must be prepared to go the limit."[22]

Others were less than happy with this bipartisan concord and expressed dismay over the president's broadening of the War on

Terror. They were even more vocal in their displeasure at the term "Axis of Evil," much as they had been with Ronald Reagan's "Evil Empire" speech during the Cold War with the Communist bloc. Daschle was the leader again, telling PBS newsman Jim Lehrer: "I think we've got to be very careful with rhetoric of that kind." According to Daschle, such language would squander the goodwill of "moderates in Iran."[23]

Once again the Left set a marker with even stronger attacks. During a February 17 forum in southern California attended by antiwar radical Tom Hayden and former Clinton labor secretary Robert Reich, Congressman Dennis Kucinich delivered a speech he called "A Prayer for America." Kucinich charged U.S. servicemen with "the bombing of civilians" and the shedding of "the blood of innocent villagers in Afghanistan." He accused the American military of operating "assassination squads" and condemned the president for issuing "national identity cards," repealing the Bill of Rights, and revoking the Constitution. He even suggested that the anthrax scare was a government conspiracy to stampede Congress into approving the operation. According to Kucinich, the White House was "in search of new enemies to create new wars,"[24] a standard radical theme.

Congresswoman Maxine Waters also spoke, expressing second thoughts about supporting America's response to the 9-11 attacks: "Some of us, maybe foolishly, gave this president the authority to go after the terrorists. We didn't know that he too was gonna go crazy with it. . . . Now we *know* that he has a problem with Saddam Hussein. We *know* that. We *know* that he's got to take revenge for what Saddam did to his daddy."[25] Fellow House California Democrat Diane Watson added, somewhat incoherently, "We never declared war, so when the president says we need more money to fight the war, it is a ruse to keep his ratings up."[26]

The opponents of the president, cowed by his popularity with the public, began questioning the war effort off the record. A few weeks after 9-11, *New York Times* columnist R. W. Apple Jr. reported that "the ominous word 'quagmire' has begun to haunt conversations among government officials and students of foreign policy, both here and abroad. Could Afghanistan become another Vietnam?"[27] Six months later Daschle and several other senators criticized the war as too open-ended.[28] It was developing, Daschle said, "without clear direction," and he warned: "the jury is still out on future success."[29]

The jury is typically out on future successes, but Daschle was not merely philosophizing: "Congress has a constitutional responsibility to ask questions. We are not a rubber stamp to this president or to anybody else." He was joined now by Senator Byrd, who was reconsidering his previous support. Byrd warned that the White House's war plan could "keep us going beyond doomsday." He wanted to know, "How long can we afford this?"[30] Two days after these remarks, American forces launched Operation Anaconda to squeeze the remnants of the Taliban in Afghanistan. To retrieve his political *faux pas*, Daschle wrote a resolution declaring that the Senate "stands united with the president in the ongoing effort to destroy al-Qaeda."[31]

Unable to gain traction on Afghanistan, the Left searched for a way to hang security failures on President Bush. It began with the off-kilter congresswoman from Georgia, Cynthia McKinney, who in April 2002 insinuated that the Bush White House knew in advance that America was going to be attacked on 9-11 and did nothing to prevent it: "We know there were numerous warnings of the events to come on September 11th. . . . What did this administration know and when did it know it, about the events of September 11th? Who else knew, and why did they not warn the innocent people of New York who were needlessly murdered? . . . What do they have to hide?"[32]

When challenged, McKinney conceded she had no evidence to back up her accusations but refused to retract them.[33] White House spokesman Scott McClellan said McKinney's tirade "shows a partisan mindset beyond all reason,"[34] but McClellan apparently failed to understand exactly how partisan the atmosphere had become. A month later, the drumbeat began. A press report declared that the

White House might have received hints in advance that Osama bin Laden wished to strike in the United States or hijack domestic flights. On the floor of the Senate, Hillary Clinton brandished a newspaper emblazoned with the headline "BUSH KNEW!"[35] House Minority Leader Dick Gephardt threw down another gauntlet, demanding to be told "what the president and what the White House knew about the events leading up to 9-11, when they knew it and, most importantly, what was done about it at that time."[36] The same day, Senate Majority Leader Daschle held his own press conference, at which he said, "I don't know that a direct question—'What did you know and when did you know it?'—was ever asked of the president of the United States."[37] These, of course, were the familiar words that had summed up the charges against Richard Nixon during Watergate.

The president's forbearance in refusing to open an inquiry into the Clinton security failures before 9-11 was now repaid by the Democrats with a frontal attack. The White House could have answered the finger-pointing with a parallel challenge, or by accusing the Democrats of dividing the home front. Instead, the president and his staff again maintained stiff upper lips, hoping to preserve what was left of the unity on the war.

In a defensive statement to the press, White House spokesman Ari Fleischer noted that Senator Clinton and her colleagues had failed to first check the facts with the White House before going public. This presumed that their intention was not political but a sincere inquiry into the truth.[38] When the basis for the original press report was eventually revealed, the "warnings" about an attack turned out to be excessively vague, not something to which the government could make an active response.[39] On the other hand, the failure of the White House to reply in kind was a signal to the Democrats to escalate their attacks.

PART II

THE WAR IN IRAQ

— 3 —

Why America Went to War

I N POLITICS, PERCEPTION IS REALITY. All the arguments over Iraq are shaped by the perception that America went to war to remove Saddam's weapons of mass destruction. This is the heart of the opposition's case: the White House "manipulated" intelligence in order to deceive Americans about the necessity of war. This perception lies behind the accusation that the president and his advisers plotted the war in advance, and deliberately failed to pursue diplomatic avenues to contain Saddam by peaceful means. It is the basis for the charge that America went to war in arrogant disregard for the United Nations and the international community at large.

The well-worn bill of indictment against the White House is summarized in Al Gore's book *The Assault on Reason*, which the former vice president wrote in the fourth year of the war:

- "The first rationale presented for the war was to destroy Iraq's Weapons of Mass Destruction."[1]

- "Five years after President Bush made his case for an invasion of Iraq, it is now clear that virtually all the arguments he made were based on falsehoods."[2]

- "We were told by the president that war was his last choice, when it was his first preference."[3]

In this perception of what happened, America's prosecution of the war in Iraq is an unprovoked aggression, a criminal act. It was justified and authorized by the president's deception—in other words, another criminal act.

This is the extreme perception of the war—advanced in the midst of battle—which has been promoted by the leaders of the Democratic Party. This is the perception that has shaped the views of the Democrats' constituencies, with devastating effect on support for the war at home.

A survey of both Democratic and Republican voters conducted two-and-a-half years after the onset of the conflict asked respondents whether the war was worth fighting. Only 4 percent of Democrats said yes, compared to 84 percent of Republicans.[4]

The survey, conducted by the Massachusetts Institute of Technology, then asked respondents what circumstances would make it appropriate for America to use troops abroad. Among Democrats only 7 percent agreed that America should go to war to spread democracy, compared to 53 percent of Republicans. Asked if they would approve a military action to defend America's oil supplies, only 10 percent of Democrats said yes, compared to 41 percent of Republicans.[5]

In only one area of military action covered by the survey did more Democrats than Republicans support the use of force: 71 percent of Democrats approved military action to help the United Nations "uphold international law," compared to only 36 percent of Republicans. The fact that Democratic voters supported the use of force to uphold international law undoubtedly reflected the emphasis Democratic leaders had placed on "multilateralism," "international opinion," and alleged violations of international law.

Yet the one indisputable fact about the origins of the war was that the trigger of America's decision and the legal basis for its action was UN Security Council Resolution 1441 and Saddam's defiance of its ultimatum. In other words, the White House's rationale for the war was precisely to "uphold international law"—specifically, the seventeen UN resolutions that Saddam Hussein had violated, and that were designed to enforce the Gulf War truce.

When France declared that it would veto any attempt by the Security Council to enforce its own resolutions, British prime minister Tony Blair commented: "This is such a foolish thing to do at this moment in the world's history. The very people who should be strengthening the international institutions are undermining [them]."[6] Yet, the Democrats' political spin—and the Bush administration's determined failure to counter it—has persuaded Democratic voters, accounting for half the American electorate, that the White House violated international law, when in fact it went to war to enforce international law.

THE UN RESOLUTIONS AND THE CASE FOR WAR

The critics of the White House have so distorted the reasons for going to war that a brief review of those reasons is in order. UN Security Council Resolution 1441 was the culmination of an eleven-year effort to use diplomatic means to secure Iraq's compliance with international law, specifically with the arms-control agreements that had constituted the Gulf War truce, which allowed Saddam to stay in power. Resolution 1441 was passed unanimously by the fifteen members of the Security Council. It declared Iraq to be in "material breach" of the sixteen previous UN resolutions that had sought to enforce the truce. The Security Council ruled that Iraq had broken the terms of the truce and was in violation of international law.

UN Security Council Resolution 1441 was also an ultimatum designed to end Iraq's eleven-year series of breaches of the agreements by holding out the threat of force. The ultimatum offered Baghdad "a final opportunity" to comply with the truce or face "serious consequences." Even so staunch an opponent of military action as UN chief weapons inspector Hans Blix recognized the ultimatum as "diplomatic language for possible armed action."[7]

Resolution 1441 gave Saddam a thirty-day deadline to comply with its terms. The deadline expired on December 7, 2002. When the deadline passed, Blix commented, "Iraq appears not to have come to a genuine acceptance—not even today—of the disarmament which was demanded of it and which it needs to carry out to win the confidence of the world and to live in peace."[8] Twelve days after the deadline's expiration, on December 19, 2002, President Bush and Prime Minister Blair issued a joint statement that Iraq was in "material breach" of the ultimatum. Three months later a coalition of America, Britain, and nineteen other nations went to war to enforce it.

These are the facts of how and why America went to war. Yet it is remarkable just how consistently those who condemn the war ignore them. All the arguments against the war are made as though these facts didn't exist, and as though Saddam Hussein's violations of international law and the Gulf War truce and his defiance of Security Council Resolution 1441 were not part of the decision to go to war, let alone its centerpiece.

Iraq's violations of the UN resolutions and the Gulf War truce are not addressed in any Democratic leader's arguments against the war: not John Kerry's, not John Edwards's, not Barack Obama's, not Hillary Clinton's.

Nor are they addressed in the articles and books written by the liberal and radical opponents of the war.

Speaking for the antiwar media, for example, *New York Times* columnist Frank Rich has written an entire book, titled *The Greatest Story Ever Sold*, which (in Rich's own words) "retraces the elaborate propagandistic stagecraft with which the administration rolled out and prosecuted the war in Iraq." In its 352 pages, Rich's book does not mention UN Security Council Resolution 1441 or its sixteen violated predecessors, or their role in President Bush's decision to go to war.[9]

Left-wing journalists David Corn and Michael Isikoff have written a parallel tract of 458 closely argued pages, in which they claim to describe the "hubris" of the Bush administration and to relate "The Inside Story of Spin, Scandal, and the Selling of the Iraq War." Their text, which is titled *Hubris*, purports to dissect the rationale for the war in elaborate detail and refute its arguments. Corn and Isikoff do mention Resolution 1441, but just barely, referring to it briefly in only two paragraphs.

In the first of these paragraphs, they fail to explain its context or to mention the fact that Resolution 1441 was a last-ditch effort to enforce the sixteen previous resolutions that had attempted to compel Saddam to observe the arms-control agreements he had signed and then violated. Nor do they examine the implications of his defiance, which had already resulted in the placement of a hundred thousand U.S. troops on the Iraqi border. Instead they argue, in their second paragraph, that Saddam's failure to comply with the December 7 deadline was unimportant, and that the Bush administration was bent on war.[10]

Similar lacunae undermine the arguments of a library of books, written for the 2006 congressional election campaign, calling for the impeachment of the president over the war. These include *The Impeachment of George W. Bush*, by former congresswoman Elizabeth Holtzman and Cynthia L. Cooper; *The Case for Impeachment*, by Dave Lindorff and Barbara Olshansky, written for the Marxist "Center for Constitutional Rights"; *U.S. v. Bush*, by former federal prosecutor Elizabeth de la Vega; and *George Bush versus the Constitution*, edited by Anita Miller, and produced by the staff of the House Judiciary Committee for its current chairman, Democrat John Conyers. In more than a thousand pages making the case against the war in Iraq, not one of these books mentions the Gulf War truce, or the systematic violation of its provisions by Saddam Hussein, or the expulsion of the UN arms inspectors in 1998, or the call for Saddam's removal by the Clinton administration because these violations were a breach of the truce. In other words, not one of them deals with the actual considerations that led to the war.

In *The Greatest Story Ever Sold*, Frank Rich does manage to discuss one related UN resolution. This was a last-minute measure, submitted by the United States *after* Resolution 1441, and less than two weeks before the onset of the war. It was submitted at the request of Prime Minister Tony Blair, who was under enormous pressure from the Labour Party's anti-war Left. The White House regarded the new resolution as redundant from a legal point of view. Its sole purpose was to reinforce the 1441 ultimatum, and provide Blair with political support.

This last-ditch resolution had to be withdrawn, however, when the French foreign minister, Dominique de Villepin, told Colin Powell that although France had voted for the original ultimatum with its implicit threat of force, it would now veto any use of force "under any circumstances."[11] In other words, France would oppose any attempt to enforce the seventeenth UN resolution, whether Saddam complied with the ultimatum or not. It was evident that Russia and China, both of which were arms suppliers to Saddam and allies that had helped him circumvent the UN sanctions, would provide vetoes as well.

Rich fails to mention any of these crucial facts, as do other critics of the president and the war generally. Instead, Rich describes the failed last-minute resolution in the following single sentence: "The next day, March 7, the United States, Britain, Spain and Bulgaria put forth a UN resolution—opposed by the major powers France, Russia, Germany and China—to give Iraq a March 17 deadline to disarm completely or go to war."[12] By neglecting to mention that these "major powers" were Saddam's arms suppliers and allies, Rich reinforced the Left's myth that the president was willfully "unilateralist," while misrepresenting what actually took place. Rich also misrepresents the UN resolution, which did not call for anything so unreasonable of Iraq as complete disarmament, but only compliance with 1441. This called for a complete *disclosure* of Saddam's holdings of weapons that had been banned by the arms-control agreements and the destruction *of these weapons.*

Rich's text then describes events that took place between March 7 and the onset of the war. According to Rich, these developments indicated that Saddam was sincerely attempting to comply with the UN demands. Moreover, in Rich's view, they also refuted the arguments Colin Powell had made to the UN on February 5. On March 7, the resolution designed to reinforce 1441 and help Tony Blair was submitted. On that day, Rich comments, UN inspector Hans Blix "said that a series of searches had found 'no evidence' of the mobile biological production facilities in Iraq that had been so highly touted by Powell in his presentation to the UN."[13]

Leaving aside the facts that the alleged production facilities were mobile, and that Iraq is a large country, and that the UN inspectors were still restricted by the Saddam government from the complete access required by the Gulf War truce and the seventeen disregarded UN resolutions, the issue raised by Rich is entirely irrelevant to the rationale for sending American troops to Iraq, which was Saddam's violation of those agreements and his continuing determination to defy them.

PROGRAMS VERSUS STOCKPILES

The same studied disregard for the central facts in the administration's case for the war is evident in all the arguments made by opponents of the war. These arguments focus on the existence of stockpiles of WMDs, the search for yellowcake uranium in the African state of Niger, and the purchase of aluminum tubes allegedly for use in building nuclear centrifuges. References to the Niger uranium deal occupy one hundred of the four hundred pages of the Isikoff and Corn book, and the aluminum-tube purchase another forty. (Niger is discussed on thirty of the three hundred–plus pages of Frank Rich's text.)

Niger and aluminum tubes were indeed cited in the administration's efforts to sell the war politically. But the administration's case for the war was something else again and did not depend on either. The administration's rationale for the war was (1) that Saddam had broken the 1991 truce and defied seventeen UN resolutions designed to prevent him from pursuing *programs* to develop weapons of mass destruction; and (2) that since Saddam had shown over a twelve-year period that he would not comply with these arms-control agreements, the only way to stop him from continuing in his defiance was to remove him from power.

To clear up the false impressions created by the propaganda and distortions of the war's opponents, it is instructive to recall some of the findings of the government task force that was sent to Iraq by President Bush after he had removed Saddam. The task force was called the Iraq Survey Group and was headed by David Kay. It was instructed by the White House not only to find Iraq's WMDs but, equally crucial, to find evidence of Saddam's programs to develop WMDs. Kay's report was made public in October 2003. No one has challenged his findings, which instead have been selectively cited or ignored.

In regard to nuclear weapons, the report could not have been clearer or more disturbing:

> With regard to Iraq's nuclear program, the testimony we have obtained from Iraqi scientists and senior government officials should clear up any doubts about whether Saddam still wanted to obtain nuclear weapons. They have told ISG [Iraq Survey Group] that Saddam Husayn remained firmly committed to acquiring nuclear weapons.[14]

Here are some other findings of the Kay report:

- "We have discovered dozens of WMD-related program activities and significant amounts of equipment that Iraq concealed from the United Nations during the inspections that began in late 2002."

- "A clandestine network of laboratories and safe houses within the Iraqi Intelligence Service that contained equipment subject to UN monitoring and suitable for continuing CBW [chemical and biological weapons] research."

- "A prison laboratory complex possibly used in human testing of BW [biological weapons] agents, that Iraqi officials working to prepare for UN inspections were explicitly ordered not to declare to the UN."

- "Reference strains of biological organisms concealed in a scientist's home, one of which can be used to produce biological weapons."

- "New research on BW-applicable agents, Brucella and Congo Crimean Hemorrhagic Fever (CCHF), and continuing work on ricin and aflatoxin were not declared to the UN."

- "Documents and equipment, hidden in scientists' homes, that would have been useful in resuming uranium enrichment by centrifuge and electromagnetic isotope separation (EMIS)."

- "Continuing covert capability to manufacture fuel propellant useful only for prohibited SCUD variant missiles, a capability that was maintained at least until the end of 2001 and that cooperating Iraqi scientists have said they were told to conceal from the UN."

- "Plans and advanced design work for new long-range missiles with ranges up to at least 1,000 km—well beyond the 150 km range limit imposed by the UN. Missiles of a 1,000 km range would have allowed Iraq to threaten targets throughout the Middle East, including Ankara, Cairo, and Abu Dhabi."

- "Clandestine attempts between late 1999 and 2002 to obtain from North Korea technology related to 1,300 km range ballistic missiles, probably the No Dong, 300 km range anti-ship cruise missiles, and other prohibited military equipment."[15]

The Kay Iraq Survey Group's findings show, beyond any reasonable doubt, that Saddam Hussein was determined to break the terms of the Gulf War truce; that, in defiance of international law, he was determined to proceed with programs to develop chemical, biological, and nuclear weapons; and that only force would stop him.

THE RATIONALE FOR THE WAR

The basic misrepresentation made by opponents of the war is to confuse the *rationale* for going to war with the *selling* of the decision to the American public. Selling any political program to an audience of hundreds of millions inevitably involves over-simplification and the use of symbolic representations in place of complex arguments and detailed historical constructions.

The distinction can be seen by recalling the role that the Japanese attack on Pearl Harbor played in America's decision to go to war in 1941. At the time, the Japanese imperialists had overrun all of Southeast Asia, and Hitler's armies had conquered all of Europe except Russia and the British isles. Yet the American public was so confirmed in its isolationism at the time that a Gallup poll conducted in April 1941 found that fully 81 percent of Americans wanted to stay out of the war.[16]

From the perspective of President Roosevelt, a decision to go to war in April 1941 (or on December 6, 1941) would have been perfectly justified. No American president could regard such aggression, by powers determined on world domination, as anything but a threat to American security. The United States could not afford to wait until the armies of the fascist Axis appeared on American soil.

In other words, the reality of the threat to the United States was clear before the Japanese sneak attack on Pearl Harbor on December 7, 1941. Roosevelt recognized it, but the American electorate did not. The attack on Pearl Harbor was a crucial event in allowing Roosevelt to *sell* the war to the isolationist American public. But it was not the reason why America needed to go to war. The rationale for going to war in 1941 was to stop the fascist military advance, and it would have been just as valid if there had been no Pearl Harbor.

All the arguments against the war in Iraq begin with the claim that since no weapons of mass destruction were found, there was no reason to go to war. In the words of former vice president Al Gore, "The first rationale presented for the war was to destroy Iraq's Weapons of Mass Destruction."[17] Behind this argument is a second, more sinister, insinuation: that for Bush the claim that there were weapons of mass destruction was merely a pretext to invade Iraq, which was something he had made up his mind to do directly following the September 11 attacks. "Not long after the attacks of 9-11," Gore explains, "President Bush made a decision to start mentioning Osama bin Laden and Saddam Hussein in the same breath, in a cynical mantra designed to fuse them together as one in the public's mind."[18] According to Gore, this was "a deliberate campaign to mislead America" in order to wage an aggressive, unnecessary war against Iraq, which only "neoconservatives" desired.[19]

The argument against the war is an accusation of criminal intent. It is a claim that the White House chose to launch a war without moral or legal justification. But this argument can be made only by ignoring the twelve years of failed diplomacy that led up to the war—that is, the inability of the UN and of both the Clinton and Bush administrations to persuade Saddam Hussein to keep his commitments in the Gulf War truce and to observe the Security Council resolutions. It was Saddam's refusal to observe the arms-control agreements designed to allow UN inspections and prevent him from *building* weapons of mass destruction that made the war necessary—not yellowcake in Niger, or aluminum tubes for centrifuges, or actual stockpiles of WMDs.

A further principle was involved: the dangerous precedent that allowing Saddam to escape these obligations would create. When the time came to prevent Iran or Syria from developing nuclear or chemical or biological weapons, there would be a counterargument provided by the failure to enforce the agreements with Iraq. Moreover, the effort to prevent other nations from developing these weapons would start on much weaker ground than an effort that began with international agreements that the regime had already signed.

The argument that America invaded Iraq on a false pretext is also refuted by the formal ultimatum Bush presented to Saddam on the eve of the war. If the president were determined on war with Iraq regardless of the facts, if it were the first agenda of the Bush administration, as the Democrats claim, then the president would not have provided Saddam with the loophole he offered on March 17, two days before U.S. forces entered the country: "It is not too late for the Iraq military to act with honor and protect your country, by permitting the peaceful entry of coalition forces to eliminate Weapons of Mass Destruction. Our forces will give Iraqi military units clear instructions on actions they can take to avoid being attacked and destroyed."[20]

This statement was accompanied by a second offer to allow Saddam and his two sons to leave the country for exile in a friendly nation such as Russia.

If Saddam had complied with this eleventh-hour request, there would not have been a war with Iraq. This is a conclusive refutation of the Democrats' case. It is proof that, while destruction of WMDs was indeed a goal of American policy, the war was triggered by Saddam Hussein's refusal to cooperate with the UN inspectors, his refusal to observe the UN resolutions, and his failure to show any readiness to comply with international law. The Bush ultimatum made it clear that the United States was prepared to deal with an Iraqi government it did not like, provided that government would observe the terms of the Gulf War truce—that is, provided it would cooperate with the international inspectors and disarmament agencies. This is the big truth, the elephant in the room that all the opponents of the decision to go to war—without exception—ignore.

The United States went to war because it had concluded that Saddam Hussein could not be trusted to observe the arms agreements embedded in the UN resolutions. Twelve years of defiance and obstruction leading up to and including the December 7 deadline had established that fact. Even then, the Bush administration was prepared to forgo war if Saddam and his sons left the country and went into exile, thus allowing the terms of the UN resolutions to be met.

The president's eve-of-war ultimatum of March 17, which is universally ignored by antiwar critics, was motivated by the administration's belief that Saddam's defiant behavior made further negotiations with him futile and regime change necessary. On March 18, Prime Minister Blair made his final statement to the House of Commons before going to war and provided a chapter-and-verse statement of this case.

Blair began by explaining the importance of the Iraq issue: "So why does it matter so much? Because the outcome of this issue will now determine more than the fate of the Iraqi regime and more than the future of the Iraqi people, for so long brutalized by Saddam. It will determine the way Britain and the world confront the central security threat of the 21st Century. . . ."[21] The threat he had in mind was the one posed by rogue states that had shown their determination to acquire weapons of mass destruction and use them.

Blair's speech continued with a capsule lesson on the history of Saddam's relations with the rest of the world, particularly with the United Nations, whose efforts to gain his compliance with the terms of the 1991 truce had failed. Saddam had been given fifteen days at the end of the Gulf War to provide a full declaration of the weapons of mass destruction he possessed. He had already used these weapons against Iran and against his own people, killing tens of thousands. The UN set up a special inspections team to verify that when Saddam made the declaration, he would be telling the truth.

As Blair explained, "The declaration when it came was false—a blanket denial of the [WMD] program, other than in a very tentative form. So the 12-year game began." The inspectors went to work, and eleven months later Iraq admitted that it indeed had WMDs when it said it had destroyed them. Iraq then provided another "full and final declaration."

But in October 1994 Iraq stopped cooperating with the UN inspectors, breaking the truce. The United States threatened military action, and the inspections resumed. In March 1995, another "full and final declaration" was made. By July, Iraq had admitted that this declaration was also false. Another "full and final declaration" was made in August. A week later, Saddam's son-in-law defected to Jordan and disclosed a crash program to produce nuclear weapons and an extensive program to weaponize various biological and chemical agents, something the Iraqis had always denied.

These developments forced Iraq to release documents that showed how extensive those programs were. In June 1996, another "full and final declaration" was made by Iraq, which also was false. Saddam now prevented the UN inspectors from visiting specific sites, a further violation of the 1991 truce. In September, Iraq made another "full and final declaration," which was also false. Now, UN inspectors discovered equipment for producing VX nerve gas. In October, the United States and Britain again threatened military action.

The obstructions continued. In February 1998 UN Secretary General Kofi Annan went on a mission to Baghdad to persuade Saddam to allow the UN inspectors to resume their job. In August Iraq stopped all cooperation, and in December the inspectors left. The inspectors' final report, in Blair's words, was "a withering indictment of Saddam's lies, deception and obstruction, with large quantities of WMD unaccounted for."

The UN inspectors were unable to return to Iraq for three years. Then, on September 11, 2001, terrorists attacked the United States. The threat posed by Saddam's determination to thwart the arms-control agreements took on a new dimension. Given the power and portability of deadly biological, chemical, and nuclear weapons—all of which Saddam had either developed or attempted to develop, and some of which he had actually deployed—the existence of a rogue regime such as Saddam's could not be tolerated. Its defiance of international order, if successful, would set a dangerous example for other rogue states, of which there were already several. Since Saddam's regime was a violator of international law and a two-time aggressor (the invasion of Kuwait had been preceded by the grueling eight-year war with Iran, which Iraq had instigated), it was also the most obvious candidate for reform.

In January 2002, President Bush identified Iraq as part of an "Axis of Evil," and began putting the Saddam regime on notice. The policy of the United States would be to see that Iraq complied with the UN resolutions and the arms-control agreements. It would do so by diplomatic means if possible but by force if necessary. In September 2002 Bush spoke to the UN and put the international body on notice that if it did not enforce its own resolutions it would become "irrelevant," and the United States would have to enforce the law itself. The White House began placing a hundred thousand U.S. troops on the Iraqi border. It was then—and only then—that Saddam signaled he would be willing to allow the UN inspectors to return.

However, it was not until months later, after the Security Council passed UN Resolution 1441, with its ultimatum to comply or else, that Saddam allowed the inspectors to return. When the December 7 deadline arrived, Saddam produced another "full and final" report that was also false.

"What is the claim of Saddam today?" Tony Blair asked the House of Commons three months after the deadline had passed. "Why exactly the same claim as before: that he has no WMD. Indeed we are asked to believe that after seven years of obstruction and non-compliance finally resulting in the inspectors leaving in 1998, seven years in which he hid his program, built it up even whilst inspection teams were in Iraq, that after they left he then voluntarily decided to do what he had consistently refused to do under coercion. When the inspectors left in 1998, they left unaccounted for: 10,000 liters of anthrax; a far reaching VX nerve agent program; up to 6,500 chemical munitions; at least 80 tons of mustard gas, possibly more than ten times that amount; unquantifiable amounts of sarin, botulinum toxin and a host of other biological poisons; an entire Scud missile program."

Summing up the situation that confronted the United States and Britain on March 18, 2003, Blair said: "We are now seriously asked to accept that in the last few years, contrary to all history, contrary to all intelligence, he decided unilaterally to destroy the weapons. Such a claim is palpably absurd." While hindsight shows that Blair should not have stressed the weapons themselves, no responsible British prime minister or American president could have rested the safety of his citizens on Saddam's words, or considered Saddam's claim adequate security for his countrymen and a reason *not* to go to war.

But this very claim is the sole and entire basis of the case against the war that took place. The claim is first that no stockpiles of WMDs existed or had been squirreled away in the territory of friendly regimes such as Syria and Russia, and second that no stockpiles meant no threat, and therefore no reason to go to war. But this begs the critical question of Saddam's intentions and demonstrated capabilities for resuming his programs to build weapons of mass destruction once the obstructionist UN inspectors were out of the way.

There is no one in a position to demonstrate that if the United States had failed to remove Saddam by force, he would not have resumed his programs to build weapons of mass destruction, or that he would not have used them. Nor can anyone seriously maintain that the United States would have been able to keep a hundred thousand war-ready troops on the Iraqi border indefinitely, at the cost of $1 billion per week, which is what the peaceful "containment" of Saddam would have required.

What then was the alternative to the use of military force against Saddam? In fact, the belief that there was no alternative is what led the Clinton administration, including Vice President Gore, to call for regime change in Iraq in 1998, and to authorize support for any group willing to accomplish this by force. That is why Democrats and Republicans alike voted to authorize the Bush administration to use force to achieve regime change; and that is why, when Saddam rejected the UN Security Council's offer of a "final opportunity" to comply with the UN resolutions, Britain and the United States decided it was time to go to war.

CRITICISMS OF THE DECISION

Are there legitimate arguments for opposing the policy that led to the war in Iraq? There may be, but to be taken seriously, such arguments would need to balance the costs of inaction, or of alternative action, with the costs incurred by the policy adopted. No Democratic politician has made a serious attempt to do so.

One line of criticism has contended that Iraq was a "distraction" from the War on Terror and that American military attentions should have focused on the al-Qaeda forces in Afghanistan. As Gore articulated this argument, "Defeating Saddam was conflated with bringing war to the terrorists, even though it really meant diverting attention and resources from those who actually attacked us."[22] Frank

Rich even warned before the war began that there would be more al-Qaeda attacks in the United States if Iraq was invaded, noting that since "major al-Qaeda attacks are planned well in advance and have historically been separated by intervals of 12 to 24 months, we will find out how much we've been distracted soon enough."[23]

As of September 2007, no such attacks had occurred. Frank Rich has not offered any second thoughts on the matter. Nor has he acknowledged that the failure of al-Qaeda to attack the American homeland during those years was more than likely, as the president has pointed out, proof that the strategy of taking the battle to the enemy camp has been effective. The White House had put the jihadists on the defensive, killed or captured many of their leaders, degraded their networks, and made the attacks that Rich warned about too difficult to carry out.

But even if the arguments about the war being a "distraction" were correct, they would be irrelevant to the question of how the administration should have dealt with an Iraqi regime that had broken the Gulf truce and systematically defied attempts to bring it into line. In short, the argument that al-Qaeda terrorists should be pursued in Afghanistan was not a response, sufficient or otherwise, to the issues posed by Saddam Hussein. If American forces were unable to fight wars on two fronts, that was an argument for increasing those forces, not for allowing Saddam to remain in power.

Twelve years of failed UN resolutions had made clear that without a military option, Saddam would soon be free to resume developing his weapons programs. One practical alternative to this prospect was the course chosen by the Bush administration, which entailed diplomatic overtures, followed by a massive military buildup on Saddam's border, followed by invasion when he refused a final ultimatum to comply. Another option—air strikes without a ground invasion—had already been tried by the Clinton administration and failed. That was why Clinton and his entire national-security team supported Bush's plan.

Instead of offering practical alternatives for dealing with the problem of Iraq, Democratic leaders have resorted to the complaint that there was no debate on the war—as though the Bush administration had kept its plans secret—and, even less plausibly, that their opposition was "silenced." In a statement on the Senate floor (cited approvingly in Al Gore's book), Senator Robert Byrd complained shortly before the war began: "This Chamber is, for the most part, silent—ominously, dreadfully silent. There is no debate, no discussion, no attempt to lay out for the nation the pros and cons of this particular war."[24]

But if there was no debate (and the claim itself is suspect) it was through no fault of the White House. In September 2002—six months before the war—the White House published a national-security White Paper laying out the reasoning behind the president's policies in the War on Terror and towards the rogue state of Iraq:

> The gravest danger our Nation faces lies at the crossroads of radicalism and technology. Our enemies have openly declared that they are seeking Weapons of Mass Destruction, and evidence indicates that they are doing so with determination. *The United States will not allow these efforts to succeed.* We will build defenses against ballistic missiles and other means of delivery. We will cooperate with other nations to deny, contain, and curtail our enemies' efforts to acquire dangerous technologies. *And, as a matter of common sense and self-defense, America will act against such emerging threats before they are fully formed.* We cannot defend America and our friends by hoping for the best. So we must be prepared to defeat our enemies' plans, using the best intelligence and proceeding with deliberation. History will judge harshly those who saw this coming danger but failed to act. In the new world we have entered, the only path to peace and security is the path of action.[25]

This was the plan for Iraq, laid out in advance of the congressional vote to authorize the use of force to remove Saddam Hussein. If Democrats had a problem with the strategy that led to war, they had a perfect opportunity to express their opposition when this document was published. They did not. On the contrary, by voting for the Authorization for the Use of Military Force against Iraq resolution the next month, they endorsed it.

Leaders of the Democrats' later campaign against the war, such as John Kerry, went on the Senate floor at the time to support it. Significantly, the Authorization for the Use of Military Force had twenty-three "whereas" clauses providing the rationale for the war. Of these only two mentioned stockpiles (as opposed to programs) of weapons of mass destruction. Fully twelve referred to UN resolutions that had been defied.[26] Thus, the failure to find weapons of mass destruction did not in any way obviate the reasons for voting in favor of the war. The argument for war was based on Saddam's determination to build such weapons, not on the assertion that he had already built them.

The reversal of their position by Democrats who voted for the authorization, at the first signs of difficulty American troops encountered in the field, is one of the most cowardly and dishonorable episodes in American political annals. In John Kerry's case it was not the first. Another Democratic claim was that the president had misled the nation into believing Saddam was an imminent threat. "There was no imminent threat," Ted Kennedy declared (echoing many other Democrats). The war, he said, had been manufactured in a Texas-based conspiracy.[27]

In fact, the president never claimed that Saddam was an imminent threat. He said precisely the opposite—that it was a matter of national security to stop him before he became one: "Some have said we must not act until the threat is imminent. Since when have terrorists and tyrants announced their intentions, politely putting us on notice before they strike? If this threat is permitted to fully and suddenly emerge, all actions, all words, and all recriminations would come too late. Trusting in the sanity and restraint of Saddam Hussein is not a strategy, and it is not an option."[28]

Most bizarrely, Democrats attacked the Bush policy on the grounds that Iraq under Saddam Hussein was no threat at all. (It was a bizarre argument because the Clinton administration had itself declared Saddam a threat that required forcible removal.) Summing up the Democrats' attacks, Al Gore wrote: "History will surely judge America's decision to invade and occupy a fragile and unstable nation that did not attack us and posed no threat to us as a decision that was not only tragic but absurd."[29]

But by Gore's logic, Afghanistan under the Taliban—a fragile and unstable nation that had not attacked us before 9-11—was not a threat either. Moreover, Gore did not attempt to explain why his own administration had conducted an air war against Saddam, firing more than four hundred cruise missiles into Iraq and dropping six hundred bombs to degrade his nuclear-, chemical-, and biological-weapons facilities, or why in February 2002 he himself had said Iraq was "a virulent threat in a class by itself," and America "must be prepared to go the limit" to stop it.[30]

THE BUSH DOCTRINE

The central point of the "Bush Doctrine," as outlined in the September 2002 White Paper, was that the twin developments of modern terrorism and modern weapons technologies made unstable totalitarian nations—such as Afghanistan, Iraq, North Korea, Libya, and Iran—threats. Indeed, it could be argued that the United States, as an open, highly developed society, dependent on vulnerable communications systems, was more fragile than the underdeveloped Third World states that posed these threats.

The threats, moreover, were being posed on a potentially ever-widening front. As Tony Blair noted in his speech on the eve of the conflict, "I know there are several countries—mostly dictatorships with highly repressive regimes—desperately trying to acquire chemical weapons, biological weapons or, in particular, nuclear weapons capability. Some of these countries are now a short time away from having a serviceable nuclear weapon. This activity is not diminishing. It is increasing."[31]

In conjunction with their dismissal of the idea that Saddam was a threat, Democrats also argued that the Iraq war was a "war of choice" and, by implication, "unnecessary."[32] But such an argument would also apply to the Civil War (since Lincoln had the choice of allowing the South to secede), and the First World War (since Germany posed no imminent threat to the United States), and the war in Bosnia (since this was a "humanitarian war" and not a matter of the national interest). Indeed, it could be said of any war short of one provoked by an invasion.

The choice to go to war in Iraq was made only because the alternative—allowing Saddam to continue as an outlaw—was unacceptable. If there was a choice, it was Saddam's. He always had the option of honoring his agreements, complying with the terms of the truce he had signed, and heeding the Security Council resolutions. In the final days before the fighting began, President Bush gave him the additional option of leaving the country. Saddam chose war. These facts render the arguments of Bush's critics hollow and—because they impugn the motives of their own country—much worse.

The Democrats' attacks have also focused on the alleged lack of connection between the regime in Iraq and the War on Terror. Al Gore has summed up the argument: "September 11 had a profound impact on all of us. But after initially responding in an entirely appropriate way, the administration began to heighten and distort public fear of terrorism to create a political case for attacking Iraq. . . . Defeating Saddam was conflated with bringing war to the terrorists, even though it really meant diverting attention and resources from those who actually attacked us."[33]

Gore's argument misunderstands the nature of the Islamic jihad against the West, as well as the realities in Iraq. The attacks of September 11 demonstrated the ability of a group of stateless terrorists to inflict massive damage on the world's greatest power, and the potential to increase that damage by incalculable degrees. What if al-Qaeda—or Hezbollah, or Hamas, or any number of other terrorist groups associated with the Islamic jihad—should acquire biological, chemical, or nuclear weapons from a rogue state such as Iraq or Iran? It was precisely this possibility that Bush had in mind when he informed the nation, in his 2002 State of the Union address, that America's "second goal," after shutting down terrorist camps, was "to prevent regimes that sponsor terror from threatening America or our friends and allies with Weapons of Mass Destruction."[34]

The president had ample reason to fear the regime of Saddam Hussein in this regard. For a dozen years, Saddam had cultivated ties to Islamic terrorism. After the Gulf War, he had the battle cry of the jihad, *Allahu Akbar* ("God is Great") placed on Iraq's national flag. He hosted one of his Popular Islamic Conferences in June 1990, as the United States began assembling the coalition that would carry out Operation Desert Storm. These gatherings of Islamic terrorists included Shi'a as well as Sunni organizations, aiming to promote their violent agendas in the Fertile Crescent.

During the Gulf War, Iraqi intelligence attempted to launch terrorist attacks against Western targets, with little success. These embarrassments taught Saddam the importance of professional expertise in the realm of terror. Accordingly, he began to position himself as protector and financier of proven Islamic terrorists. He gave sanctuary to the 1993 World Trade Center bomb maker, Abdul Rahman Yasin, as he did many others, including the notorious terrorists Abu Nidal and Abu Abbas, the mastermind of the *Achille Lauro* hijacking.[35]

Nor were Hussein's contacts believed to be entirely unrelated to "the terrorists who committed these acts" in America on 9-11.[36]

In March 2002, CIA director George Tenet told the Senate Armed Services Committee of Iraqi "contacts and linkages to the al-Qaeda organization" and even raised the concern that Iraq might have sponsored 9-11, though this hypothesis eventually went unconfirmed.[37] Numerous intelligence sources stated, and Tenet confirmed, that Sudanese terrorist Hassan al-Turabi had facilitated an entente between Osama bin Laden and the Iraqi government in the mid-1990s. Tenet wrote of additional "high-level Iraqi intelligence service contacts with bin Laden himself."[38] The Clinton administration's 1998 indictment of bin Laden for the U.S.-embassy bombings in Africa asserted, "Al-Qaeda reached an understanding with the government of Iraq that al-Qaeda would not work against that government and that on particular projects, *specifically weapons development*, al-Qaeda would work cooperatively with the government of Iraq."[39] (Emphasis added.)

U.S. Attorney Patrick Fitzgerald declared that al-Qaeda and Iraq "went from a position where they were working against each other to standing down against each other, and we understood they were going to explore the possibility of working on weapons together."[40] High-ranking al-Qaeda officials corroborated the statement that bin Laden "would work with whomever could help him, so long as al-Qaeda's independence was not threatened,"[41] and following 9-11, a parade of nearly a score of al-Qaeda terrorists—including Abu Musab al-Zarqawi, the leader of Ansar al-Islam, the seedling of al-Qaeda in Iraq—operated from Baghdad.[42]

THE MARCH TO WAR AND THE OPPOSITION

In June 2002, Bush stepped up the pressure on Saddam, who at that point was still barring the UN inspectors. In a graduation speech the president gave at West Point in June 2002, he warned, "If we wait for threats to fully materialize, we will have waited too long. . . . T]he War on Terror will not be won on the defensive. We must take the battle to the enemy, disrupt his plans, and confront the worst threats before they emerge."[43]

Following the West Point speech, the media began stirring speculation about an imminent war with Iraq. On July 5, 2002, the *New York Times* published details of a plan for a three-pronged invasion involving "up to as many as 250,000 troops."[44] Two senior fellows at the liberal Brookings Institution published an op-ed piece in the *Washington Post* warning the president against unilaterally declaring war without congressional approval, claiming that it would constitute "an unprecedented, even unconstitutional, expansion of presidential authority."[45]

On September 12, 2002, Bush went before the UN General Assembly to make his case for bringing Saddam into line: "Iraq has answered a decade of UN demands with a decade of defiance," he told the world body. The central question was: "Are Security Council resolutions to be honored and enforced, or cast aside without consequence? Will the United Nations serve the purpose of its founding, or will it be irrelevant?"[46] If the UN would not act to enforce international law, he warned, the United States would.

As Bush began to organize the international coalition that would rein in the rogue regime, the international Left began mobilizing to thwart his efforts. In October 2002, International ANSWER, a coalition formed by the pro–North Korean Workers World Party, organized a hundred thousand protesters against the Authorization for the Use of Military Force resolution.[47] Because the power behind International ANSWER was a Marxist sect that overtly supported Saddam, a second coalition, United for Peace and Justice, was created by other radicals to make the movement more palatable and provide it with a wider popular base. In January 2003, the two organizations staged the largest demonstrations since Vietnam, which were joined by the international Left. One political scientist has estimated that between January and April 2003, the effort to prevent the United States from overthrowing Saddam included more than three thousand protests worldwide, with a combined turnout of more than thirty-five million.[48]

On September 23, with the midterm congressional elections approaching, Al Gore addressed the San Francisco Commonwealth Club in a very different vein from the way he had spoken the previous spring. Now the titular head of the Democratic Party, Gore used the platform to withdraw the support he had previously given to the president on Iraq. Instead, he launched into an unprecedented partisan attack on the war policy. In typical fashion, Gore began by speculating on "the role that politics might be playing in the calculations of some in the administration," insinuating that it was the president whose motivations were partisan rather than Gore himself. Acknowledging that the UN resolutions were "completely sufficient" to warrant regime change, Gore described the president's effort in regard to Iraq as a "distraction" from the War on Terror. "I do not believe," he said, "that we should allow ourselves to be distracted from this urgent task simply because it is proving to be more difficult and lengthy than was predicted. Great nations persevere and then prevail. They do not jump from one unfinished task to another."[49]

Gore specifically condemned the Bush doctrine of pre-emption. The problem with pre-empting terrorist threats was that "if Iraq is the first point of application, it is not necessarily the last. . . . [T]he implication is that wherever the combination exists of an interest in Weapons of Mass Destruction together with an ongoing role as host to or participant in terrorist operations, the doctrine will apply." This, of course, was the *point* of the Bush Doctrine, which was to discourage nations with WMDs from harboring terrorists, sponsoring terrorism, breaking arms-control agreements, or defying international law.

Gore's attack on pre-emption was unconstrained by the considerations that normally temper the criticism of foreign policy by leaders of the opposition. He equated the Bush Doctrine with the Soviet aggression in Afghanistan: "Two decades ago," he observed, "the Soviet Union claimed the right to launch a preemptive war in Afghanistan," as though there could be any comparison between a pre-emptive war to disarm an outlaw regime and a war of aggression and conquest.

Gore extended his indictment to "the administration's attack on fundamental constitutional rights that we ought to have and do have as American citizens." This employed the extreme rhetoric of the Left, which had been claiming that the Patriot Act infringed the civil liberties of Americans and that enemy combatants who had fought for the Taliban and were incarcerated in Guantanamo were being denied their human rights. As the widely perceived leader of the Democratic Party and "rightful" president whose victory had been "stolen" by an unscrupulous usurper Gore was issuing a battle cry to the influential constituencies of the Left in the American mainstream.

Far from being an eccentric outburst, Gore's attack was one of the first signs of a deep schism in the political landscape. It was preceded by an even more vitriolic barrage from Jimmy Carter. In a September 5 op-ed piece in the *Washington Post*, the former president declared that the Bush administration's "actions are similar to those of abusive regimes that historically have been condemned by American presidents." In his best conspiratorial prose, Carter added that "belligerent and divisive voices" were determined to go to war and had diminished the opportunity for unrestricted UN inspections, "perhaps deliberately."[50]

The two Democratic leaders had introduced bitterly partisan politics into a foreign-policy debate over issues of war and peace. It was the first time this had happened since the Second World War, and it opened a Pandora's box of partisan bitterness whose malign influences would have a profound impact on America's effort in the war to come.

Lesser Democratic voices quickly rallied to the new standard— and some felt mere rhetoric insufficient. With war clouds looming, three Democratic congressmen—Jim McDermott, David Bonior, and Mike Thompson—flew to Baghdad, the capital city of the enemy, to meet with Iraqi officials and oppose their own country's policy. On September 29, they appeared via satellite link on ABC's *This Week with George Stephanopoulos.*

Bonior, a senior Democratic leader in the House, accused America of "trying to push and dictate" to the rest of the world. McDermott claimed that Tariq Aziz and other Iraqi officials "said they would allow us to go look anywhere we wanted," even though Iraq was still off-limits to the UN weapons inspectors. Then he indicated that in his view it was his own president and not the Iraqi dictator who was a liar. "I think the president would mislead the American people," McDermott told the ABC viewers. By contrast, "I think you have to take the Iraqis on their face value."[51] Summing up their effort to undermine their country's case, McDermott said, "We assert from here that we do not want the United States to wage war on any peace-loving countries. As members of Congress, we would like diplomatic efforts to continue so as not to launch any aggression."

Television commentators on the Iraq Satellite Channel explained that the congressmen would "visit hospitals to see the suffering caused by the unjust [UN] embargo." At the time, of course, the UN's Oil for Food program was providing food for every Iraqi man, woman, and child, although (as would be revealed later) the Iraqi regime had stolen billions from the effort.[52] When CNN's Jane Arraf asked McDermott whether he had not been used by the Iraq dictatorship, McDermott said, "If being used means that we're highlighting the suffering of Iraqi children, or any children, then, yes, we don't mind being used."[53]

When asked to comment on this extraordinary episode, House Minority Leader Dick Gephardt replied, "[E]very member, as I've said over and over again, has to reach their own conclusion."[54] When asked if he would "condemn" McDermott's statement, conservative

Democratic congressman Martin Frost replied tersely, "No."[55] Other Democratic leaders refused to offer an opinion. It was a signal for Democrats to begin criticizing their own country and commander-in-chief in other overseas capitals. In early October, former president Bill Clinton told a meeting of the British Labour Party, "The West has a lot to answer for in Iraq. . . . [W]e are not blameless in the misery under which [Iraqis] suffer."[56]

At this point a disturbing effort to blame Israel for American war policy—already a propaganda theme of the Iraqis and the American Left—began to spread from the fringes to the mainstream. Democratic senator Ron Wyden, himself of Jewish origin, worried about his co-religionists' pulling America into a wider war. "[W]hile I am not privy to the administration's war plans," he confessed, "I am of the belief the administration is . . . preparing for a potential enlargement of the conflict with Israel or other allies. I am concerned this issue has not been adequately addressed."

Five months later, on the eve of the war, Congressman James Moran, a Democratic regional whip, told an antiwar rally in Reston, Virginia: "If it were not for the strong support of the Jewish community for this war with Iraq, we would not be doing this." He explained that Jewish power was so immense that foreign policy could pivot on a dime, if the Jews wanted it. "The leaders of the Jewish community are influential enough that they could change the direction of where this is going, and I think they should."[57] This produced enough alarm that House Minority Leader Nancy Pelosi forced Moran to resign from his leadership position.

In fact Israel was not enthusiastic about the focus on Iraq, fearing instead the much larger Middle Eastern power, Iran, whose proxy army, Hezbollah, was situated on Israel's northern border. Former State Department planner Lawrence Wilkerson called Israel's warnings *against* the invasion of Iraq "pervasive." Israelis reportedly told Bush administration officials, "If you are going to destabilize the balance of power, do it against the main enemy," that is, Iran.[58]

Senator Edward Kennedy, who was becoming the party's chief alarmist, speculated that a war "could run through battalions a day at a time" and would look "like the last 15 minutes of the movie *Saving Private Ryan*."[59] Senator Robert Byrd worried: "What about my health insurance? What about us older folks? What about prescription drugs? You do not hear much about that now. Everything is tuned to Iraq."[60] On the eve of the war, Barack Obama, then an Illinois state senator, informed a radical antiwar rally that he was not opposed to all war: "What I am opposed to is the attempt by political hacks like Karl Rove to distract us from a rise in the uninsured, a rise in the poverty rate, a drop in the median income, to distract us from corporate scandals and a stock market that has just gone through the worst month since the Great Depression."[61]

Many on the Left had their own international policy concerns. They began warning that if pre-emption became law, there would be massive casualties around the world, inflicted, of course, by bloody-minded Americans. Senator Russ Feingold warned that the doctrine of pre-emption "could well represent a disturbing change in our overall foreign and military policy. . . . [S]uch a doctrine could trigger very dangerous actions with really very minimal justification."[62]

Democratic congressman Pete Stark was less guarded. He described an America that would "exercise brute force anywhere in the world without regard to international law or international consensus." Referring to Saddam's failed assassination attempt against the president's father, he wondered, "Is the president's need for revenge for the threat once posed to his father enough to justify the death of any American?" Then he warned: "The entire nation will pay as Bush continues to destroy civil rights, women's rights and religious freedom in a rush to phony patriotism and to courting the messianic Pharisees of the Religious Right."[63]

At this juncture in the buildup to a final confrontation with the defiant Saddam, the position of most Democrats was still substantially removed from such radical sentiments. On October 11, 2002, most Democrats in the Senate voted to authorize the president to use force against Saddam Hussein, although a majority of House Democrats voted no.

On the day of House vote, Jimmy Carter was awarded a Nobel Peace Prize. Gunnar Berge, a member of the Norwegian Nobel Committee, said Carter's selection "should be interpreted as a criticism of the line that the current administration has taken. It's a kick in the leg to all that follow the same line as the United States."[64]

Carter welcomed the opportunity to deliver a slap in the face to his president and his countrymen and to lend his support to the outlaw regime the United States was making a last-ditch effort to control. On learning of the Nobel honor, he embraced it as an occasion for another political statement. He told the listening world that he opposed any effort to "unilaterally . . . begin a conflict or war, which I think would be a direct violation of international law."[65] Far from planning to violate international law, the United States was, at the time, appealing to the UN Security Council for a resolution to enforce international law. It would be passed unanimously and give Saddam a "final opportunity" to abide by the law. In attacking his own country, Carter had stood the issue exactly on its head. In the Nobel lecture he delivered in Oslo in December, the ex-president hailed the "commitments to freedom and human rights" by "the former Soviet empire," and took a moment to warn that "preventive war may well set an example that can have catastrophic consequences."[66]

The UN Security Council had unanimously passed Resolution 1441 in November, with its ultimatum to Saddam to comply or else. Thus began the final steps towards a war that would take place when Saddam defied the resolution. On March 17, 2003, Bush gave Saddam a *final* final ultimatum to leave Iraq with his sons and avoid the necessity of war. The ultimatum was ignored. Two days later, American troops entered Iraq.

— 4 —

The War Against the War

I N EVERY PREVIOUS INTERNATIONAL CONFLICT, American soldiers went to war backed by a unified political leadership. Even
if some elected officials had opposed the war decision, once
the troops were in the battle zone, the leaders of both parties supported them. In all previous wars, America's troops could go into
battle secure in the knowledge that their country was behind them.
But in the war to remove an oppressive tyrant who had committed
two armed aggressions and murdered hundreds of thousands of his
own citizens, America's soldiers would have no such support.

With combat less than a week away, Senator Robert Byrd went
to the Senate chamber to denounce the impending conflict: "The
case that this administration tries to make to justify its fixation with
war is tainted by charges of falsified documents and circumstantial
evidence. We cannot convince the world of the necessity of this war
for one simple reason: this is not a war of necessity, but a war of
choice."[1]

On March 17, two days before the war began, Bush had given
Saddam and his two sons forty-eight hours to leave the country. If

they had complied, there would have been no war. But that same evening, Senate Minority Leader Tom Daschle told an audience of union members, "I'm saddened, saddened that this president failed so miserably at diplomacy that we're now forced to war, saddened that we have to give up one life because this president couldn't create the kind of diplomatic effort that was so critical for our country."[2] Daschle didn't bother to explain how Bush could have persuaded Saddam's allies and collaborators—France, Russia, and China—to get Saddam to comply with the UN ultimatum that they had voted for and he had defied.

The American military executed a lightning-fast liberation of Iraq, beginning with a "Shock and Awe" bombing campaign and completed in three weeks with a loss of only 139 U.S. servicemen.[3] Yet even as American soldiers were helping Iraqis pull down the statues of the dictator on April 9, House Democratic leader Nancy Pelosi was attacking its cost: "We could have probably brought down that statue for a lot less."[4] Not wishing to mislead anyone about her intentions, which were entirely political, Pelosi added, "I have absolutely no regret about my vote on [i.e., against] this war."

Meanwhile the American Left, which had mobilized to prevent the overthrow of the Saddam regime, now began a campaign against the American reconstruction effort, which it denounced as an "imperialist occupation." In July 2003, Code Pink leader Medea Benjamin and longtime Communist Party activist Leslie Cagan, head of the antiwar coalition United for Peace and Justice, traveled to Baghdad to launch what they called the Iraq Occupation Watch. It was an organization set up to conduct a propaganda campaign against the American presence and to induce U.S. soldiers to declare themselves conscientious objectors so they could leave the field of battle. The goal was to deprive the "occupation" of necessary manpower.[5]

Just before American troops entered Iraq, Saddam emptied the nation's prisons. When looting followed the chaos of war, the Western media reported that 170,000 artifacts had been stolen from the

Baghdad Museum. The figure was based on misinformation and was wildly exaggerated. In fact, the museum only housed 170,000 pieces total. In their apparent haste to report bad news from the front, some journalists had confused that figure with the number of items stolen.[6] It was only weeks later that the initial story was corrected by the facts: the museum's curators had moved the artifacts to safety vaults before the war, and only *a few dozen* items had disappeared; these may even have been stolen before the invasion.[7]

It was a small indication of what was in store. Despite the factual correction, the false story became part of the lore of the conflict and an item in the indictment of the Bush administration by its opponents. A year later, Democratic congressman Neil Abercrombie recalled on the House floor how U.S. soldiers "were unable to prevent looting, mass looting not just of the Baghdad museums, the history of the entire Middle East . . . in virtually every area of Baghdad and throughout Iraq." [8]

Abercrombie's indictment included the Left's favorite slander of the war as a sacrifice of "blood for oil." As Abercrombie put it, U.S. troops had failed to guard "hospitals, schools, businesses . . . [but] was it not interesting the Oil Ministry was guarded? And I wonder how that took place. I wonder what the emphasis was." [9]

THE WILSON AFFAIR

This was an early instance of the trope that came to dominate opposition to the American war effort—the shift of the blame for the conflict and its tragedies away from Saddam Hussein, whose defiance had made it necessary, away from the Iraqi criminals and Ba'athist fascists, away from the Fedayeen diehards and al-Qaeda jihadists who were already there or had streamed into the country from Syria, Jordan, and Iran to confront American troops.

The efforts of the Left to sabotage a war already in progress began in earnest less than a month after American troops entered the capital. It was then that the first serious accusation surfaced charging that the president had manipulated the intelligence on Saddam's weapons of mass destruction and had lied to the nation about Iraq's efforts to secure fissionable uranium in Niger. In short, that the White House had deceived the nation into war.

On May 6, 2003, *New York Times* columnist Nicholas Kristof wrote the first in a series of articles in which he alleged, on the basis of a then-anonymous government source, that the White House had lied to the nation about Iraq's efforts to secure uranium in Niger on the eve of the war. Kristof's column was followed by a front-page story in the *Washington Post*, which relied on the same anonymous source, triggering a general press frenzy over the mystery.

Less than a month after Kristof's first column appeared, the indictment became the theme of a national TV spot placed by the Democratic National Committee; it was titled "Read His Lips: President Bush Deceives the American People." The theme was taken up by the Democrats' presidential candidates, who were then engaged in a hotly contested primary fight in which the war in Iraq was a divisive issue. The charge that Bush had lied about the Niger uranium deal provided a way for those who had previously supported the war to find common ground with the party's radicals who had opposed it, and who were then being led by Vermont governor Howard Dean.

The charge and the arguments it gave rise to were grave. They attacked the very rationale for the war, implying that the decision was based on phony information and therefore groundless, and thus that the war itself was an American aggression, a violation of international law, and a war crime.

The source for Kristof's articles, and for the charges that now became the centerpiece of the Democrats' opposition to the war, was an obscure diplomat with a left-wing bent named Joseph Wilson. Kristof had referred to him as a "former U.S. ambassador to Africa who was dispatched to Niger" to check out the stories of Saddam's interest in yellowcake uranium.[10]

Significantly, Kristof had met Wilson at a meeting of the Senate Democratic Policy Committee, a committee composed of Democratic legislators whose purpose was to plan political strategy. A political activist himself, Wilson had contributed to Democratic candidates, including Al Gore, Ted Kennedy, Charles Rangel, and Barbara Mikulski.[11] In the same month that Kristof's first column appeared, Wilson took a position as a foreign-affairs adviser to John Kerry's presidential campaign.[12] None of these facts were a focus of the articles Kristof and like-minded colleagues wrote about Wilson, nor did these facts cause them to wonder about the reliability of the source, or to question his motives for discussing a classified mission with the press. Nor did these facts cause them to investigate a possible connection between Wilson's revelation and the Democrats' partisan campaign against the president.

Wilson told Kristof that he had been sent to Africa as a result of an inquiry into the Niger deal by Vice President Cheney. His mission was to investigate whether Saddam had sought fissionable uranium, as British intelligence was reporting. Wilson claimed that he had found nothing to support the British report. Far more sinister, he claimed to have seen the documents on which the intelligence about the Niger uranium deal was based, and to have recognized immediately that they were forged. Moreover, he claimed that long before the 2003 State of the Union address, he told the Bush administration that the documents were forged and the British report was false. According to Wilson, the administration ignored his report and lied to the American people to justify the war.[13] As Wilson himself put it in a *New Republic* story that appeared in June 2003 and was titled "The Selling of the Iraq War": "They knew the Niger story was a flat-out lie."[14] In October, *The Nation* magazine gave Wilson the "Ron Ridenour Award for Truth-Telling."[15]

Virtually every aspect of Wilson's accusations, however, was false. A year later, when the damage to Bush's credibility and the rationale for America's war effort was well advanced, the Senate's Select Committee on Intelligence investigated Wilson's claims and refuted them. In particular, Wilson could not have known that the documents about uranium were forgeries at the time he made his report, nor could he have described them as forgeries to the Bush administration. The reason was that the CIA had not even received the documents until eight months after Wilson's mission was completed and he had left the government's employ.

When the Senate Intelligence Committee confronted him on how he could tell the *Washington Post* he knew the "dates were wrong and the names were wrong" on documents he had never seen, Wilson sheepishly confessed he must have "misspoken." This did not prevent him from publishing a book, titled in part *The Politics of Truth: . . . Inside the Lies That Led to War . . . .* The Senate committee concluded that Wilson had provided "misleading" information to the media, which was to put it mildly.[16] The committee actually found that contrary to what Wilson claimed, his own oral report on Niger "lent more credibility" to the existence of a proposed Iraqi deal for Niger uranium. At the same time, British intelligence was standing by the Niger report. *The Butler Report*, commissioned by the British government at the same time as the Senate inquiry, stated, "We conclude also that the statement in President Bush's State of the Union Address . . . was well-founded."[17] However, neither Wilson's confession nor two governments' consensus caused any of Wilson's promoters to reconsider their support for a man who had lied in such consequential ways.

When a press leak had identified Wilson's wife, Valerie Plame, also a Democratic Party donor, as the CIA officer who recommended the anti-Bush Wilson for the Niger mission, Wilson had denied it. This denial was also exposed as a lie when the committee uncovered documents in which Plame proposed Wilson's name to her superior. It was further revealed that she had arranged a meeting to facilitate his assignment. Under oath, Plame confessed to the Senate Intelligence Committee that she privately told her husband there was "this crazy report" about Iraq trying to purchase uranium from Niger, indicating that she and her husband shaped intelligence based on their preconceived political views, the very thing they were accusing the president of doing. [18]

A year earlier, in July 2003, as an armed terrorist resistance was picking up steam in Iraq and Saddam was still unaccounted for, the Democrats' attack on the president and the war, fueled by Wilson's false claims, was in full force. Representative Henry Waxman, a member of the Democratic leadership who had voted in favor of the war, wrote a letter to the White House complaining that the Niger uranium story had been "a central part of the U.S. case against Iraq," an element that had "particularly influenced" his vote. Waxman accused President Bush of citing evidence about Niger he knew to be false, "a breach of the highest order" that represented either "knowing deception or unfathomable incompetence."[19] In fact, as the inquiries into the Wilson case made clear, if any party to the dispute over the war was operating on false intelligence, it was the Democrats themselves.

BLAME AMERICA FIRST

In July 2003, Representative Ellen Tauscher, a California Democrat who had also voted for the war, told a crowd at the University of California at Berkeley, "I believe that this administration cooked the books on the intelligence that caused us to believe that Iraq was an imminent threat." In fact, the president had said the opposite, that Iraq was *not* an imminent threat, but that America could not afford to allow Iraq to become one. But Tauscher barreled on. "This administration took part fact and part supposition—subjective information delivered to them by the intelligence community—and they shaped it to reach a preconceived conclusion for the use of force, something that they had determined to do sometime well before March of this year." She called for a congressional investigation into her charges. But, since the war had just begun, she, like Abercrombie, felt it politically prudent to say she still thought her vote for the war had been the right thing to do.[20]

One month later, former vice president Al Gore appeared before the far-Left group MoveOn.org to condemn the war he had so recently supported. "[B]y now, it is obvious to most Americans that we have had one too many wars in the Persian Gulf," he said. According to Gore, Bush had "engaged in a systematic effort to manipulate the facts in service to a totalistic ideology."[21] As Gore was well aware, "totalistic ideologies" generally refer to fascism, Nazism, and Communism.

The floodtide of indictments continued to swell. Carl Levin, the ranking Democrat on the Senate Armed Services Committee, concluded that because the president had referred to the Niger uranium deal more than once (and since Joseph Wilson had declared the claim to be an invention), its appearance in the sixteen words in the State of the Union address "makes it more than a mistake."[22] In fact, Levin knew better. The day after the State of the Union, Levin had written to CIA director George Tenet instructing him to produce "what the U.S. [intelligence community] knows about Saddam Hussein seeking significant quantities of uranium from Niger." The CIA responded on February 27, 2003, that "reporting suggest[s] Iraq had attempted to acquire uranium from Niger."[23]

This didn't prevent Bob Graham, the number-two Democrat on the Senate Intelligence Committee and a presidential candidate, from repeating Wilson's falsehoods. Said Graham, "I have to believe that the president knew or should have known that this information [about Niger uranium] had been classified as unreliable by the CIA."[24] In September, as the Democrats' attacks on the White House continued to escalate, Senator Edward Kennedy said that Operation Iraqi Freedom, as the war was officially named, "was made up in

Texas, announced in January to the Republican leadership that the war was going to take place and was going to be good politically. This whole thing was a fraud."[25]

PLAME AND KWIATOWSKI

Wilson's disinformation campaign—orchestrated at the highest levels of the Democratic Party—had done its work, persuading Democratic constituencies that the war was based on a lie. Along the way, it acquired a second plot line after Wilson's wife's identity was leaked in a column written by Robert Novak, a conservative who, like Plame and Wilson, was opposed to the war. Novak identified his anonymous source as two senior administration officials. (Later it would be revealed that the leaker was a State Department official, Richard Armitage, who also opposed the war and concealed his role in the leak while the press and the Democrats pursued the president.)[26]

On September 26, 2003, an investigation by a special prosecutor was ordered to determine the source of the leak. Over the next two weeks the *New York Times* ran more than three dozen stories on the case and the *Washington Post* more than forty.[27] Every story focused on the White House and the office of Vice President Cheney as the putatively vindictive source for the leak. The search kept the story intermittently on the front pages for more than four years, raising the same questions about whether the White House had lied to the American people and whether, therefore, the war was "unnecessary" and an American aggression. More immediately, the Plame leak allowed Democrats who had been critical of national-security measures taken after 9-11 to appear uncharacteristically concerned about security issues.

The template of the drama, which was to extend over the course of the war, was now fixed: the White House had lied about the prewar intelligence on weapons of mass destruction and had "outed" a covert CIA operative, Valerie Plame, in revenge for exposing its duplicity. Democratic House member Louise Slaughter summed up the indictment: "At its worst, treason was committed by high ranking White House officials. At its best, we have witnessed a startling abuse of power by this administration. One which has seriously compromised our National Security . . . jeopardized the war on terror . . . and placed the lives of a covert CIA operative and her contacts in danger . . . All for what so far appears to be a reprehensible act of political retribution."[28]

Joseph Wilson and Valerie Plame were not the only government insiders to provide the Left with a sharp-edged weapon against the administration and the war. Like Wilson, Karen Kwiatkowski began as an anonymous whistle-blower, blogging more than thirty articles during 2002 and 2003 under the heading "Deep Throat Returns," all attacking the president. Deep Throat claimed to be a Pentagon employee with first-hand knowledge of how a "cabal" of "neoconservatives" manipulated intelligence to push the United States into war. Typical of her writing was a column titled, "The 'No Oil Bidness Left Behind' Act." In it she claimed "a Zionist political cult has lassoed" the Pentagon in an effort to acquire Iraq's oil for Halliburton.[29] Elsewhere, she wrote of "the Likud-leaning thinktankers determined to create a new Middle East direct from the Pentagon."[30]

Kwiatkowski's theories attracted the attention of Jeffrey Steinberg, editor of the crackpot LaRouche publication *Executive Intelligence Review* (EIR), who interviewed her and distributed the interview to his network of sympathizers.[31] Following the interview, Kwiatkowski's work appeared on LewRockwell.com, a right-wing antiwar website, and then on the influential left-wing websites Huffington Post and Salon.com. By now Kwiatkowski had retired from active service and was operating under her own name. On the first anniversary of the Iraq war, speaking on the Senate floor, Kennedy cited her testimony in approving terms: "Lt. Colonel Karen Kwiatkowski, a recently retired Air Force intelligence officer who served in the Pentagon during the buildup to the war, said, 'It wasn't intelligence—it was propaganda

... they'd take a little bit of intelligence, cherry-pick it, make it sound much more exciting, usually by taking it out of context, usually by juxtaposition of two pieces of information that don't belong together."[32]

The false charges made by Plame and Kwiatkowski joined a series of left-wing canards, which included rumors that Vice President Cheney had pressured CIA analysts to twist intelligence before the war, and allegations that Under Secretary of Defense Douglas Feith had run a private pro-war intelligence service to advance a neoconservative agenda of promoting the interests of Israel. The charges were taken seriously enough by Democrats to prompt them to demand congressional investigations into pre-war intelligence, including Cheney's purported role in shaping it.

The Senate Intelligence Committee addressed these issues in the already mentioned report, which was released in the summer of 2004. The report concluded that Karen Kwiatkowski "could not provide any examples" to substantiate her allegations, "had no direct knowledge to support any claims that intelligence analysts were pressured, and much of what she said is contradicted by information from other interviews."[33] The Senate concluded there was no underlying basis for the Left's overheated and irresponsible charges that the president pressured agents or fabricated intelligence to lead the nation into war. The two main sources of the charges were found to be fabricators themselves. To borrow from Senator Kennedy, "This whole thing was a fraud." But it took a damaging toll on the president's credibility and on the public's support for the war nonetheless.

THE RADICALIZED DEMOCRATS

It was but one of many signs that extreme views were becoming integral to the Democrats' attack on the war. In December 2003, U.S. forces caught Saddam Hussein hiding in a spider hole near one of his palaces, and placed him under arrest pending trial by a democratically elected Iraqi government. After the capture, Congressman Jim McDermott, still a member of the Democratic caucus in good standing, told a Seattle radio station that the capture was staged, and that U.S. servicemen could have snared the despot "a long time ago if they wanted." Former secretary of state Madeleine Albright was soon asking *Roll Call* editor Mort Kondracke, "Do you suppose that the Bush administration has Osama bin Laden hidden away somewhere and will bring him out before the election?" Although she later claimed to be joking, Kondracke observed that "She was not smiling when she said this," a fact confirmed by others present. Kondracke surmised: "This is not some kid in sandals . . . This is the former Secretary of State. That's irrational. But they will believe anything about George Bush, the Democratic Party."[34]

The party's increasing radicalization was also marked by the success of Howard Dean in the 2004 presidential primary contest, which forced an about-face on the war by its eventual winners, Kerry and Edwards. Dean was then elected chairman of the Democratic National Committee. Dean's antiwar fervor also helped to spawn a new force in the Democratic Party, the "netroots," so called because of its organization through the Internet. The term is somewhat misleading, as it implies a populist movement, organized from the bottom up. One of its main elements, the radical group MoveOn.org, however, received its start from two dot.com millionaires and was given millions more by George Soros and his elite "shadow party" network.[35]

In February 2004, former vice president Al Gore again appeared on a MoveOn.org platform. This time he denounced Bush as a traitor, an accusation the White House had so far refrained from making against the ferocious opponents of the war both inside the Democratic Party and beyond it.

"He betrayed us!" Gore screamed at the cameras. It was a strange moment from more than one perspective, since Gore had himself advocated regime change in Iraq and the forcible toppling of Saddam

Hussein and had characterized Saddam's regime as "evil." But he was now equating such sentiments and actions with high political crimes. Gore claimed that the war had been "preordained and planned before 9-11" and decried Bush as the man responsible,[36] although his own administration had called for such action four years before.

The Democrats' presidential nomination was won by John Kerry, a man who had voted for the war but turned against it the moment it became apparent that he would lose the primary contest to Howard Dean if he did not reverse his pro-war stance. Kerry was now referring to the Iraq conflict as "the wrong war, in the wrong place, at the wrong time," a message certain to demoralize any American troops who were listening.[37]

THE ANTI-WAR MEDIA

The Left's campaign against America's war was now joined by a crucial ally: the national media. Two months after Gore's outburst, *60 Minutes* II aired a segment on the abuse of inmates in the Iraqi prison at Abu Ghraib. Although a military investigation of the incident was already in progress, CBS chose to break the story and make it an international scandal, causing major damage to America's standing abroad and enraging Muslims throughout the world. The eventual result of the coverage was to deliver a body blow to America's ability to wage the war.

The CBS broadcast featured photos of a handful of U.S. soldiers harassing prisoners, piling them into naked pyramids, forcing them to pose nude, and pointing at their genitalia. What would normally be counted as a minor incident in any war, however, was elevated to a national and then a global scandal by editors determined to exploit it without regard for its potential impact on the national interest or the security of American troops in Iraq.

Realizing that it had in its hands a powerful weapon to derail America's war effort, the antiwar media, led by the *New York Times*, first exaggerated the implications of the story and then refused to let it go. Comparing the incident to such real atrocities as My Lai and Saddam's own crimes, the *Times* ran at least one front-page story about the Abu Ghraib incident every day for thirty-two days in a row, and more than sixty days total. This set the standard for the rest of nation's press, which was accustomed to following the *Times*'s lead.[38] It was exactly the kind of psychological-warfare campaign that would normally have been conducted by an enemy propaganda machine.

On the floor of the Senate, Edward Kennedy equated American troops with Saddam's Ba'athist thugs who tortured and executed his opponents in their cells, often after forcing them to watch the rape, torment, and murder of their wives and children. What Kennedy said was: "Shamefully, we now learn that Saddam's torture chambers reopened under new management: U.S. management."[39] In one statement, the senator had confirmed the darkest intimations of the conspiratorial Islamist mind.

The day of Kennedy's speech, al-Qaeda's leader in Iraq, Abu Musab al-Zarqawi, beheaded American contractor Nicholas Berg in alleged retaliation for Abu Ghraib. At the same time, the Grand Ayatollah, Ali al-Sistani, the spiritual leader of Iraq's Shi'a majority, kept his silence, preferring American warders at Abu Ghraib to those of Saddam Hussein. The barbaric execution of Berg was put on video to demonstrate Islamic justice for the American invaders.

The anti-American outrage fanned by the Abu Ghraib photos did not cause domestic critics a moment's pause or second thoughts. Two weeks after Kennedy's speech, with the Abu Ghraib stories still front-page news, Al Gore stood before another MoveOn.org audience denouncing the prison as "an American gulag . . . Bush's gulag." What happened at Abu Ghraib, said Gore, was "not the result of random acts by 'a few bad apples'; it was the natural consequence of the Bush administration policy."[40]

If the excesses were not the actions of a few bad apples, as Gore maintained, the implication was clear. Every uniformed American soldier was under a cloud of suspicion, particularly among those international audiences ready to believe the worst about American purposes and practices. With the entire Muslim world listening, Gore added an indictment, declaring that the American military was deliberately incarcerating innocent people for its soldiers to torture: "According to the Red Cross," Gore claimed, "70 to 90 percent of the victims are totally innocent of any wrongdoing."[41]

In fact the Red Cross had made no study of American prisoners allegedly tortured. Moreover, the statement was not referring to the prisoners in Abu Ghraib. The quotation came from an anonymous source who estimated that 70 to 90 percent of those detained in Iraq"—whether for a short or a long period of time—"had been arrested by mistake."[42] To underscore the false accusations he had made against his countrymen, Gore then called for the resignations of Donald Rumsfeld, Condoleezza Rice, George Tenet, Paul Wolfowitz, Douglas J. Feith, and Under Secretary of Defense for Intelligence Stephen Cambone for their alleged offenses in regard to Abu Ghraib.

A month later, candidate John Kerry would formally take up Gore's demand for heads to roll. An Independent Panel to Review Department of Defense Detention Operations had been convened to investigate the Abu Ghraib matter. Headed by former defense secretary James Schlesinger, it issued its report in August and concluded that "No approved procedures called for or allowed the kinds of abuse that in fact occurred. There is no evidence of a policy of abuse promulgated by senior officials or military authorities."[43] In other words, Rumsfeld and other administration officials were cleared of any wrongdoing. But this did not persuade Kerry or other administration critics to suspend their attacks. Two days after the findings were released, Kerry renewed his call for Rumsfeld's resignation "for failure to do what he should have done" at Abu Ghraib.[44]

ANTI-AMERICAN PROPAGANDA

One effect of the opposition's effort to present Abu Ghraib as a symbol of American malignity was that it lent credence to anti-American propaganda efforts such as those of Michael Moore. In April 2004, Moore, a pro-Castro leftist, had publicly compared the terrorist resistance in Iraq with America's founding fathers: "The Iraqis who have risen up against the occupation are not 'insurgents' or 'terrorists' or 'The Enemy,'" Moore proclaimed; "they are the REVOLUTION, the Minutemen, and their numbers will grow—and they will win. Get it, Mr. Bush?"[45]

Moore had produced a propaganda film against the war, timed for the November election, called *Fahrenheit 9-11*. The film won a *Palme d'Or* at Cannes and an Academy Award in Hollywood, which were thinly veiled promotions for its message from communities whose politics were well to the left. At Cannes it received the longest ovation in memory. The pseudo-documentary presented Iraq as a sleepy hamlet where children and their families gamboled and flew kites in the parks before the oil-greedy Americans began raining death on them. Two months after Moore's comments declaring his own country the enemy, Democratic Party leaders flocked to the *Fahrenheit 9-11* premiere in Washington. The enthusiastic audience included Senate Majority Leader Tom Daschle, Senator Barbara Boxer, Senator Tom Harkin, and Democratic National Committee Chairman Terry McAuliffe. Harkin explained, "It's important for the American people to understand . . . what led us to this point," calling Moore's mendacious construction of events an "unvarnished presentation" of the facts.[46]

After the screening, Moore told *Time* magazine that Daschle "gave me a hug and said he felt bad and that we were all gonna fight [against the war] from now on."[47] To show his appreciation for Moore's attacks on his own country, former president Jimmy Carter invited the filmmaker to sit beside him at the Democratic National Convention in July.

Osama bin Laden was also an admirer of Michael Moore's work. Just days before the election, bin Laden released a taped message that seemed to have been cribbed from the script of Moore's film. On the tape, bin Laden discussed "the size of the contracts acquired by the shady Bush administration–linked mega-corporations, like Halliburton," which had been heavily referenced in the film. Moore had reproduced video clips of Bush reading a story about a goat to elementary-school children in Florida when news of the 9-11 attack was brought to him, implying that Bush was not up to his day job of defending the American people. Bin Laden picked up the theme and said that Bush thought "occupying himself by talking to the little girl about the goat and its butting was more important than occupying himself with the planes and their butting of the skyscrapers." Lifting a page from the "No Blood for Oil" theme of American leftists, featured in Moore's film, bin Laden said that "the darkness of the black gold blurred [Bush's] vision."[48]

Bin Laden concluded his *fatwa* with a thinly veiled threat to the American people: vote for the presidential candidate most likely to withdraw from Iraq and retreat from the War on Terror, or else. "In conclusion, I tell you in truth, that your security is not in the hands of Kerry, nor Bush, nor al-Qaeda. No. Your security is in your own hands. And every state that doesn't play with our security has automatically guaranteed its own security." Walter Cronkite found Osama's statement so overtly political that it might "tilt the election," adding, "I'm a little inclined to think that Karl Rove . . . probably set bin Laden up to this thing."[49] The speculation was all too typical of opponents of the war: the devil Bush made them do it.

Kerry lost the election, but the antiwar Left gained an institutional host in the Democratic Party. A December 9, 2004, email signed by "Eli Pariser, Justin Ruben, and the whole MoveOn PAC team" told the organization's membership: "In the last year, grass-roots contributors like us gave more than $300 million to the Kerry campaign and the DNC, and proved that the Party doesn't need corporate cash to be competitive. Now it's our Party: we bought it, we own it, and we're going to take it back."[50] The first step towards securing formal control took place with the installation of Howard Dean as head of the Democratic National Committee.

DEMOCRACY IN AMERICA AND IRAQ

Meanwhile, the president and the American military were moving forward with their agenda of stabilizing Iraq and helping its people establish democratic self-government. Simultaneously, Islamic terrorists were streaming into the country from Syria, Jordan, and Iran in a crusade to sabotage the reconstruction effort. The terrorist leader Zarqawi issued a *fatwa* declaring "a fierce war against this evil principle of democracy" and warning Iraqis who voted for the "demi-idols" running for election that they would be regarded as "infidels" and hunted down.[51]

On the Thursday before the election, Senator Kennedy gave a speech at the Johns Hopkins School of Advanced International Studies. In it he made clear that in his view the problem in Iraq was not Zarqawi but us: "We must recognize what a large and growing number of Iraqis now believe. The war in Iraq has become a war against the American occupation. . . . The U.S. military presence has become part of the problem, not part of the solution." To begin to solve this problem, he suggested that we should allow Iraqi "insurgents" a place in the new government.[52]

Despite the threats of the terrorists and the warnings of doubters that the insecure conditions in Iraq would doom the experiment, the White House pushed forward with the first truly democratic election in Iraq's history. On January 30, 2005, despite terrorist attacks, which

killed sixty Iraqis, 58 percent of the Iraqi population turned out to
vote and elected a Transitional National Assembly that would draft
a new constitution.[53]

It was a stunning victory for the anti-Saddam and anti-terror
forces both in Iraq and in Washington. Speaking on *Meet the Press*
that same day, however, defeated presidential candidate John Kerry
could not find much to praise in the result. The process, he said, had
only "a *kind* of legitimacy—I mean, it's hard to say that something is
legitimate when a whole portion of the country can't vote and doesn't
vote."[54] Kerry was referring to the fact that some Sunnis, who had
been the privileged caste under the Saddam regime, had refused to
vote. But this hardly undermined the legitimacy of an election that
turned out a higher percentage of voters than his own. Even International Occupation Watch had to note the higher-than-expected
Sunni turnout, including among residents of the most hostile city,
Fallujah.[55] Not Kerry. "No one in the United States should try to
overhype this election," he warned.[56] Kerry was seconded by Edward
Kennedy, who commented: "[W]hile the elections are a step forward,
they are not a cure for the growing violence and resentment of the
perception of an American occupation."[57]

Others, too, found the positive result disturbing. California Democrat Lynn Woolsey said on the House floor, "The U.S. military
presence in Iraq is nothing short of stifling to the prospect of
democracy. How can democracy possibly take root if forced upon
the Iraqi people by the barrel of a gun?"[58] But if the election was
under the barrel of a gun, that particular gun was held by Zarqawi and
his al-Qaeda fighters, not the United States. Moreover, Woolsey had
a "gun" of her own. Ignoring the expressed will of the Iraqi people,
Woolsey introduced a plan for immediately withdrawing American
troops and, with them, any hope of support for Iraqi democracy.
Woolsey's plan was supported by twenty-four other Democrats. A
similar plan was submitted by Massachusetts congressman Martin

Meehan, who called for the withdrawal of tens of thousands of troops immediately after the election, and all troops by January 2006.[59]

For Democrats the elections in Iraq were a distraction from their war against the war. Thus the Democrats' new leader in the Senate, Minority Leader Harry Reid, demanded that the Bush administration immediately make public an exit strategy, while taunting the president to "come clean" with the American people, evidently by admitting that he had manipulated intelligence to involve Americans in an unnecessary war.[60]

Weeks later, the investigation of the intelligence rumors that had been demanded by the Democrats came to an end, and concluded that there was no such manipulation. This was the report of the Silberman-Robb Commission, co-chaired by former senator and liberal Democrat Chuck Robb and Republican judge Laurence Silberman. Their investigation found that no pressure had been put on intelligence officials by Vice President Cheney or the Bush administration in order to produce a desired result. CIA analysts, hampered by the lack of agents in the field, had merely misread the facts in regard to Iraq's weapons programs. "These errors stem from poor tradecraft and poor management," the report stated. "The Commission found no evidence of political pressure to influence the Intelligence Community's pre-war assessments of Iraq's weapons programs."[61]

CIVIL RIGHTS FOR TERRORISTS

Abu Ghraib was not the only American prison targeted by the Left in its efforts to make America the guilty party in the War on Terror. Directly after 9-11, attorney Michael Ratner began an effort to organize lawyers behind a campaign to defend the terrorists detained in Guantanamo, with the political objective of demonizing the government that had put them there. Ratner, who is president of the Center for Constitutional Rights, later recalled: "I became involved back in November 2001. The president had just issued a military order saying he had the power to indefinitely detain any non-citizen who he believed was involved in international terrorism. The idea that you could pick up people anywhere in the world and hold them forever without a trial is outrageous. We at [the Center for Constitutional Rights] decided that we would represent the first people who were detained under that military order. . . . Once we won in the Supreme Court case [*Rasul v. Bush*], we got authorizations from family members to represent about 100 detainees."[62]

Ratner then organized teams of attorneys from prestigious Wall Street and Washington law firms to sue on behalf of the detainees, and he coordinated their efforts. The firms, with large resources to devote to the effort, included Wilmer, Cutler, Pickering, Hale & Dorr; Clifford Chance; Covington & Burling; Dorsey & Whitney; and Allen & Overy.[63]

Ratner himself was a veteran leftist. He was the former head of the National Lawyers Guild, an old Soviet front, and he had been active in the solidarity campaigns with Communist guerrillas in Central America during the Cold War. The Center for Constitutional Rights is a radical group that has represented Fidel Castro, the terrorist organization Hamas, and Omar Abdel Rahman, the blind sheikh who organized the World Trade Center bombing in 1993. Attorney Lynne Stewart—a protégé of William Kunstler, who founded the Center for Constitutional Rights—was convicted of providing material aid to the blind sheikh in a federal court.[64]

In addition to defending Stewart's actions both before and after her conviction, Ratner has condemned the Patriot Act, profiling techniques, the establishment of the Department of Homeland Security, the granting of greater surveillance powers to the FBI and CIA, and the war against the Taliban in Afghanistan.[65] His efforts have succeeded in freeing more than a dozen Guantanamo detainees, many of whom returned immediately to the field of battle, rejoining their terrorist comrades.[66]

With the help of media allies such as the *New York Times*, and cooperative Democrats in Congress, Ratner's campaign is one of the most successful efforts to open up a domestic front against the War on Terror, conducted by political means. Ratner's campaign has led to multiple legal defeats for the United States government in court. The alleged abuses that Ratner's attorneys have unearthed have been the focus of major news features condemning the Guantanamo procedures, and causing further damage to America's image abroad.

Since the Bush administration was unwilling to pay the political costs of ignoring the attacks, one result of the campaign has been that Guantanamo's inmates are among the best treated prisoners anywhere. They are provided with Korans in thirteen languages, prayer rugs and beads, hot meals that observe Islamic dietary laws, and prayers broadcast five times daily over the prison public-address system.[67]

One surprisingly effective method of interrogation that is still permitted apparently consists in feeding detainees doughnuts while women in long dresses attend to them and provide a sympathetic ear.[68] The detainees are allowed to eat as much as they want; some are reportedly eating four thousand calories a day, and one terrorist has nearly doubled his weight. The government also provides inmates exercise equipment to keep in shape, but apparently this inmate took insufficient advantage of the stationary bikes.[69] Aside from the holy text they believe commands them to kill Americans, the terrorists can avail themselves of the Harry Potter books and Agatha Christie detective stories in a library soon to rival those of many small American communities. "We want to have 20,000 books within the next five years," a prison librarian told the *Washington Times*, adding that many detainees have become avid fans of the Potter series. "We've got a few who are kind of hooked on it," she added. "A couple have asked if they can see the movie."[70] According to a separate report, inmates caught passing secret messages in the books, attempting to start a riot, will lose their library privileges for one week.[71]

Despite no evidence to support the claim, the International Committee of the Red Cross has called the treatment terrorists receive at Guantanamo "tantamount to torture" (note the slippery qualification).[72] The left-wing organization Amnesty International referred to the detention facility as "the gulag of our time,"[73] likening it to the infamous Siberian concentration camps described by Alexander Solzhenitsyn. Another left-wing group, Human Rights Watch, repeated these claims verbatim.[74] Its U.S. Advocacy Director, Wendy Patten, called Guantanamo "the Bermuda Triangle of human rights."

Following the lead of these leftist rights groups, Dick Durbin— the second highest-ranking Democrat in the Senate—read a list of unsubstantiated reports of atrocities (many of them subsequently refuted) on the Senate floor. Durbin compared American officials at Guantanamo Bay to "Nazis, Soviets in their gulags or some mad regime—Pol Pot or others—who have no concern for human beings."[75] Senator Durbin did not know or did not care that the al-Qaeda handbook instructs its detainees to invent stories of torture and abuse, and that by repeating their lies he was helping to spread terrorist propaganda around the world. All the wildly exaggerated statements of the anti-Guantanamo activists were breathlessly repeated to the Arab world by Al Jazeera television, confirming the jihadists and their sympathizers in the belief that America was indeed "the Great Satan."[76]

Meanwhile, twelve official investigations of Guantanamo, which took place within a span of fifteen months, turned up no evidence of the extreme abuses claimed by the critics. In July 2005, for example, Lt. Gen. Randall Schmidt and Brig. Gen. John Furlow testified before the Senate Armed Services Committee that "No torture occurred." Their testimony mirrored the conclusions of a 2004 investigation, which declared that Guantanamo's interrogation model "does not lead to detainee abuse" and "is a model that should be considered for use in other interrogation operations in the global War on Terror."[77]

Secretary of Defense Donald Rumsfeld was found to have authorized the use of "extreme" methods for exactly one detainee: Mohammed al-Qahtani, the "twentieth hijacker." Interrogators called the would-be mass murderer a homosexual, subjected him to strip searches, and forced him to wear a bra and dance with another man. He also had to bark like a dog and hear GIs impugn the virtue of his female relatives. Rumsfeld authorized the tactics after al-Qahtani resisted all other methods of interrogation.

The new methods proved successful. Schmidt testified that under this duress al-Qahtani broke his silence and "proved to have intimate knowledge of [terrorists'] future plans," providing "extremely valuable intelligence."[78] The news media reported that interrogators also subjected the mastermind of the 9-11 attacks, Khalid Sheikh Mohammed, to "waterboarding," which resulted in notable success.[79] A year later, the Senate passed an amendment sponsored by Senator John McCain that banned some of the techniques by which interrogators elicited this "extremely valuable intelligence."[80]

Speaking for the more moderate anti-administration forces, former president Bill Clinton declared that Guantanamo "either needs to be closed down or cleaned up. It's time that there are no more stories coming out of there about people being abused. . . . I think sooner or later you've got to move or let them go . . . it is just inimical to a free society."[81] Speaking for the consensus, former president Jimmy Carter and 2008 presidential hopeful Senator Joe Biden called for shutting down the Guantanamo prison immediately. [82]

These demands overlooked the character of the Guantanamo captives and the dangers they posed. A study published by the Combating Terrorism Center at West Point in 2007, and ignored by virtually all media outlets except the *Washington Times*, concluded that "between 73 and 95 percent of the Guantanamo Bay prisoners represented a threat to U.S. forces; they include veterans of terrorist training camps, al-Qaeda fighters and men who have experience with explosives, rocket-propelled grenades and sniper rifles."[83]

Writing in the *Wall Street Journal*, two former Justice Department officials warned:

> The most important cost of closing Guantanamo would be strategic. From the start of the conflict, al-Qaeda's strategy for victory had been to take maximum advantage of Western sensibilities and institutions, including public opinion and legal rules which limit what states can do in their own defense. The Bush administration had attempted to minimize the impact of this strategy by adopting a wartime legal paradigm and declaring a war against terror. This made it possible to use the authority and prerogatives of the United States military, rather than simply relying on American law-enforcement resources against al-Qaeda and its allies. Detaining captured al-Qaeda and Taliban operatives as enemy combatants at Guantanamo Bay was, and remains, a central aspect of that policy and there is little doubt that abandoning it will be seen by al-Qaeda as a failure of American nerve and a vindication of their strategic vision. Closing Guantanamo would also be a victory for al-Qaeda because the other alternatives for detaining captured jihadists give terrorists a legal advantage. The status quo is the best option we have.[84]

COLLATERAL DAMAGE

Playing on Americans' concern about civil liberties and sympathy for the underdog, even the terrorist underdog, is only one of the tactics the Left has deployed in its campaign to undermine America's war in Iraq. Playing on America's sympathies for those who bear the burdens of the war, particularly children, is another. Thus, shortly after the Gulf War truce, Saddam's regime had begun a propaganda campaign claiming that the United Nations and the United States were responsible for the deaths of five hundred thousand Iraqi children as the result of economic sanctions they had imposed.

The UN had instituted these sanctions after Saddam's aggression in the Gulf was thwarted and his regime refused to comply with the arms-control agreements that were part of the truce. To protect Iraq's civilian population from the hardships that sanctions would impose, the UN offered the regime an "Oil for Food" program, which would allow Iraq to sell oil in exchange for food and medical supplies. Saddam rejected the proposal and launched the propaganda campaign instead.[85]

Seeing an opportunity to discredit the allied cause, American radicals began an anti-sanctions movement based squarely on the Iraqi regime's propaganda. The founder of the movement was Texas journalism professor and jihadist sympathizer Robert Jensen, who claimed that "each month 5,000 to 6,000 children die because of the sanctions." Another radical group, the Center for Economic and Social Rights, made a "fact-finding" tour of Iraq, courtesy of the Iraqi regime. The tour was filmed, courtesy of *60 Minutes* and its correspondent Lesley Stahl, who was a willing accessory to the scheme. When the tour was concluded, Stahl confronted then UN Ambassador Madeleine Albright: "We have heard that a half million children have died. I mean that's more children than died in Hiroshima. And—and, you know is the price worth it?"[86]

The actual facts were quite different. In March 1997, six years after the sanctions were put in place, Saddam finally agreed to the "Oil for Food" program, through which the UN offered to provide every man, woman, and child in Iraq with twenty-four hundred calories a day. Not surprisingly the institution of the new program caused no let-up in the Left's attacks on the United Nations and the United States. In 1999, Jensen and his three major colleagues in the anti-sanctions movement—Noam Chomsky, Howard Zinn, and Edward Said—issued a joint statement, which ignored the fact that the United States and the United Nations were providing billions in food for the Iraqi population. Instead, the four men blithely condemned the situation in Iraq as "sanctioned mass murder that is nearing Holocaust proportions."[87] Five years later, it was revealed that Saddam, abetted by corrupt UN officials, including Kofi Annan's son, had misappropriated an estimated $21 billion of the proceeds, in what is undoubtedly the largest theft on record.[88]

In the months after Saddam's regime fell, antiwar activists mounted a similar propaganda attack, with the same massively inflated statistics of civilian deaths. This time the deaths were attributed to allegedly indiscriminate American bombing, or deliberate raids on civilians. Just before the 2004 election, an epidemiologist named Les Roberts provided the statistical basis for the claim that more than a hundred thousand civilians had been killed as the result of "collateral damage" in the war, more than ten times the generally accepted figure.[89]

This claim was useful in "balancing" the three hundred thousand innocent civilians that Saddam had murdered and buried in mass graves, thus creating the impression that the solution to the Saddam problem was a greater evil than the problem itself. It was an impression that Roberts explicitly endorsed: "The bottom line is that by any measure the death rate after the invasion was far higher than the death rate before. Most of the deaths were violent and most of those deaths were caused by Coalition forces."[90] Ironically, Roberts's inflated estimates were challenged by an antiwar group called the Iraq Body Count project. The project issued a report in the summer of 2005 that put the figure at only eight thousand civilian deaths since the start of the war, or one-twelfth of Roberts's total. Of these, Iraq Body Count held the U.S. military responsible for only 3.8 percent of the casualties, or as many deaths in almost two years as Saddam had averaged in ten days.[91]

On the eve of the 2006 midterm elections, Roberts released a new study claiming that coalition forces had killed 650,000 civilians, or more than 450 civilians every day of the war.[92] Roberts's partisan motivations were by now in the open, as a result of his unsuccessful effort that year to become the Democratic Party's candidate for a seat in the House from the 24th District of New York. Roberts ran on a platform that called for an American withdrawal "on a short timetable."[93]

Osama bin Laden was impressed enough with Roberts's statistics that he cited them in one of his taped *fatwas*, observing that "American statistics speak of the killing of more than 650,000 of the people of Iraq as a result of the war and its consequences."[94] Once again, however, the Iraq Body Count project came out with figures that discredited Roberts's report. The project issued a series of "Reality Checks," which dismissed the report's conclusions as "extreme and improbable."[95] Nearly a year later, the Iraq Body Count estimates amounted to barely one-tenth of Roberts's claims.[96]

Radicals undertook to highlight the allegedly wanton destructiveness of the American war effort by sending missions to Iraq to repair the damage they accused U.S. forces of causing. In July 2003, Medea Benjamin had traveled to Baghdad for the purpose of opening an office of Iraq Occupation Watch. In December 2004, another Benjamin operation, Code Pink, delivered $600,000 in cash and medical supplies to the residents of Fallujah, which journalist Bob Woodward described in his book on the war as "terrorism central."[97]

Half −a million of these dollars came from Operation USA and the Middle East Children's Alliance, one of whose founding organizers was Yasser Arafat's brother Fathi.[98]

Commenting on these activities, Benjamin said, "I don't know of any other case in history in which the parents of fallen soldiers collected medicine . . . for the families of the 'other side.'"[99] That was probably because, in most other wars, parties to the conflict generally did not tolerate activists such as Benjamin committed to their own country's defeat. During the Cold War, American leftists did collect money and medical supplies for the Communist enemy in Vietnam and for Communist guerrillas in El Salvador. One of Benjamin's Code Pink colleagues, Sand Brim, had recruited a surgeon to operate on the hand of Salvadoran Communist leader Nidia Diaz, who claimed to have killed four Marines. Antiwar activist and *M*A*S*H* star Mike Farrell assisted in the surgery.[100]

In the case of the visit to Fallujah, how did such a collection of radicals gain passage through a war zone to deliver supplies to a terrorist stronghold? One of the participants, Fernando Suarez del Solar, told an interviewer, "I have a letter from Congressman Henry Waxman to the consular officer for Jordan, Daniel Goodspeed, in support of the mission. He also sent a letter to military commanders in Iraq saying we won't go into dangerous areas, only refugee camps."[101]

MOTHER SHEEHAN

Another opportunity to manipulate the heartstrings of American compassion presented itself in the person of Cindy Sheehan. Sheehan's son Casey had been killed in Iraq, and she had decided to hold a "peace" vigil outside President Bush's ranch in Crawford, Texas. The Left, aided by a compliant media, instantly deified her and made her an icon of the hopes for peace and for shaking off the unbearable burdens of war. The *New York Times*'s Maureen Dowd wrote that as a grieving mother, Sheehan possessed "absolute" moral authority.[102] Code Pink leader Medea Benjamin became her handler. The Daily Kos website said activists should always refer to her as "Mother Sheehan."[103] Forty congressmen signed a letter encouraging the president to meet with her.

Responding to these pressures, Bush dispatched National Security Adviser Steve Hadley and Deputy White House Chief of Staff Joe Hagin to speak with Sheehan for forty-five minutes, to no avail. Former Howard Dean campaign strategist Joe Trippi joined California Democratic Party fundraiser and Code Pink organizer Jodie Evans to produce a webcast from Crawford featuring a call from Illinois Democratic congresswoman Jan Schakowsky, who called in to express her solidarity with Cindy.[104]

Then, as with Wilson, Plame, and Kwiatkowski, Mother Sheehan's true colors began to show. A year prior to her political coming out, she had met with Bush and chosen not to raise any political issues. In fact, she had glowing words to say about the president and their meeting at the time. But now, under the influence of Medea Benjamin and her comrades, Sheehan began accusing the president of murdering her son Casey. In fact, Casey had volunteered not for one but for two tours of duty, the second after the Iraq war was already in progress. He also had volunteered for the mission in which he was killed, against the advice of his sergeant. The mission was to rescue his comrades who were under attack.[105] Instead of honoring her son's courage and paying tribute to him as a hero despite their political differences, Mother Sheehan chose to exploit and abuse his memory, falsely presenting him as an unwitting pawn in the president's evil scheme to colonize Iraq.

Sheehan soon was referring to the terrorists as "freedom fighters," saying that "America has been killing people on this continent . . . since it was started," and sounding just like the leftist Medea Benjamin had trained. "This country is not worth dying for," Mother Sheehan declared, calling the president a "lying bastard" and "the biggest terrorist in the world." According to Sheehan, who picked up the latest conspiracy theory from the political circles around Benjamin, "9-11 was their Pearl Harbor to get their neocon agenda through."[106] Her son Casey, she wrote, echoing the Left's anti-Semitic prejudices, "was killed for lies and for a . . . Neo-Con agenda to benefit Israel." When this comment drew a critical blast, she attempted to lie about writing it.[107]

Even after Sheehan had exposed herself, Democrat Lynn Woolsey provided her with the rare privilege of being a guest of Congress at the 2006 State of the Union address. The House gallery is not large, and every member of Congress is provided with exactly two tickets for the event, with the second ticket usually going to a spouse. Woolsey gave her spare ticket to Sheehan, who used it to stage a one-woman protest against the president, and was arrested by Capitol police. When asked why she had facilitated Sheehan's protest, Woolsey claimed she "didn't see [the invitation] as a political statement at all."[108]

THE CALL FOR WITHDRAWL

One of the subjects of the president's State of the Union address that evening was a second remarkable outpouring by Iraqi citizens, who had defied terrorist violence in October 2005 to vote for a new constitution. More than 60 percent of Iraq's voters had dipped their fingers in purple ink to cast their ballots.[109] The provisional government had even offered thirteen thousand prisoners, including Saddam Hussein, the right to vote. To permit them to accept the offer, the U.S. military, whom the terrorists and the Sheehan Left were portraying as brutal "occupiers," set up voting booths in the "gulag" of Abu Ghraib.[110] In a remarkable display of unity, 79 percent of Iraqis, including inhabitants of most of the Sunni-dominated provinces, voted their approval of the document.[111]

Nonetheless, the eve of the vote provided Senator Kennedy with yet another opportunity to attack the president, this time for not spelling out an exit plan. He claimed that the scheduled vote "pushed victory further from our reach."[112] Kennedy was not alone in defining American withdrawal—i.e., defeat—as victory. Just before the election, the United States intercepted a letter written to the terrorist leader Zarqawi by the number-two figure in al-Qaeda, Ayman al-Zawahiri. The letter contained the terrorists' four-point plan for the Middle East, and beyond:

> The first stage: Expel the Americans from Iraq.
>
> The second stage: Establish an Islamic authority or amirate, then develop it and support it until it achieves the level of a caliphate—over as much territory as you can to spread its power in Iraq . . .
>
> The third stage: Extend the jihad wave to the secular countries neighboring Iraq.
>
> The fourth stage: It may coincide with what came before [stage three]: the clash with Israel, because Israel was established only to challenge any new Islamic entity.[113]

Zawahiri informed his ally Zarqawi that his organization had to begin planning immediately because "things may develop faster than we imagine." What he was referring to was the prospect of the "victory" Kennedy was contemplating, which the terrorist leader correctly saw as a victory *for them*: "The aftermath of the collapse of American power in Vietnam—and how they ran and left their agents—is noteworthy. Because of that, we must be ready starting now, before events overtake us . . . We must take the initiative and impose a *fait accompli* upon our enemies, instead of the enemy imposing one on us."[114]

Meanwhile, the Democratic Party's left wing was working hard to ensure that there would be no possibility of the United States imposing anything on the al-Qaeda warriors in Iraq. It was nearly a year since Woolsey had introduced her bill for a unilateral American withdrawal. In June 2005, forty members of the House—including Maxine Waters, Barbara Lee, Dennis Kucinich, Charlie Rangel, James Moran, Jan Schakowsky, and John Conyers—had formed the "Out-of-Iraq Congressional Caucus" to remove U.S. troops from Iraq and Afghanistan, regardless of the consequences.[115]

In November 2005 Jack Murtha, a former Marine and a House leader, introduced a plan to "redeploy" (the term was itself a political stratagem) all U.S. troops out of Iraq within six months. Murtha suggested that the Armed Forces redeploy "to Okinawa," which is forty-two hundred nautical miles from Baghdad, about six times the distance an F-16 can fly without re-fueling.[116] This would effectively remove American forces from the Middle East, the heartland of Islamic terrorism. Notwithstanding this reality, Murtha attempted to reassure skeptics, saying "you know, our fighters can fly from Okinawa very quickly."[117]

Such an illogical policy would have been dismissed if it had come from anyone other than a military veteran. Recognizing this, Minority Leader Nancy Pelosi and other backers decided to let Murtha take the heat. As *Newsweek*'s Howard Fineman reported, the plan was that "Pelosi and the other liberals would keep their distance, while their own Marine charged up the Hill."[118] Just as they had trusted in presidential candidate John Kerry's military service to shield the party from charges it was weak on defense, so they hoped Murtha's status as a "war hero" and a "hawk" on defense issues would inoculate them as they pushed for unilateral surrender, even as the citizens of Iraq were defying death to ratify a constitution.

The irony was that, as a politician, Murtha had another war record—as a cut-and-run activist. Murtha had indeed voted for the war before it started. But his support was short-lived. Only six months after it began, he had already declared the war "unwinnable." This made it difficult to claim that events two years later had turned him into a dove.[119] Just days after the death of al-Zarqawi in June 2006—a death that would not have taken place had the Murtha plan been adopted—Murtha told Tim Russert: "If you're not winning, [then] you're losing, and that's what's happening. . . . [A]t some point you got to reassess it like Reagan did in Beirut, like Clinton did in Somalia, you just have to say, 'OK, it's time to change direction.'"[120]

Murtha's choice of historical precedents was unfortunate. Osama bin Laden had cited each of these foreign-policy reversals as indications that America lacked the will to fight a real war and was therefore doomed in its conflict with Islam. For Osama bin Laden, America's unwillingness to stay the course was an encouragement to attack. Murtha had, in fact, supported both the surrenders mentioned above, following his mentor, longtime House Speaker Tip O'Neill. In 1967, before the Tet Offensive, O'Neill told President Johnson that Vietnam was lost.[121] Twenty-six years later, after American Rangers had been massacred in Mogadishu, Murtha told the *Today* show, "Our welcome has been worn out. There's no military solution."[122] A month later, he assured the *Pittsburgh Post-Gazette* that he could not "see any achievable goal or national security interest in this operation."[123] In his June 2006 *Meet the Press* appearance, Murtha recalled that "When we went to Beirut, I said to President Reagan, 'Get out.'"[124] It's one thing to be wrong, even consistently wrong; it's another to have learned nothing from events or from the reading of those events by America's enemies. Yet when the Democrats took control of the House after the 2006 elections, Murtha was the new Speaker's personal candidate for Majority Leader.[125]

"TREASONGATE"

Meanwhile, the Joseph Wilson–Niger uranium case was gaining new life. After a two-year investigation of the Valerie Plame leak, Special Prosecutor Patrick Fitzgerald indicted Vice President Cheney's top aide, Lewis Libby.[126] Libby had not leaked Plame's identity, but in answering prosecutors' questions, he had perjured himself.

When the dust began to clear, however, following years of media-fueled speculation that a vindictive White House had planted the Plame leak as a revenge whose intent was to intimidate others, the leaker turned out to be neither a neoconservative nor a supporter of the Bush war strategy, but Deputy Secretary of State Richard Armitage, a Bush critic. Armitage and journalist Robert Novak had concealed this information while the investigations went on, allowing the speculation to metastasize and further undermine the president's ability to wage the war. In other words, the entire affair was concocted out of whole cloth by opponents of the war. Fitzgerald never indicted Armitage or anyone else for the "crime" of leaking Plame's identity, much less for manipulating intelligence to begin a war.

The fact that Libby was innocent of the leak, and that the White House was therefore also innocent of seeking to punish Plame's husband for making false accusations about the Niger case, failed to dissuade Senate Minority Leader Harry Reid from attempting to reinvigorate the same charges. Invoking a rarely used Senate provision, he closed the Senate doors in order to discuss classified "national security" issues, specifically, how—in his words—"The Libby indictment provides a window into what this is really about: How the administration manufactured and manipulated intelligence in order to sell the war in Iraq, and attempted to destroy those who dared to challenge its actions. As a result of its improper conduct, a cloud now hangs over this administration."[127]

Ignoring the results of the investigations that had refuted these charges and put a damaging taint on the American mission in Iraq, Reid claimed yet again that Bush had "consistently and repeatedly manipulated the facts" before the war.[128] Senator Dick Durbin seconded Reid's corrosive claim. Without any supporting evidence other than the irrelevant Plame case and the false Wilson accusations, Durbin declared, "Intelligence information was distorted, was misused, and we have seen as late as last week the lengths [to] which this administration has gone to try to silence and discredit their critics of the misuse of this intelligence information."[129]

WHAT THEY KNEW AND WHEN THEY KNEW IT

Five months later, in April 2006, the Bush administration declassified portions of the "key findings" of the National Intelligence Estimate that had been submitted by Clinton appointee George Tenet to provide the rationale for the war in Iraq. The idea of publishing the information was to persuade the Democrats to desist from continuing their defamatory campaign, which had shredded America's image abroad and undermined its morale at home. By publishing the classified intelligence reports on which the war was based, the administration hoped to lay to rest the issue of why America had gone to war.

The hope was futile. Instead of diminishing the attacks, the release of the findings merely provided another occasion for the Democrats to repeat them on even flimsier grounds.

Among the conclusions to be found in the report—which had been submitted in support of the vote to authorize the use of force in Iraq in October 2002, and which had been provided by the White House to every member of the Senate, Democrats included—were the following:

- We judge that Iraq has continued its Weapons of Mass Destruction (WMD) programs in defiance of UN resolutions and restrictions. Baghdad has chemical and biological weapons as well as missiles with ranges in excess of UN restrictions; if left unchecked it probably will have a nuclear weapon during this decade . . .

- We have solid reporting of senior level contacts between al-Qaeda and Iraq going back a decade . . .

- Since Operation Enduring Freedom, we have solid evidence of the presence in Iraq of al-Qaeda members, including some that have been in Baghdad . . .

- We have credible reporting that al-Qaeda leaders sought contacts in Iraq who could help them acquire WMD capabilities. The report also stated that Iraq has provided training to al-Qaeda members in the areas of poisons and gases and making conventional bombs.[130]

Since it was the intelligence community and not the White House that produced this report, it should have been obvious to every Democratic leader, that Bush had neither manufactured nor manipulated the intelligence on which a reasonable decision to go to war was based. With the release of the report, it could be said that if there were large untruths that had been told about the war—untruths, for example, defaming the president and damaging the security of the American people—it was the Democrats who had told them.

When the findings were published, however, the Democrats ignored their contents and went back on the attack. Far from expressing their own chagrin or second thoughts, they reacted with a familiar *faux* outrage that once again the president had disrespected America's security concerns. Majority Leader Pelosi was shocked, *shocked*, that the president would declassify classified information: "I served for 13 years on the House intelligence committee, and I know intelligence must never be classified or declassified for political purposes. One of the constants in the Bush administration's miserable record on Iraq has been the manipulation of intelligence precisely for political purposes."[131] In other words, the publication of a report that showed that the Bush administration had *not* manipulated intelligence was presented as proof that it had.

Although the National Intelligence Estimate obviously did not mention Valerie Plame, the Democrats deliberately conflated the two anyway. "Two and a half years ago, President Bush . . . said he'd fire whoever leaked classified information," declared an indignant Senator Kerry (Bush had pledged to fire anyone who *broke the law* in the Valerie Plame case); "and now we know the president himself authorized it [i.e., the "leak" of the intelligence report]. Now we know that the president's search for the leaker needs to go no further than a mirror." [132] Kerry went on to imply that Bush should resign over the controversy.

Invoking the Plame affair only because it seemed politically clever to do so, Senator Chuck Schumer detected conspiracies behind the administration's declassification of the intelligence report. "The more we hear, the more it is clear this goes beyond Scooter Libby," Schumer declared. "At the very least, President Bush and Vice President Cheney should fully inform the American people of any role in allowing classified information to be leaked."[133] Democratic National Committee Chairman Howard Dean concluded the president "can no longer be trusted to keep America safe."[134] Senator Dick Durbin called for disciplinary action: "The president and the vice president must be held accountable. Accountable for misleading the American people, accountable for the disclosure of classified material for political purposes. It is as serious as it gets in this democracy."[135]

Summing it all up, the new Democratic chairman of the House Judiciary Committee, John Conyers, held *faux* impeachment hearings, calling Bush's presidency "Treasongate."[136]

DESTROYING AMERICA'S SECURITY PROGRAMS

The Democrats demonstrated just how seriously they took the actual leaking of classified information when the *New York Times* and the *Washington Post* decided to publish information about the government's top-secret anti-terrorism programs. The entire left side of the political spectrum supported the leaks, even though the leakers had violated the espionage laws (as, of course, the president had not), destroying vital national-security programs in the process (as the president had not).

The first leak came in November 2005, when Dana Priest of the *Washington Post* revealed the existence of CIA "black sites" in the Middle East and Eastern Europe. Priest reported that the CIA had engaged in "rendition" with a number of countries, including the Kingdom of Jordan. This was the practice of sending suspected terrorists overseas, where they could be questioned more harshly than in the United States. It was in itself an indication that coercive methods were effective, unless one believed that American officials supporting the program were simply sadists.[137]

Exactly one week after the *Post* disclosed the program's existence, al-Qaeda launched terrorist attacks in Jordan, killing more than fifty people in coordinated bombings of Western hotels. The victims included Syrian-born American citizen Moustapha Akkad, the producer of the *Halloween* horror movies as well as a film about the life of Mohammad.[138]

The CIA identified the leaker as Mary McCarthy, a senior CIA policy adviser who had served on President Clinton's National Security Council. Both she and her husband had given the maximum legal campaign contribution to John Kerry, and also gave money to the Democratic Party of Ohio and other Democratic candidates.[139] Despite the grave consequences of her leak and the fact that she had violated the espionage laws, McCarthy was never prosecuted. Perhaps government officials were fearful of the political repercussions such a "partisan" act might have in the atmosphere of division and recrimination that prevailed; perhaps they were daunted by the difficulties they would face in convicting anyone on such serious charges when half the political establishment was cheering her on.

The political Left responded to these events with bristling outrage, but not towards the leaker whose political zeal had led to the murder of innocent people, or towards her abettors in the press. Instead, their indignation was directed at the Bush administration for pursuing policies designed to prevent such leaks and the murders they led to. Perhaps forgetting that the captives in the program that McCarthy had exposed were *terrorists*, Massachusetts Democrat Ed Markey scorched the nation's security establishment, saying that the American government "kidnaps innocent people around the world, tortures detainees in secret prisons, and then constructs cynical legal arguments to cover it all up."[140]

Following his outburst, Markey introduced legislation co-sponsored by seventy-seven Democrats titled "Torture Outsourcing Prevention Act," which was designed to stop the practice of rendition.[141] Senator Bob Menendez, Democrat of New Jersey, used the occasion of this leak, which had led directly to the deaths of fifty innocent people in the Middle East, as an opportunity to say someone should be fired—over the Valerie Plame affair.[142]

A few days later, undoubtedly encouraged by the public reaction to the McCarthy leak, the *Los Angeles Times* published a leak of its own. The *Times* exposed the fact that the U.S. government was attempting to conduct its own propaganda war in Iraq. As the *Times* story revealed, the U.S. government was using the Lincoln Group, a private public-relations firm, to place stories favorable to the American war effort in the Iraqi media.[143] It was something that Iran was already doing, and a common practice in war, but in the eyes of the *Times* it was interfering with the freedom of the Iraqi press. After all, America had to maintain a higher standard, even in regard to war propaganda, than its enemies.

The *Times* leak led to the termination of the program, depriving American troops of valuable support on the battlefront. This produced no regret among those who had come to regard their own government as the threat. In Senator Kennedy's view, the Iraqi

program "speaks volumes about the president's credibility gap. If
Americans were truly welcomed in Iraq as liberators, we wouldn't
have to doctor the news for the Iraqi people."[144] But there was no
indication that any information had been "doctored." And conducting propaganda operations is standard practice for any nation at
war, including America. During World War II the Office of Facts
and Figures, and later the Office of War Information, published
mountains of propaganda in support of the war effort at home and
abroad. In the interests of victory—something that was obviously not
on Senator Kennedy's mind—broadcasting legends Walter Cronkite
and Eric Sevareid submitted their reporting to routine censorship
by the military, while the novelist John Steinbeck, who contributed
to the war effort, censored himself.[145]

There was little need to invent good news in Iraq at the time
of the leak. The *Times*'s disclosure appeared in November 2005, just
after the Iraqi vote for a new constitution. In December, Iraqis voted
again—their third vote in a year—to elect the 275 members of the
new parliament (25 percent of whom were required by law to be
women).

Previously, the Left had voiced skepticism about Iraq's elections
because of the decision of the Sunni minority not to participate,
although some Sunnis inevitably did. By the December vote, this
situation had changed dramatically. This time the Sunnis participated
in significant numbers, embracing the new democratic order. *New
York Times* reporter John Burns reported "a new willingness [among
the Sunnis] to distance themselves from the insurgency, an absence
of hostility for Americans, a casual contempt for Saddam Hussein, a
yearning for Sunnis to find a place for themselves in the post-Hus-
sein Iraq."[146] Sunni militants went into local neighborhoods to
encourage their co-religionists to vote. The Iraqi "Islamic Army,"
which was an anti-American Sunni militia group, safeguarded the
polls in Ramadi, as a result of which Sunni turnout in Ramadi
increased 4,000 percent over the October referendum.[147] Polls

stayed open an extra hour to accommodate the long lines, which included some 80 percent of the population of Saddam Hussein's home province.[148] In the former terrorist stronghold of Fallujah 70 percent of the populace cast ballots. Mayor Dari Abdul Hadi Zubaie said, "Right now, the city is experiencing a democratic celebration." He compared the municipal euphoria to the Arab world's most joyful celebration, a wedding.[149] Equally heartening, Iraqi troops "took the lead" in keeping the peace.[150]

Unimpressed as usual by American success, congressional Democrats responded to these developments by stepping up their calls for withdrawal from Iraq. Conscious that this meant withdrawing American support from a fledgling democracy and turning a blind eye towards the clearly expressed aspirations of the Iraqi people, the Democrats presented their proposed retreat as a reward for a job well done. At a press conference, House Minority Leader Nancy Pelosi said, "I think the Iraqi people are ready and willing now to take matters into their own hands."[151] Hillary Clinton wrote to her constituents, "the December 15th elections . . . should, if successful, allow us to start bringing home our troops in the coming year."[152] Senator Kennedy concurred: "If America wants a new Iraqi government to succeed, we need to let Iraqis take responsibility for their own future."[153] Speaking for the party's left-wing, Representative Louise Slaughter observed that the problem was the Americans, not the jihadists. "Our forces are drawing fire, not suppressing it," she said. "Their presence on foreign soil is serving as a catalyst for all those who wish to do us, and Iraq, harm." Slaughter decried "shameful acts of torture," which she alleged were committed by American troops, and dismissed any potential critics of retreat as "name-calling, sand-throwing bullies."[154]

Republicans responded with a resolution condemning withdrawal as "fundamentally inconsistent with achieving victory" and promising that American troops would remain on the battlefield "until Iraqi forces can stand up so our forces can stand down [but] no longer than is required for that purpose." Without a hint of irony, a spokes-person for Nancy Pelosi described the resolution as "playing politics with the Iraq war."[155]

The day after the House vote, the *New York Times* ran a front-page story leaking classified information about yet another national-security program. What the *Times* described as a "domestic wiretapping program" had been instituted immediately after 9-11. It allowed the National Security Agency to listen to phone calls between previously identified foreign terrorists and their contacts in the United States without obtaining a warrant in advance.[156] The *Times*'s leak about the program alerted the terrorists to its existence, ensuring that they would find other ways to communicate with their agents in the United States and plan their war against its citizens.

Both the White House and congressional leaders had pleaded with the editors of the *Times* not to run the story by its reporter James Risen, but their pleas fell on deaf ears. The *Times* merely delayed the article to make its appearance coincide with the publication of Risen's book, *State of War: The Secret History of the CIA and the Bush Administration*. Risen was rewarded by the academic Left for his breach of national security with a Pulitzer Prize.

Legislation to reauthorize the Patriot Act, which was pending be-fore the Senate the weekend the *Times* chose to publish Risen's story, stalled over the controversy. This pleased Senate Minority Leader Harry Reid, who exulted, prematurely, "We killed the Patriot Act!"[157] Senator Barbara Boxer thought the president should be impeached and asked four presidential scholars to submit their opinions "as soon as possible" as to whether the exposed NSA program would justify such a move.[158] Representative Jim McDermott hailed the breach of security that destroyed the wiretapping program—along with the previous leak about the rendition of prisoners— for "breaking through the administration's secrecy." In McDermott's view, "the president and his administration [were] doing everything possible to impose censorship."[159] Of course, there was no censorship, since Democrats on the congressional intelligence committees had been briefed about the program, and not even classified information could be kept secret. Moreover, it was a peculiar complaint on its face, since "wartime censorship" was so accepted a practice as to be a cliché.

Edward Markey, the ranking Democrat on the House Telecommunications and Internet Subcommittee, took a different tack: "We have reached a privacy crisis," he said. "The NSA stands for 'Now Spying on Americans.'"[160] This barb disregarded the fact that the program was specifically designed to spy on terrorists who had been identified as such through telephone numbers on the captured computers of al-Qaeda operatives and agents of similar organizations, and also the fact that at least one of the parties being wiretapped had to be located overseas.

Senator Robert Byrd introduced a bill to establish a commission that would investigate the now-crippled surveillance program. In his words, the investigation "will lift the fog of secrecy and clandestine government activity misaimed at law-abiding citizens."[161] How a citizen taking an international call from a previously identified member of a terrorist organization would qualify as "law-abiding," the senator didn't explain.

As though conscious that a line had been crossed when classified programs designed to protect Americans from enemy attacks were sabotaged by the nation's media, the Democrats sought to appear extra patriotic in defending the betrayal. In a Martin Luther King Day speech at Constitution Hall, former vice president Al Gore rose "to sound an alarm . . . in demanding that our Constitution be defended and preserved" from a government program that "seemed so clearly to violate the Bill of Rights."[162]

Notwithstanding Gore's concern, most legal experts agreed that the president had the inherent constitutional authority to wiretap terrorists and other enemy combatants during a time of war. Gore conveniently failed to mention his own administration's Echelon program, which intercepted a massive number of phone calls, not between known terrorists and their American contacts, but between American citizens, including the late senator Strom Thurmond.[163] Instead, in honor of Martin Luther King Day, he now called for civil disobedience against the government's anti-terrorism program, urging telecommunications companies to "immediately cease and desist their complicity in this apparently illegal invasion of the privacy of American citizens."[164]

Gore made additional unwarranted charges, claiming that the president had pressured the CIA to break the law and that he had authorized the brutal murder of captured enemy soldiers. "Over 100 captives have reportedly died while being tortured by Executive Branch interrogators," he claimed, "and many more have been broken and humiliated." The real fact, which Gore grossly distorted, was that 108 prisoners had *died* while in U.S. custody, hardly the same thing as being tortured to death or murdered. Homicides and abuses, not unusual on the battlefields of war, accounted for only a quarter of the 108 cases.[165]

In four years, on two fronts—Afghanistan and Iraq—the United States had captured sixty-five thousand prisoners. Of these, twenty-seven were victims of abuse or homicide, or 0.04 percent.[166] None of the twenty-seven cases had been authorized by President Bush or by any U.S. agency, as Gore irresponsibly claimed. The government had already prosecuted or punished most of the perpetrators, reflecting the very opposite of the impression Gore sought to create in his zeal to condemn his own countrymen. Gore's slander of American servicemen was an eerie echo of the unfounded charges John Kerry had made on returning from the Vietnam War thirty-five years earlier.

Six months after the wiretapping leak, another classified government security program was exposed on the front pages of three of the nation's leading newspapers, the *Los Angeles Times*, the *Wall Street Journal*, and the *New York Times*. All three detailed the workings of the secret Terrorist Finance Tracking Program, which allowed Treasury agents to trace the bank transactions of terrorist groups through private international financial institutions. Once again the public disclosure of the information destroyed the program by alerting the terrorists to its existence.

The Terrorist Finance Tracking Program had been established by President Bush within two weeks of 9-11. As per standard operating procedures, the White House had briefed both Democrats and Republicans on the House and Senate intelligence committees about the existence of the program. Officials who knew about the program said it tightly circumscribed the information available for government scrutiny, which is why there were no objections from the bipartisan congressional committees that reviewed it. As White House spokesman Tony Snow explained, "If you're not a member of al-Qaeda . . . you're safe."[167] In short, the security breach by the press in the name of constitutional order was completely unwarranted.

Republican congressman Peter King of New York was incensed by the leak and its brazen promotion by the three papers, which coordinated its release. He called on the Bush administration to prosecute the editors of the *New York Times*.[168] The White House, however, failed once again to enforce the law. A week later, the Republican House passed a measure that "condemns the unauthorized disclosure of classified information" and "expects the cooperation of all news media organizations in protecting the lives of Americans." During debate on the bill, Congresswoman Maxine Waters rose to defend those who had breached American security and broken the espionage statutes. She identified the government as the true culprit: "I think this government is spinning out of control. The government is violating the United States Constitution and federal law in the name of fighting terrorism."[169] The Republicans' resolution passed on a nearly party-line vote, 227 to 183, with more than 100 Democrats voting no.[170]

PREPARING FOR RETREAT

The Democrats' assault on the American mission in Iraq was ratcheted up as the November 2006 mid-term elections approached. In May, Congressman Murtha held a press conference to announce that U.S. Marines in Haditha had "killed innocent civilians in cold blood." An investigation was already ongoing, but Murtha's agenda—to discredit the American presence in Iraq—was apparently more pressing than traditional considerations of due process, or of showing loyalty to the men who had served their country by providing them with the benefit of the doubt. In his rush to judgment, Murtha claimed to have inside sources who assured him the military would conclude that the Marines had ruthlessly executed twenty-four innocent Iraqis. (Such sources constituted another form of political leakers whose purpose was to undermine the war effort.) "There was no firefight," Murtha told the press; "there was no IED [improvised explosive device] that killed these innocent people. Our troops overreacted because of the pressure on them."[171] Like other domestically generated propaganda against the American war effort, Murtha's irresponsible attack on his own country's troops reverberated throughout the Arab world.[172]

Four Marines had indeed been charged with "unpremeditated murder." But investigators quickly became suspicious when relatives would not allow doctors to autopsy the bodies, while the house where the alleged murders had taken place had been freshly repaired and painted.[173] Defense attorneys claimed photographs of the scene revealed that the curtains and walls were riddled with bullet holes, indicating that a firefight had taken place. As the evidence built up, the government's case against its own troops began to collapse. A year later, the government dismissed charges against one defendant in exchange for his testimony. In June 2007, one of the hearing officers, Lt. Col. Paul Ware, told the prosecution, "The account you want me to believe does not support unpremeditated murder. Your theories don't match the reason you say we should go to trial."[174] Then on August 9, the military dismissed charges against another of the Marines, Lance Cpl. Justin Sharratt.[175] In dismissing the charges, Lt. Gen. James Mattis went further, pronouncing the twenty-two-year-old Sharratt "innocent."[176] In short, to advance his political agendas, Murtha had slandered at least two (and perhaps more) U.S. Marines, claiming they had wantonly killed Iraqi women and children.[177]

The U.S. military in Iraq pressed on, despite the attacks from the rear. In June 2006, American troops killed the terrorist leader Abu Musab al-Zarqawi. Had the president followed Murtha's advice for immediate withdrawal, Zarqawi would still be alive, directing terrorists on the ground, and not merely in Iraq. European investigators found that Zarqawi had built a terrorist network on the continent, recruiting European extremists. One of these, a Belgian woman, blew herself up while attacking Americans in Iraq.[178]

But most immediately, Zarqawi's death deprived al-Qaeda of its leader in Iraq. John Kerry greeted the news of Zarqawi's death by calling again for an American withdrawal. "With the end of al-Zarqawi and the confirmation of the final vital cabinet ministries in Iraq's new government, it's another sign that it's time for Iraqis to stand up for Iraq, bring the factions together, end the insurgency, and run their own country," he said. "It's time to work with the new Iraqi government to bring our combat troops home by the end of this year."[179] The "end of this year" was just six months away, meaning the withdrawal would have to begin immediately.

As the midterm elections in America approached, the radical activists who believed they now "owned" the Democratic Party disowned anyone who did not toe their line. Hillary Clinton addressed their "Take Back America" conference and told the attendees, "There must be a plan that will begin to bring our troops home."[180] But this was not enough for a group of Code Pink protesters, who booed Clinton loudly because she opposed setting "a date certain" for withdrawal. The radicals mounted a successful primary campaign to defeat

Senator Joe Lieberman in Connecticut, because he had remained consistent in his support for the war. Lieberman was challenged in the Democratic primary by left-wing neophyte Ned Lamont.[181] Lamont had the backing of the "netroots" organized by MoveOn.org, and won the primary. Lieberman refused to concede defeat and ran as an independent in the general election. In this race Lamont had the backing of Hillary Clinton, who gave him $5,000 from her political-action committee, HILLPAC, and loaned him one of her senior strategists, Howard Wolfson. Wolfson told the press, "It's vitally important that we elect a Democrat to that seat."[182] The people of Connecticut thought differently, and Lieberman won.

While room for supporters of the war in the Democratic Party was diminishing, the reverse was true for those who opposed it, no matter how extreme. A Daily Kos blogger, and self-described poet and "Mayanist," Jeeni Criscenzo, ran as a Democratic candidate for Congress in the mid-term elections. She traveled to Iraq in August 2006, under the auspices of Code Pink, to meet with anti-American politicians there, some of whom had endorsed killing Americans. The Code Pink group met with Sheikh Ahmad al-Kubaysi, a Baghdad-based figure who said of the terrorists, "These young men who came here from other Muslim countries to defend Iraq are very brave. They left their homes and comfortable lives to protect fellow Muslims. That is the most important form of *jihad*. These *mujahideen* are guaranteed Paradise."[183] Kubaysi's group, the Association for Muslim Studies, reportedly had given $50 million to Shi'ite terrorist Muqtada al-Sadr.[184]

The Iraq National Dialogue Front served as Code Pink's prime Iraqi sponsor during the Criscenzo trip. Its leader, Saleh al-Mutlaq, complained that "biased people are trying to shuffle cards to brand as terrorists the honorable national resistance movements."[185] Before the end of the trip, the leftists and the terrorists coalesced on a message for the American government: Get out but leave your wallet behind. Code Pink elaborated: "The common thread among this diverse group of Iraqis and Americans was a desire to set a timetable for the withdrawal of U.S. troops, ensure no permanent bases in Iraq, and secure a U.S. commitment to pay for rebuilding Iraq."[186]

Congressional candidate Criscenzo blogged upon her return: "If justice is to ever come to the people of Iraq, the people we call insurgents will have to be recognized as the ones who are actually defending their homeland."[187] She added, "Some of the things I heard in the past few days made me sick and ashamed of my country." Criscenzo suggested that "the United States was deliberately instigating the conflicts so they would have an excuse to stay," and would continue torturing "tens of thousands" of Iraqis.[188] Before and after the trip, Criscenzo was endorsed by such Democratic Party heavyweights as Senator Barbara Boxer, former senator Max Cleland, Congresswoman Maxine Waters, Congressman Bob Filner, and California's lieutenant governor, treasurer, and attorney general, plus at least three state senators.[189] Mercifully, Criscenzo lost the election.

Not all the party's 2006 candidates had gravitated to the far Left. Democratic Party chairman Howard Dean, the netroots' favorite, was determined to recruit candidates who could win outside the progressive enclaves. Among them were soon-to-be senators Jim Webb of Virginia and Jon Tester of Montana. Tennessee Senate candidate Harold Ford Jr., who failed to win election, called himself "a Jesus-loving, gun-supporting believer that families should come first, that taxes should be lower and America should be strong."[190] Harry Mitchell defeated Republican congressman J. D. Hayworth of Arizona by running to his right on illegal immigration, no small feat. The Democrats had another factor working for them: a variety of scandals, both real and imagined, that plagued the Republican Party. A key issue dispiriting the Republican base was the failure of the White House to secure America's borders, a concern heightened by the ongoing War on Terror.

In November, three million fewer Republicans voted than in the previous midterm election, and the party lost.[191] For the first time in twelve years, Democrats took control of both houses of Congress. As 2006 drew to a close, Jack Murtha, who was slated to become the new House majority leader, pronounced the U.S. Army "broken"[192] and declared, "This war cannot be won militarily."[193] The new Senate majority leader, Harry Reid, steeled his party's resolve by instituting conference calls with the radical netroots "to discuss party strategy."[194] Among those consulted was Markos Moulitsas Zúniga, founder of Daily Kos, who had said of four American contractors murdered in Fallujah, "I feel nothing over the death of mercenaries . . . Screw them."[195] Democratic Party chairman Howard Dean told a radio audience in Texas that the "idea that we're going to win the war in Iraq is an idea which is just plain wrong."[196] A contemporary poll showed that 59 percent of Democrats agreed.[197] The same poll also showed that 69 percent of Democrats believed Iraqis could not defeat the terrorists without American help, and 46 percent thought Iraq would be "worse off if U.S. troops left." But a majority still wanted the troops withdrawn.[198]

DILEMMAS OF POWER

Once in office, the Democrats were forced to confront their new reality. Until now, they had been able to attack the war without having to own the consequences of their policy. If they contributed to the war's going badly, the Republican White House and Congress would still be blamed for the results. But now, if they did not act on their proposals to end the war, there was no one to hold accountable but themselves. Since they had the power, they could not avoid the responsibility for exercising it. On the other hand, if they cut off funding for the war and a bloodbath ensued, they would have to live with the results. The one factor that alleviated their dilemma was that they did not have the votes to override a presidential veto.

The first leadership battle brought these issues to the surface. The new Speaker, Nancy Pelosi, had handpicked Jack Murtha to fill the majority-leader post. But when the caucus voted, House Democrats selected the more moderate Steny Hoyer of Maryland, handing Pelosi and Murtha a resounding defeat. Pelosi retaliated by taking Murtha into her inner circle and freezing out Hoyer, a gesture designed to mollify her radical constituencies, who were determined to bring the war to an end.

Moving beyond the symbolic resolutions that had expressed their antiwar sentiment to date, Pelosi and Murtha devised a "slow-bleed strategy," hoping to pass rules that would prevent units from being deployed to Iraq unless they met unreachable levels of training and "readiness."[199] Murtha was not coy about the intentions of the plan: "They won't have the equipment, they don't have the training, and they won't be able to do the work."[200] A majority of Democrats in both houses was now ready to approve a war-funding bill that set a timetable for withdrawal. In April, Harry Reid, who had once pledged, at a politically opportune juncture, never to "limit funding or cut off funds" for the troops, joined Russ Feingold in offering legislation to eliminate all war funding within a year.[201]

"Redeployment" could have begun as early as July 1, regardless of conditions on the ground or the unlikelihood of avoiding a catastrophic defeat. Senior Democratic congressman Howard Berman called it "an entirely incoherent bill. They have a provision to set goals, but there's no follow-up to see whether we've met them." Thus, regardless of success or failure on the ground, "we withdraw either way."[202] All freshman Democrats, including those who had run on platforms opposing precipitate withdrawal, voted for the bill.[203] Bush responded with only the second veto of his presidency.[204]

The serious nature of the Democrats' threat brought a sharp response from Vice President Cheney. Commenting on the Pelosi-Murtha plan to place crippling restrictions on the funding request for an additional $93 billion for the Iraq war, Cheney told ABC News: "I think if we were to do what Speaker Pelosi and Congressman Murtha are suggesting, all we will do is validate the al-Qaeda strategy. The al-Qaeda strategy is to break the will of the American people . . . try to persuade us to throw in the towel and come home, and then they win because we quit."[205] The Democrats were outraged. Pelosi phoned the president to complain about Cheney's remarks: "You cannot say as the president of the United States, 'I welcome disagreement in a time of war,' and then have the vice president of the United States go out of the country and mischaracterize a position of the Speaker of the House and in a manner that says that person in that position of authority is acting against the national security of our country."[206] On the other hand, if the Speaker is sponsoring legislation to cut off funding for the troops in the middle of a war, what was a vice president who believed the war was necessary to protect American security supposed to say?

Bush had recently appointed Lt. Gen. David H. Petraeus to be the new commander in Iraq. Petraeus was authorized to preside over a strategy that the White House described as a "new way forward in Iraq." It called for coalition forces to partner with Iraqis to "protect the population," target al-Qaeda forces that were fomenting sectarian violence, "take more vigorous action against death squad networks," and provide the security necessary for political reconciliation among Iraq's rival Sunni and Shi'a factions.[207] A "surge" of 21,500 new troops into Iraq was to be a key component of this strategy, precisely the force that Pelosi and Murtha had sought to abort.

The surge force was designed to spearhead an effort to secure Baghdad, a city of six million people, and also to pacify Anbar province, an al-Qaeda stronghold.[208] In previous campaigns in Najaf, Sadr City, and Baghdad, understaffed U.S. forces had cleared a region of terrorists, only to withdraw and see them re-enter.[209] The new plan was designed to give the coalition enough manpower to hold the ground it had won. Reinforcements would gradually enter Iraq starting in January 2007 until the surge reached its full strength on June 15. Military spokesman Lt. Col. Christopher Garver estimated it would take thirty to sixty days after all units were in place before they would be sufficiently acclimated to the environment. This meant the surge would not be at full strength until mid-August.[210]

Not a single congressman of either party voted against Petraeus's confirmation. On both sides of the aisle there were glowing endorsements. Senator Hillary Clinton said, "I want the very best leadership for the young men and women who are going to be put in harm's way to implement this strategy, and I have no doubt General Petraeus is the person to try to pull this off."[211] Senate Armed Services Committee chairman Carl Levin, a harsh critic of the war, said, "General Petraeus is well-qualified for this command, widely recognized for the depth and breadth of his education, training and operational experience."[212] Months after the confirmation, Harry Reid said, "He's the man on the ground there now. . . . I stick with General Petraeus."[213]

From the moment the new troops arrived in Iraq, the sectarian violence that had erupted with the bombing of the Golden Mosque in February 2006 began to diminish. After the first month, Maj. Gen. William Caldwell reported that "there has been an over 50 percent reduction in murders and executions," and the number of civilian deaths declined from 1,440 to 265.[214] There had been a dramatic reduction of Shi'ite death squads, the arrest of seven hundred guerrilla leaders aligned with Shi'ite fanatic Muqtada al-Sadr, and the detention of more than a thousand more.[215] Sadr quietly ordered his Mahdi Army to cooperate.[216]

Yet before all the assigned troops had reached the field, and against all evidence on the ground, the Democrats' congressional leaders, Reid and Pelosi, were already declaring the surge a failure. "This war is lost, and this surge is not accomplishing anything," Reid told the nation on April 19.[217] When asked how he could make such a judgment in advance of the facts, Reid explained that he felt no remorse in announcing defeat: "[M]y conscience is great," he said.[218] On June 13, as the surge forces were reaching their full complement, Reid and Pelosi co-signed a letter to the White House. "As many had foreseen," they wrote, "the escalation has failed to produce the intended results." Instead of the surge policy, they recommended a "phased redeployment of our troops from Iraq so that Iraqis could take responsibility for their own security." At the same time, they claimed that "after years of effort," Iraqi forces remained "uneven in their quality and reliability."[219] In other words they were conceding that a bloodbath was possible, but apparently the prospect didn't bother them.

The surge continued. By August, major terrorist attacks had fallen by 50 percent. In July alone, General Petraeus reported, hundreds of al-Qaeda leaders had been captured or killed.[220] The insurgent Mahdi Army announced "a total suspension" of activities for the next several months, while some twenty-five thousand Sunnis re-aligned themselves *against* al-Qaeda. A U.S. military commander called the situation on the ground "a tectonic shift."[221] In an article in the New York Times, two liberal critics of the war noted that "the Sunni sheikhs [in Anbar] are close to crippling al-Qaeda and its Salafist allies." The title of their piece reflected their reassessment: "A War We Just Might Win."[222]

Mindful that an American victory in Iraq might increase the prospects of a Republican victory in the next presidential election, Democrats refused to be impressed. Only one antiwar Democrat changed his position on the surge. In 2002, Congressman Brian Baird had voted against the war, and as of early 2007 he still described the invasion as one of "the largest foreign policy mistakes in the history of our nation." However, a trip to Iraq in August 2007 convinced him that U.S. soldiers needed to stay there until at least early 2009. Whatever one's view of going to war, he said, "we're on the ground now. We have a responsibility to the Iraqi people and a strategic interest in making this work."[223]

He might have added that America's leaders—Democrats as well as Republicans—had a parallel responsibility to the American people: to defeat the jihadists and their enablers, Syria and Iran, on the battlefields of Iraq. But Baird was virtually alone among Democrats in acknowledging American successes. Only Senator Joseph Lieberman, no longer a member of the Democratic Party, whole-heartedly embraced the American cause in Iraq.

"GENERAL BETRAY US"

General Petraeus was scheduled to give his first progress report in September 2007, even though the surge had been at full strength for only a month. Unwilling to wait for the results, the Left launched a pre-emptive strike in an attempt to discredit him. The day Petraeus was scheduled to testify, MoveOn.org took out a full-page ad in the *New York Times*. The ad was headlined "General Petraeus or General Betray Us?" It was accompanied by an equally unsubtle subhead: "Cooking the Books for the White House?"[224]

The only difference between this attack on the commander of American forces in Iraq and the attacks on the president that had been ongoing since the summer of 2003 was that Petraeus was not even given a chance to speak his piece before his integrity and truthfulness were questioned. Unlike the president, Petraeus is not a politician. He is a public servant responsible to both parties, who was putting his own life and that of his military son on the line to protect his fellow citizens, including those at MoveOn.org. That this made no difference to radicals was no surprise. But it was a sign of how far things had gone that none of the Democratic leaders who had confirmed Petraeus's appointment and spoken so highly of him during his confirmation hearings were willing to condemn the ad as a slur on an American war hero and a disservice to his troops in the field.[225]

Petraeus's two-day testimony coincided with the sixth anniversary of the attacks of 9-11. In his report, the general presented a guardedly optimistic picture of events on the ground. Sectarian violence still took place at "disturbing levels," he noted; "al-Qaeda and its affiliates in Iraq remain dangerous," and the political situation is "sometimes downright frustrating." Notwithstanding these cautions, "the military objectives of the surge are, in large measure, being met"; sectarian killings were down "substantially," and the new way forward had produced "significant change," denying al-Qaeda a new base of operations.[226]

Petraeus told the legislators that some U.S. troops could begin returning home by year's end. However, he also warned that "a rapid withdrawal would result in the further release of the strong centrifugal forces in Iraq and produce a number of dangerous results," including the collapse of local security forces, "al-Qaeda [in] Iraq regaining lost ground and freedom [to] maneuver," and a stronger alliance between Iraqi Shi'ites and Iran. He presented hard data to support all his claims and vouched that the testimony he offered was his own, saying that it had "not been cleared by, nor shared with, anyone in the Pentagon, the White House, or Congress."While congressional Democrats kept a prudent distance from the "Betray Us" ad, without actually condemning it, they seemed to follow its script nonetheless. During her questioning of General Petraeus, Senator Clinton dressed him down and essentially accused him of lying: "I think that the reports that you provide to us really require a willing suspension of disbelief," she said.[227] On hearing Petraeus's cautious but positive assessment of the surge, her colleague Carl Levin, now chairman of the Senate Armed Services Committee, called it a "litany of delusion."[228]

Harry Reid had offered his negative judgment months before Petraeus's report, saying in June that the general was not "in touch with what's going on in Baghdad."[229] On the eve of Petraeus's testimony, Reid used the Democrats' weekly radio address to warn the public not to believe the general, in terms that suggested that if he hadn't read the MoveOn.org ad in advance, he was certainly in tune with its message. "Before the [Petraeus] report arrives in Congress," Reid advised his audience, "it will pass through the White House spin machine, where facts are often ignored or twisted, and intelligence is cherry-picked. It's not his report anymore. It's Bush's report."[230]

Dick Durbin, the assistant majority leader in the Senate, also could not wait to hear Petraeus's report before attempting to discredit it. "By carefully manipulating the statistics," he said, "the Bush-Petraeus report will try to persuade us that violence in Iraq is decreasing and thus the surge is working." Durbin then demonstrated just how determined the Left was to seek defeat in Iraq, whatever the facts, whatever the consequences: "Even if the figures were correct," he said referring to Petraeus's still undelivered report, "the conclusion is wrong."[231]

Conclusion

O N SEPTEMBER 11, 2001, war was brought to America's shores by religious fanatics who regarded their innocent victims as "infidels" and their own deaths as a passage to paradise. In response, President Bush warned Americans "not [to] expect one battle, but a lengthy campaign, unlike any other we have ever seen."[1] This warning has been borne out. Four years after Pearl Harbor, the Axis powers had been defeated. Four years after 9-11, the war with the Islamofascists was still raging in the Middle East, and jihadists were launching attacks across the globe with no end in sight.

There have been many consequences of the campaign to discredit the president and the war, some of which will not become apparent until the war is over. Others are already manifest. The decision to attack the morality of America's war effort has dealt a severe blow to the American cause. It has undermined American unity in the face of the enemy, profoundly damaged the clarity with which the war is understood, and diminished Americans' ability to defend themselves.

The partisan attacks have distracted attention from a crucial reality: the enemy is not just the specific party, al-Qaeda, that attacked us on 9-11, and the war is not merely in Afghanistan and Iraq. It is global. If America were to abruptly quit the battlefield in Iraq, as many Democrats demand, there would be no peace; nor would the vacuum created remain unfilled. Iran would immediately reap the spoils, and become the dominant power in the Muslim Middle East. A precipitate American withdrawal would mean an escalation of the war against us, not its end.

On the evidence of their pronouncements, leaders of the Democratic Party have not understood this. When Nancy Pelosi became Speaker of the House in January 2007, she said: "My highest priority, immediately, is to stop the war in Iraq."[2] She did not say, "My highest priority is victory in Iraq." She said "stop the war," as though America could do so merely by leaving the battlefield, or in some way other than defeating the terrorists.

In arguing that the war in Iraq is a distraction from the War on Terror and that America could stop it through a military withdrawal, the Democrats are in denial as to what the war is about. This failure of the Democratic leadership to understand the war is America's most dangerous vulnerability in the war itself. Al-Qaeda's leaders, to name only one among many Islamic adversaries, have made their plans clear: First, expel America from Iraq; then establish a caliphate and military base in Baghdad; then spread radical Islam to the neighboring countries, and ultimately to the world.[3] Osama bin Laden himself has said that the war in Iraq is only the beginning of World War III: "The most important and serious issue today for the whole world is this Third World War, which the Crusader-Zionist coalition began against the Islamic nation. It is raging in the land of the two rivers. The world's millstone and pillar is in Baghdad, the capital of the caliphate."[4]

Iraq, however, is only one crucible of the war waged by radical Islam; Iran is another. The Iranian mullahs have already extended their power into Iraq, waging a proxy war authorized and directed at the highest levels of the regime. One U.S. Army commander, noting the confluence of Islamofascists throughout the Middle East, concluded, "Iranian operatives are using Lebanese surrogates to create Hezbollah-like capabilities [in Iraq]."[5] The mullahs armed these newly minted "insurgents" with improvised explosive devices (IEDs) and explosively formed penetrators (EFPs), the "deadliest bomb in Iraq."[6] Teheran also sponsors and funds America's deadliest Shi'ite foe, Muqtada al-Sadr and his Mahdi Army, sheltering its top- and middle-tier leaders when they fled from the incoming surge.[7] A practical result of the Democrats' attacks on the war has been to make it far more difficult for the White House to confront key elements of the enemy axis, such as Iran.

When the Bush administration belatedly began exposing Iran's surrogate war against the United States in Iraq, Iranian leaders seized on arguments already made by American leftists in their psychological war against the United States. Iran's ambassador to the United Nations, Javad Zarif, wrote that America had "invaded Iraq on false pretenses" and was now "trying to make Iran its scapegoat and fabricating evidence of Iranian activities in Iraq."[8] Iranian Foreign Ministry spokesman Mohammad Ali Hossaini similarly assured reporters: "Lots of this evidence is fake, artificial. For example, when they wanted to start a war in Iraq, they made [up] plenty of evidence that there were lots of weapons in Iraq."[9]

The deadly chickens of the attacks on the war are coming home to roost. As early as July 2003, even as the Democrats launched their campaign to tar the president as a liar, Congresswoman Ellen Tauscher told a Berkeley audience: "I hear the drumbeat and the rhetoric coming from the administration about Iran and their nuclear program. And it all sounds vaguely familiar. I am not going to sit idly by and be duped."[10]

Iran is, in fact, America's self-declared enemy. Iran's sainted Ayatollah Khomeini identified America as the very incarnation of evil, the "Great Satan," and its current dictator, Mahmoud Ahmadinejad, has called for its elimination from the world. At a conference in Teheran in 2005, called "A World without Zionism," while the audience chanted "Death to Israel" and "Death to America," Ahmadinejad promised, "With the help of the Almighty, we shall soon experience a world without America or Zionism, notwithstanding those who doubt."[11] Taking one's enemy seriously is the first step towards survival in war.

Ahmadinejad and his fellow jihadists look forward to the day when America will disappear from the face of the earth. They view nuclear war as an Armageddon that will carry them to paradise. It would be hard to imagine a more dangerous scenario for America and the rest of the world than a nuclear-armed Teheran. Yet, even as the war in Iraq began, the Democrats, by discrediting their own government, were undermining any response the president might make to the Iranian threat or any other threat America might face, since it would be hard to imagine a more sinister opponent.

This is not an argument that the war policies of George W. Bush, or any president, should be above criticism. The war in Iraq has been characterized by serious errors, as wars generally are. It was probably a mistake to go into the conflict with so lean a military force. It was probably unwise to turn authority over to the fractious Iraqis before the country had been pacified. It was self-defeating to adopt rules of engagement that did not allow American forces to crush the insurgency in its lairs.

At the same time, it is important not to overlook the fact that the president's credibility and motives were under ferocious and constant attack. In these circumstances it was far more difficult for him to achieve the flexibility or assert the authority required to correct his mistakes, and the reasons would not have been only psychological. Dan Bartlett, the president's longest-serving aide, told *New York Times* reporter Todd Purdum, "My sense is that if [the president] expressed public doubt [about his policies] it would crumble, like a house of cards, what public support he has left."[12] Such considerations contributed to a "bunker mentality" that severely limited the president's options. If America had entered Iraq with five hundred thousand troops and imposed an occupation government on the Iraqis that lasted for years, if American troops had invaded the Baghdad neighborhoods of the Sunnis and Shi'a and put them under martial law for as long as was necessary, what would the global outcry have been then? How would the president have been able to defend himself politically then, against the inevitable charges of "imperialism," "despotism," and "betrayal" that would have confronted him?

A democracy at war is faced with problems dictatorships find avoidable. Its citizens have a responsibility—as the Left never tires of repeating—not to abandon the freedoms they are defending, in order to defend them. The imperative can be abused, however, as the Left's actions constantly remind us. Justice Robert H. Jackson warned Americans, following the Second World War, that they should be careful not to "convert the constitutional Bill of Rights into a suicide pact."[13] Even in peacetime, the right to other freedoms must be weighed against the primary right to life itself.

Criticism of every war, including the one in Iraq, is warranted and necessary. The military surge that began in 2007 was a belated admission that the war had been launched without sufficient forces. Equally crucial, there had been no planning for the ethnic infighting that plagued the reconstruction effort after the toppling of the Saddam regime. Four years after the initial invasion, Bush acknowledged to journalist Robert Draper that defusing Sunni-Shi'ite tensions was "something we didn't spend a lot of time planning for." He had thought that Saddam had been stoking these resentments and that, once he was apprehended, they would resolve themselves.[14] As Vice President Cheney observed privately in November 2003, the Pentagon believed that it was in a "mopping-up phase," which was an unwarranted assumption. "They fail to see that we're in a major battle against terrorists in Iraq and elsewhere," Cheney commented.[15] More precisely, they failed to see that we were in a war with Islamists who were terrorists, a failure contributed to by the Bush administration's reluctance to recognize the religious nature of the enemy we face.

But while critics are necessary and can be valuable, a line must be drawn between constructive criticism and partisan attacks that are so extreme they close the margin of compromise and undermine the support for the mission. Many Democrats criticized the Bush administration for mistakes over troop levels and postwar planning, yet partisan rancor prevented them from offering constructive alternatives. In mid-2003, Minority Leader Pelosi and six other House Democrats wrote to President Bush, asking him to send more troops—but from foreign nations that were unwilling to provide them.[16] In the 2004 campaign John Kerry also promised troops from countries that refused to send any.[17] Kerry even attacked those countries that did, deriding the dozens of nations that had joined the "Coalition of the Willing" to fight in Iraq as the "coalition of the bribed, the coerced, the bought and the extorted."[18]

Congressional leftists had no trouble introducing measures to limit or withdraw troops from Iraq and otherwise micromanage the conflict. However, at no time did any Democrat introduce a bill to *increase* the number of troops. The Democrats did not seek timetables with benchmarks to show whether more troops were needed, or promise to send additional battalions if the Iraqis approved a constitution and formed a democratic assembly. Instead, they introduced measures to *cap* troop levels,[19] regularly belittled the troops' sacrificial successes as "a failure," and offered retreat and withdrawal as their only remedy, one which would allow Iran, Syria, and the terrorists to turn Iraq into a permanent base for their jihad against the West.

There were isolated but conspicuous models of responsible dissent from other quarters. General Eric Shinseki had insisted that half-a-million troops would be needed to occupy Iraq successfully. Even though these troop levels were not met, Shinseki stood by his troops, once the course had been set. Former national security adviser Brent Scowcroft criticized the decision to go to war in Iraq and to hold democratic elections. But he supported the war effort, knowing the consequences of American failure.[20] By contrast, Senator Harry Reid's defeatist rhetoric and withdrawal schemes became so excessive that VFW Commander-in-Chief Gary Kurpius, a Vietnam veteran, reminded him that "The time to debate the war is not in front of a microphone making irresponsible statements, and it's certainly not in the funding bill that keeps our troops alive."[21]

This is the real line that divides responsible critics from those whose desire is to sabotage the war. Responsible criticism expresses policy differences without malice towards the soldiers implementing those policies or their commanders defending the national interest. The characterization of General Petraeus as "General Betray Us" by MoveOn.org encapsulates the problem. The Senate condemned the ad in a symbolic resolution, but every Democratic presidential hopeful in the 2008 field voted against the resolution or skipped the vote.

Responsible critics do not paint public servants, such as General Petraeus, in the worst possible light over policy disagreements. Nor do they destroy the credibility of the commander-in-chief over policy differences. Responsible media do not recklessly promote the enemy's goals by transforming American malfeasances, such as Abu Ghraib, into monstrous war crimes. They do not reveal classified information and destroy national-security programs to achieve private agendas or make a political point. Honorable legislators do not maliciously (and erroneously) accuse Marines of committing atrocities in advance of trial. And loyal citizens do not set out to sap the nation's war morale by making films such as *Fahrenheit 9-11* that promote the conspiracy theories and propaganda of those who wish America ill.

Navy SEAL Marc Luttrell has provided a case study of the horrendous consequences that may result from overzealous critics who are bent on holding American troops to impossible ideals. In his book, *Lone Survivor*, Luttrell gives an eyewitness account of a covert mission in Afghanistan that involved himself and three other SEALS. A group of unarmed Afghan goat-herders, one of whom was a teenager, stumbled on the SEALS in the course of their mission. The rules of war demanded, and the SEALS knew, that they should kill the goat-herders, who could betray their whereabouts, since they had no way of holding them captive. But conscious of the mounting din of antiwar sentiment at home, which had led to prosecutions of soldiers in the field, the SEALS let the goat-herders go. They reasoned that if they killed defenseless villagers, they would be defamed as war criminals and possibly tried by their own government. Within an hour, the Taliban attacked, killing a total of nineteen of America's most highly trained and bravest men—three of the original SEAL team and the sixteen men sent to rescue them. Luttrell reflected: "Look at me right now in my story. Helpless, tortured, shot, blown up, my best buddies all dead, and all because we were afraid of the liberals back home, afraid to do what was necessary to save our own lives."[22]

Taken in isolation, almost any criticism of a war policy or its leaders can be a legitimate complaint. But when one looks at the consistent pattern of the opposition's attacks on the war in Iraq—on the integrity of the commander-in-chief, on the morality of the military, on the necessity of national-security programs designed to protect American citizens, and on the justice of the American cause—it is impossible not to suspect an agenda that is either recklessly opportunistic, or hostile to America itself.

A criticism that must be made of the president and his aides is over their failure to defend America's troops in the field from the political attacks on their support at home. The failure begins with the refusal of the president to defend himself as commander-in-chief. When Democrats launched their reckless campaign against his integrity and the war's morality in July 2003, they crossed a line. But they were made to pay no political price for doing so, because there was virtually no response from the White House or its proxies holding them to account for what they had done.

The president and his advisers took the view that they should not respond in kind to the Democrats' attacks because the commander-in-chief should be kept above the fray, as though this were possible once his opponents had attacked his office and the justice of the American cause. Silence in the face of relentless assaults on the president's integrity and truthfulness, which continued without let-up for the next four years, finally destroyed the president's credibility, his most vital asset as commander-in-chief. The damage this did to America's war in Iraq—and to any war that America may have to wage in the future—is incalculable. What future president will be able to warn Americans when a hostile regime threatens, and have his warnings heeded? Or act to remove the threat before it results in harm?

President Bush failed in his responsibility to protect key national-security programs designed to defend the American people. Leaking classified information is an act of treason and should have been prosecuted as such. The editors of the *New York Times*, the *Washington Post*, and numerous other media institutions that enabled the leakers should have been subpoenaed, and ordered to reveal the names of the officials who betrayed both their office and their country. If the editors refused, they should have been jailed until the names were produced. This was the course pursued with *New York Times* reporter Judith Miller in connection with the Valerie Plame affair, although the stakes were not remotely as high and the leak jeopardized no national-security program. But in the case of the national-security programs that leaks actually destroyed, the *Times* and the other papers were allowed to wrap themselves in the Constitution and pretend that the treason they enabled was indistinguishable from ordinary American dissent.

Treason is only the outer limit of the disregard for American democracy that has marked the opposition to this war. If a policy is wrong, there are democratic institutions available for changing it. These do not include taking the law into one's own hands by disclosing classified American security programs. If a security program is unwise, there are avenues for reforming it. By the same token, when an opposition party changes its collective mind about a war in progress, the way to affect the policy is to argue its merits and persuade the electorate, not to undermine the support for the troops and the credibility of the commander-in-chief.

Perhaps the most important failure of the Bush administration in the long term has been the failure to explain to the American people, in a way they can understand, why the war is being fought, and by this means provide support for the troops who are in the field. In his speech following 9-11, the president observed of the terrorists, "They are the heirs of all the murderous ideologies of the 20th century. By sacrificing human life to serve their radical visions, by abandoning every value except the will to power, they follow in the path of fascism, Nazism, and totalitarianism." But the attackers also followed in the path of Islam, clutching the Koran as they flew into tall buildings and crying *"Allahu Akbar"* as they headed for paradise. Instead of recognizing the far-reaching implications of this fact, the president defined the war against the Islamic jihad as a "War on Terror."

Not explaining that the global war is, in fact, a war with religious fanatics, whose agencies are both Shi'a and Sunni, has allowed Democrats to pretend that America is only fighting al-Qaeda, which is Sunni, and only in Afghanistan, and that the war in Iraq is unconnected to 9-11. In fact, al-Qaeda is also in Pakistan, Iraq, Gaza, and Somalia. Moreover, even in Iraq the terrorists are being supported and supplied by fascist Syria and Shi'a Iran and by jihadists from Jordan, Saudi Arabia, and other Islamist centers. Al-Qaeda is not alone in its armed struggle, but has allied armies that include Hezbollah, Hamas, and the Palestinian Islamic Jihad. As the exiled Iranian writer Amir Taheri has noted, "this is a global war from Indonesia to Algeria, passing through Afghanistan, Pakistan, Saudi Arabia, Lebanon and the Palestinian territories."[23]

Ignoring these realities, the Democratic strategy is to discard the "war" model as merely a "political bumper sticker," and replace it with the policy of the Clinton years, which would mean treating the terrorists as criminal agents unconnected to a religious crusade. As John Kerry described the strategy during the 2004 election campaign, "We have to get back to the place we were, where terrorists are not the focus of our lives, but they're a nuisance. As a former law enforcement person, I know we're never going to end prostitution. We're never going to end illegal gambling. But we're going to reduce it, organized crime, to a level where it isn't on the rise, it isn't threatening people's lives every day, and fundamentally it's something you continue to fight but it's not threatening the fabric of your life."[24] Inspired by similar illusions, the Clinton administration ignored acts of war, including the bombing of U.S. embassies and a U.S. warship. It treated the jihadists as organized-crime units and allowed al-Qaeda to train a hundred thousand terrorists in its camps undisturbed, and eventually to put together an attack on the American homeland.

President Bush's retreat in the face of the Democrats' attacks has caused him to segregate elements of a war that can be won only if it is seen as a whole. After 9-11 the president said the United States would make no distinction between terrorists and the nations that harbor them: "Every nation, in every region, now has a decision to make. Either you are with us, or you are with the terrorists. From this day forward, any nation that continues to harbor or support terrorism will be regarded by the United States as a hostile regime." But if this was the president's policy, then American forces in Iraq should have been pursuing terrorists across the borders with Syria and Iran. Democrats are not surprisingly opposed to such a strategy and have asked for a presidential pledge that he will not attack Iran without congressional approval.[25] Only Senator Joseph Lieberman, a Democrat purged from his own party, has proposed "a strike over the border into Iran, where we have good evidence that they have a base at which they are training these people coming back into Iraq to kill our soldiers."[26]

While Democrats complain that the war in Iraq is a distraction, the enemy has explicitly said that Iraq is the central battleground of their crusade. The war we are facing is made far more dangerous by the decision of Democrats such as Carter and Gore to fracture a bipartisan unity and launch an offensive directed at their own government and commander-in-chief. Democrats have misrepresented the war as a "neoconservative" contrivance, while suppressing the facts that the call for regime change in Iraq was first made by a Democratic administration, that the Authorization for the Use of Military Force was supported by a majority of Senate Democrats, that the war itself was endorsed by the entire national-security cabinet of the Clinton White House, and that Senate Democrats were privy to the National Intelligence Estimate on which the president's policy was based. These facts make their attacks on the president, and their decision to undermine his credibility and his authority in the midst of a war, the most disgraceful episode in America's political history.

The war with Islamofascism cannot be won if its religious roots are denied or its global reach is ignored. It cannot be won if Americans deny themselves the means necessary to fight the war—whether these involve strategies to strike first, or to spy on our enemies before they attack us, or to deny terrorists the rights of American citizens—thereby turning the Constitution into a suicide pact. It cannot be won if we allow a disloyal and hostile Left to dictate the parameters of our political debate. It can be won only if Americans will put their differences aside to come together as a people, and unite as a nation, and mobilize the powers of our extraordinary civilization to confront the enemy who has attacked us.

Notes

Introduction: A House Divided

1   Cf. David Horowitz, *Unholy Alliance: Radical Islam and the American Left* (Washington, D.C.: Regnery, 2005).

2   Jimmy Carter. See Andrew Buncombe, "Jimmy Carter Savages Blair and Bush: 'Their War was Based on Lies,'" *Independent* (UK), March 22, 2004.

3   Sen. Richard Durbin: "The Patriot Act crossed the line on several key areas of civil liberties." Quoted by Associated Press, "Gore to Bush: Rescind Patriot Act," *Wired*, November 10, 2003. Online at: http://www.wired.com/politics/law/news/2003/11/61170.

4   Al Gore, "Iraq and the War on Terrorism," Commonwealth Club, September 23, 2002. Online at: http://www.commonwealthclub.org/archive/02/02-09gore-speech.html.

5   Sen. John Kerry: "Florida is the place where America's democracy was wounded . . . We had more votes; we won!" Quoted in Andrew Cline, "Failed at the Booth," *National Review*, March 11, 2004. Online at: http://www.nationalreview.com/comment/cline200403110921.asp. Also Jimmy Carter: "There's no doubt in my mind that Al Gore was elected president" in 2000. Speech at American University, September 19, 2005. Text online at: http://www.american.edu/media/speeches/carter.htm.

6   "Jimmy Carter: 'The War Has Been Unnecessary,'" interview on *Today*, NBC, September 30, 2004. Transcript online at: http://www.msnbc.msn.com/id/6138962.

7   Sen. Edward M. Kennedy. "Kennedy's 'Texas' Remark Stirs GOP Reaction," CNN, September 18, 2003. Online at: http://www.cnn.com/2003/ALLPOLITICS/09/18/kennedy.iraq.

8   Al Gore. "Bush 'Betrayed Us,'" CNN, February 9, 2004. Online at: http://www.cnn.com/2004/ALLPOLITICS/02/09/gore.bush.ap/index.html.

9   Sen. Edward M. Kennedy: "Robert Greenwald's new *Iraq for Sale* . . . is a convincing indictment of the [Bush] administration's decision to give multi-billion dollar sweetheart deals that have lined contractors' pockets while failing to meet the basic needs of our soldiers." Kennedy, "*Iraq for Sale*: Further Evidence of the Bush

Administration's Incompetence," Huffington Post, October 19, 2006. Online at: http://www.huffingtonpost.com/sen-edward-m-kennedy-/iraq-for-sale-f_b_32046. html.

10 Sen. Hillary Clinton: "I think it's particularly important to point out this is George Bush's war. He is responsible for this war. He started the war." In the New Hampshire debate, June 4, 2007. http://www.kron4.com/Global/story.asp?S=6607798.

11 Clinton signed the "Iraq Liberation Act," H.R. 4655, on October 31, 1998.

12 Sen. Robert C. Byrd. Stephen Dinan, "Byrd says Iraq was no threat to U.S.," Washington Times, May 22, 2003: "'When it comes to shedding American blood, when it comes to wreaking havoc on civilians, on innocent men, women and children, callous dissembling is not acceptable,' Mr. Byrd said. 'Nothing is worth that kind of lie: not oil, not revenge, not re-election, not somebody's grand pipe dream of a democratic domino theory.'"

13 Sen. Robert C. Byrd, "The Arrogance of Power," March 13, 2003. Online at: http://byrd.senate.gov/speeches/byrd_speeches_2003march/byrd_speeches_2003march_list/byrd_speeches_2003march_list_4.html.

14 Stephen F. Hayes, Cheney: The Untold Story of America's Most Powerful and Controversial Vice President (New York: HarperCollins, 2007), pp. 384–87.

15 www.cbsnews.com/stories/2006/10/20/60minutes/main2111089_page2.shtml. The final exchange was in the original broadcast as witnessed by one of the authors, but does not appear in the written transcript.

16 Adam Nagourney, "Democrats Say Bush's Credibility Has Been Damaged," New York Times, July 14, 2003.

17 President George W. Bush, "State of the Union," January 28, 2003. Online at: http://www.whitehouse.gov/stateoftheunion/2003.

18 According to the Senate Intelligence Committee, a CIA agent testified that "the most important fact in the [Joseph Wilson] report was that Nigerian officials admitted that the Iraqi delegation had traveled there in 1999, and that the Nigerian prime minister believed the Iraqis were interested in purchasing uranium, because this provided some confirmation of foreign government service reporting." Full report available online at: http://gpoaccess.gov/serialset/creports/iraq.html. The Butler Commission report, produced in the UK, stands by the "sixteen words." The relevant passage of the Butler report can be found in Norman Podhoretz, World War IV: The Long Struggle against Islamofascism (New York: Doubleday, 2007), p. 163.

19 Nagourney, "Democrats Say."

20 Ion Mihai Pacepa, "Propaganda Redux," Wall Street Journal, August 7, 2007.

21 Ibid.

22 Ibid.

23 William S. Cohen and Gen. Anthony Zinni, "Operation DESERT FOX Briefing with Secretary Cohen and Gen. Zinni," December 21, 1998. Online at: http://www.defenselink.mil/transcripts/transcript.aspx?transcriptid=1792.

24 Stephen Dinan and Amy Fagan, "Pelosi Stands By Vote Against Iraq War," Washington Times, April 11, 2003; Todd S. Purdum, op. cit., p. 212

25 Dean came in first in the MoveOn.org virtual primary, with nearly 44 percent of the vote. His closest competitor was Dennis Kucinich, with 24 percent. "No Candidate Wins Majority in MoveOn.Org PAC First-Ever Democratic Online 'Primary,'" Common Dreams, June 27, 2003. Online at: http://www.commondreams.org/news2003/0627-01.htm.

26 Robert Wright, "An Easter Sermon," New York Times,. April 7, 2007.

27 Matthew 12:30; Luke 11:23.
28 Laura Blumenfeld, "Soros's Deep Pockets vs. Bush," *Washington Post*, November 11, 2003, p. A3.
29 In fact, a litany of Democratic complaints about Republican attacks, three years into the war, turns up nothing so venomous: http://www.buzzflash.com/articles/releases/012.
30 http://www.whitehouse.gov/news/releases/2001/09/20010920-8.html.
31 http://www.realclearpolitics.com/articles/2007/05/special_report_roundtable_may_28.html.
32 http://www.breitbart.com/article.php?id=D8PA5VM80&show_article=1.
33 George Soros, "A Self-Defeating War," *Wall Street Journal*, August 15, 2006.

1 *The Path to 9-11*

1 "Country Reports on Terrorism," chapter 6. Released by the State Department's Office of the Coordinator for Counterterrorism, April 28, 2006.
2 Safa Haeri, "Iran on Course for a Showdown," *Asia Times*, October 28, 2005. Online at: http://www.atimes.com/atimes/Middle_East/GJ28Ak03.html.
3 George McGovern's acceptance speech to the 1972 Democratic National Convention in Miami Beach, delivered July 14, 1972.
4 Ibid.
5 Cf. Christopher Matthews, *Kennedy and Nixon: The Rivalry That Shaped Postwar America* (New York: Simon & Schuster, 1996), for insight into the partisan agendas of Watergate.
6 Anthony Lake, "At Stake in Cambodia: Extending Aid Will Only Prolong the Killing," *Washington Post*, March 9, 1975.
7 See Stephen E. Ambrose, *Rise to Globalism: American Foreign Policy since 1938* (New York: Penguin Books, 1993), pp. 281–84.
8 Gary Sick. All Fall Down: America's Fateful Encounter with Iran. (NY: Random House, 1985), p. 291.
9 Both bin Laden and his second-in-command, Ayman al-Zawahiri, state that they received no U.S. assistance; U.S. government policy forbade funding foreign-born fighters in Afghanistan. See the U.S. State Department statement, "Did the United States 'Create' Osama bin Laden?" available online at: http://usinfo.state.gov/media/Archive/2005/Jan/24-318760.html. Accessed March 9, 2007. On bin Laden's bizarre and pathetic sojourn in Afghanistan, see Lawrence Wright, *The Looming Tower: Al-Qaeda's Journey to America* (New York: Vintage, 2006).
10 Daniel Patrick Moynihan. Quoted in Dinesh D'Souza, *The Enemy at Home: The Cultural Left and Its Responsibility for 9/11* (New York: Doubleday, 2007), p. 207.
11 Hamilton Jordan, *Crisis: The Last Year of the Carter Presidency* (New York: Putnam, 1982), pp. 429–30. The phrase "directly involved" comes from "The Weekend of Crisis," *Time*, December 18, 1978. Online at: http://www.time.com/time/magazine/article/0,9171,916524-2,00.html.
12 William Shawcross, *The Shah's Last Ride: The Fate of an Ally* (New York: Simon and Schuster, 1988).
13 Although later suppressed, the Soviet-dominated Tudeh Party supported the Islamic Revolution and operated openly from 1979 to 1983. United Nations Human Rights Commission, "Iran Country Report," October 2003. Online at: http://www.unhcr.org/home/RSDCOI/402a15034.pdf.

14   Turner regrets the "Halloween Massacre" in his book *Burn before Reading: CIA Directors and Secret Intelligence* (New York: Hyperion, 2005).

15   Peter G. Bourne, *Jimmy Carter: A Comprehensive Biography from Plains to Postpresidency* (New York: A Lisa Drew Book/Scribner, 1997), p. 454.

16   Tom Hayden and Jane Fonda actually made a documentary, *Introduction to the Enemy*, in the zones of Vietnam occupied by the Communists, which they touted as forerunners of a liberated future.

17   D'Souza, *The Enemy at Home*, pp. 206-7.

18   Steven F. Hayward, *The Real Jimmy Carter* (Washington, D.C.: Regnery, 2004), p. 128.

19   "Who Will Get Blamed for What?" *Time*, November 26, 1979. Online at: http://www.time.com/time/magazine/article/0,9171,946390,00.html.

20   Iranian kidnappers played on leftist stereotypes, releasing the thirteen hostages who were women or blacks to express their solidarity with "oppressed" minorities in America. Another hostage was released in mid-1980. The remaining fifty-two hostages were held a total of 444 days and released minutes after Ronald Wilson Reagan's inauguration.

21   Meeting on Friday, May 9, 1980. No dissent was recorded. Jordan, *Crisis*, pp. 289-90.

22   The mullahs netted $3 billion of the payoff.

23   Teddy Roosevelt conducted a campaign to force Woodrow Wilson to enter the First World War. Herbert Hoover severely criticized the New Deal.

24   Hayward, *The Real Jimmy Carter*, pp. 201-2.

25   Mona Charen, *Useful Idiots: How Liberals Got It Wrong in the Cold War and Still Blame America First* (Washington, D.C.: Regnery, 2003), pp. 222, 224.

26   Ronald Reagan, "Address to the Nation on the United States Air Strike against Libya," April 14, 1986. Online at: http://www.reagan.utexas.edu/archives/speeches/1986/41486g.htm.

27   Hayward, *The Real Jimmy Carter*, p. 196.

28   "Cranston for Raid, Dymally against It," *Daily News of Los Angeles,* April 19, 1986. Quotation available online at: http://nl.newsbank.com/nl-search/we/Archives?p_product=LA&p_theme=la&p_action=search&p_maxdocs=200&p_topdoc=1&p_text_direct-0=0EF50DDB7741B472&p_field_direct-0=document_id&p_perpage=10&p_sort=YMD_date:D&s_trackval=GooglePM.

29   Dave Eberhart, "Kerry on the Record: Bashing Reagan," March 15, 2004. Online at: http://www.newsmax.com/archives/articles/2004/3/12/192323.shtml.

30   James Taranto, "If You're Happy and You Know It, Run for Office," *Wall Street Journal*, July 9, 2004. Online at: http://www.opinionjournal.com/pl/?id=110005328.

31   Cited in Lowell Ponte, "Carter Attacks the 'Road to Peace,'" FrontPageMag.com, December 12, 2003. Online at: http://www.frontpagemag.com/Articles/ReadArticle.asp?ID=11284.

32   Chris Sullentrop, "Jimmy Carter," Slate.com, May 17, 2002. Online at: http://www.slate.com/id/2065887.

33   Max Boot, "Reasons for Hope in Iraq," *New York Sun,* October 22, 2004. Online at: http://www.nysun.com/article/3644.

34   Vote held January 12, 1991. Online at: http://www.senate.gov/legislative/LIS/roll_call_lists/roll_call_vote_cfm.cfm?congress=102&session=1&vote=00002.

35   William Schneider, "The Vietnam Syndrome Mutates," *National Journal*, April 25, 2006. Online at: http://www.theatlantic.com/doc/prem/200604u/nj_schneider_2006-04-25.

36 Rep. Roscoe Bartlett, R-MD, summed up the Clinton years: "Morale . . . sucks." "Morale Goes into the Tank," *Insight on the News*, June 9, 1997. Online at: http://findarticles.com/p/articles/mi_m1571/is_n21_v13/ai_19469420.

37 Mercifully, the cyanide was burned up during the explosion.

38 David N. Bossie, *Intelligence Failure: How Clinton's National Security Policy Set the Stage for 9/11* (Nashville: Thomas Nelson, 2004), pp. 147–48, 155–59.

39 Roger Cohen, "Taming the Bullies of Bosnia," *The New York Times Magazine*, December 17, 1995. Online at: http://www.nytimes.com/books/98/05/17/daily/holbrooke-profile.html.

40 Dick Morris, *Off with Their Heads: Traitors, Crooks, and Obstructionists in American Politics, Media, and Business* (New York: ReganBooks, 2003), p.75.

41 John Miller's 1998 interview with Osama bin Laden. Originally posted on abcnews.go.com, now available at: www.freerepublic.com/focus/news/833647/posts.

42 *The 9/11 Commission Report*, chapter 3. See also Dick Morris and Eileen McGann, *Because He Could* (New York: ReganBooks, 2004), pp. 111–15.

43 Yossef Bodansky, *Bin Laden: The Man Who Declared War on America* (Roseville, CA: Forum, 1999/2001), p. 186.

44 "Bin Laden's Fatwa," PBS. Online at: http://www.pbs.org/newshour/terrorism/international/fatwa_1996.html.

45 Transcript of interview with Peter Arnett. Online at: http://www.anusha.com/osamaint.htm.

46 Lt. Col. Robert "Buzz" Patterson, USAF (Ret.), *Dereliction of Duty: The Eyewitness Account of How Bill Clinton Compromised America's National Security* (Washington, D.C.: Regnery, 2003), pp. 25–30. (Quotations on pp. 28 and 30.)

47 Bossie, *Intelligence Failure*, pp. 172–75.

48 Ibid., p. 82.

49 Quotation from *Hardball*, MSNBC, August 18, 2005.

50 Morris and McGann, *Because He Could*, p. 109. For a more complete account, see Richard Miniter, *Losing Bin Laden: How Bill Clinton's Failures Unleashed Global Terror* (Washington, D.C.: Regnery, 2003), pp. 102–5. Miniter speculates that these overtures were not reported to the officer's superiors, but Clinton's statement seems to indicate to the contrary.

51 At this time, because of Clinton's slow-moving investigation into the 1993 Twin Towers bombing, investigators did not know that bin Laden already had attacked the United States.

52 *The 9/11 Commission Report*, chapter 4.

53 Ibid. The "rogue elephant" charge was specifically made by Rep. Otis Pike, D-NY, who chaired the Pike Committee, the House counterpart to the Senate's infamous Church Committee.

54 Morris and McGann, *Because He Could*, pp. 99–100.

55 This and following quotations from *The 9/11 Commission Report*, chapter 4. Also, see the excellent summary in Morris and McGann, *Because He Could*, pp. 95–100.

56 *Hardball*, MSNBC, August 18, 2005.

57 Quoted in Miniter, *Losing Bin Laden*, p. 240.

58 Jennifer Weeks, "Will O'Leary Legacy Last?" *Bulletin of the Atomic Scientists*, vol. 54, no. 2 (March 1998), pp. 11–14. Online at: http://bcsia.ksg.harvard.edu/publication.cfm?program=STPP&ctype=article&item_id=383.

59 John B. Roberts II, "Nuclear Secrets and the Culture Wars," *The American Spectator*, May 1999. Online at: http://www.infomanage.com/womd/news/1999/nuclearpercent20secretspercent20andpercent20thepercent20culturepercent20wars.htm.

60   Hazel O'Leary, "Openness." Archived at the "Gifts of Speech" website hosted by Sweet Briar College. Online at: http://gos.sbc.edu/o/oleary.html.

61   Bossie, *Intelligence Failure*, p. 80.

62   In 2000, Sen. John McCain condemned "the disgraceful situation of more than 12,000 military families forced to use food stamps to make ends meet." Sen. John McCain, "McCain Objects to Over $900 Million Requested Spending in Mil-Con Bill," May 15, 2000. Online at: http://mccain.senate.gov/press_office/view_article. cfm?id=865. On military pay freeze, see Patterson, *Dereliction*, p. 107.

63   Bossie, *Intelligence Failure*, pp. 62–64.

64   Ibid., p. 167.

65   Online NewsHour, "Background: Bowing Out," PBS.org, September 30, 2002. Online at: http://www.pbs.org/newshour/bb/congress/july-dec02/bkgdtorricelli_09-30.html.

66   Charen, *Useful Idiots*, pp. 213–18.

67   "Speaking of Leaks," *Investor's Business Daily*. Online at: http://www.investors. com/editorial/editorialcontent.asp?secid=1501&status=article&id=156556&secure=el.

68   Jim Geraghty, "A Brief History of Classified Leaks," *National Review*, October 1, 2003. Online: http://www.nationalreview.com/geraghty/geraghty200310010843.asp.

69   Vernon Loeb, "Panel Advocates Easing CIA Rules on Informants," *Washington Post*, June 6, 2000, p. A25.

70   Bossie, *Intelligence Failure*, pp. 26–27, 49.

71   Read John Kerry's full profile at DiscoverTheNetworks.org: http://www.discover-thenetworks.org/individualProfile.asp?indid=1346.

72   *The 9/11 Commission Report*, chapter 3.

73   "Bush, Cheney to Meet with 9/11 Panel," Fox News, April 29, 2004. Online at: http://www.foxnews.com/story/0,2933,118466,00.html.

74   Debra Burlingame, "Our Right to Security," *Wall Street Journal*, January 30, 2006. Online at: http://www.opinionjournal.com/editorial/feature.html?id=110007891.

75   Bossie, *Intelligence Failure*, pp. 40–43.

76   Ibid., pp. 93–96.

77   Edward G. Shirley, "Can't Anybody Here Play This Game?" *The Atlantic Monthly*, February 1998. Online (for subscribers only) at: http://www.theatlantic.com/issues/98feb/cia.htm.

78   Bossie, *Intelligence Failure*, pp. 93–96.

79   Rep. Dana Rohrabacher, "9/11 Represented a Dramatic Failure of Policy and People." Testimony given on the House floor on June 21, 2004.

80   "Clinton Has Woman Arrested for Insulting Him!" The Daily Republican. Online at: http://www.dailyrepublican.com/clintoninsulted.html.

81   Bossie, *Intelligence Failure*, pp. 123–24.

82   The government of Slobodan Milosevic was socialist, and the Serbian Orthodox Church had condemned his policies. However, following the war, KLA Muslims began persecuting Serbia's Christian population, their centuries-long enemy.

83   Sen. Orrin Hatch, "Senate Judiciary Committee Hearing Case of Clinton Pardon of Marc Rich," CNN, February 14, 2001. Online at: http://transcripts.cnn.com/TRANSCRIPTS/0102/14/se.02.html.

84   Morris and McGann, *Because He Could*, pp. 233–34.

85   Cf. David Horowitz, "The President's Pardoned Bombers," in *How to Beat the Democrats and Other Subversive Ideas* (Dallas: Spence, 2002).

86   Rowan Scarborough, *Sabotage: America's Enemies within the CIA* (Washington, D.C.: Regnery, 2007), p. 114.

87 Ibid., p.117.

88 George Tentet, with Bill Harlow, *At the Center of the Storm: My Years at the CIA* (New York: HarperCollins, 2007), p. 9.

89 Scarborough, *Sabotage*, p. 118.

90 Bill Gertz, *Betrayal: How the Clinton Administration Undermined American Security* (Washington, D.C.: Regnery, 1999), pp. 33–166.

91 Sam Giancana once said Kennedy "wouldn't even be in the White House" without him. Richard Daley also intimated Mafia involvement. See "Flashback 1960: Kennedy Beats Nixon," BBC News, November 9, 2000. Online at: http://news.bbc.co.uk/1/low/world/americas/1015074.stm. Until his death Nixon steadfastly believed—with reason—that he had been robbed. See Monica Crowley, *Nixon off the Record: His Candid Commentary on People and Politics* (New York: Random House, 1996), pp. 30–31.

92 *The McLaughlin Group*, PBS, December 15, 2000. Online at: http://www.mclaughlin.com/library/transcript.asp?id=185.

93 The National Opinion Research Center recount was commissioned by such media heavyweights as CNN, the Associated Press, the *Wall Street Journal*, the *New York Times*, and the *Washington Post*. "Florida Recount Study: Bush Still Wins," CNN, 2001. Online: http://www.cnn.com/SPECIALS/2001/florida.ballots/stories/main.html.

94 Bossie, *Intelligence Failure*, pp. 205–6.

2 *The Response to 9-11*

1 Sean Hannity, *Deliver Us from Evil* (New York: ReganBooks, 2004), p. 198.

2 Bullock also endorsed Bush over Gore in 2000; he passed away before the 2004 elections.

3 "George W. Bush Statement," CNN, December 13, 2000. Online at: http://www.cnn.com/ELECTION/2000/transcripts/121300/bush.html.

4 See Bossie, *Intelligence Failure*, pp. 104–21. See also Gertz, *Betrayal*, *passim*, and Edward Timperlake and William C. Triplett II, *Year of the Rat* (Washington, D.C.: Regnery, 2000).

5 Gerald Posner, *Why America Slept: The Failure to Prevent 9/11* (New York: Ballantine, 2004), p. 17.

6 Karen Hughes, *Ten Minutes from Normal: Counselor to the President, Wife, and Mother: The Woman Who Left the White House to Put Family First* (New York: Viking, 2004), pp. 246–47.

7 Ibid., p. 247.

8 Ibid., p. 263.

9 Jake Tapper, "Congress Balks at Giving Bush a Blank Check," Salon.com, September 13, 2001. Online at: http://archive.salon.com/politics/feature/2001/09/13/bush/print.html.

10 Quoted in Amanda B. Carpenter, "How Hillary Played Politics with 9/11," *Human Events*, October 13, 2006. Online at: http://www.humanevents.com/article.php?id=17523.

11 "Bush Job Approval Edges Back Up," CBSNews.com, October 22, 2003. Online at: http://www.cbsnews.com/stories/2003/10/22/opinion/polls/main579524.shtml.

12 Ari Fleischer, *Taking Heat: The President, the Press, and My Years in the White House* (New York: William Morrow, 2005), p. 157. Also quoted in Fred Barnes, *Rebel-in-Chief: Inside the Bold and Controversial Presidency of George W. Bush* (New York:

Crown Forum, 2006), p. 65.

13 Tapper, "Congress Balks."

14 Bill Sammon, *Misunderestimated: The President Battles Terrorism, Media Bias, and the Bush Haters* (New York: Harper Paperbacks, 2005), p. 129.

15 The whole text of her speech is archived at: http://www.wagingpeace.org/articles/2001/09/14_lee-speech.htm. Lee's floor speech was also quoted positively by the Communist newspaper *People's Weekly Worker*. See Tim Wheeler, "Lee Shows Courage with Vote for Peace," *People's Weekly Worker*. Online at: http://www.pww.org/past-weeks-2001/Leepercent20showspercent20couragepercent20withpercent20votepercent20forpercent20peace.htm.

16 "Barbara Lee's Stand," *The Nation*, October 8, 2001. Online at: http://www.thenation.com/doc/20011008/editors2.

17 Michael Moore, "Death, Downtown." Originally posted on MichaelMoore.com; it is also found online at the website of Z Magazine: http://www.zmag.org/moorecalam.htm.

18 David Frum, *The Right Man: An Inside Account of the Bush White House* (New York: Random House Trade Paperbacks, 2005), p. 206.

19 Ibid., pp. 205–6.

20 President George W. Bush, "State of the Union," January 29, 2002. Online at: http://www.whitehouse.gov/news/releases/2002/01/20020129-11.html.

21 Al Gore, "A Commentary on the War against Terror: Our Larger Tasks," Council on Foreign Relations, February 12, 2002. Online at: http://www.cfr.org/publication/4343/commentary_on_the_war_against_terror.html.

22 Ibid.

23 "Newsmaker: Sen. Tom Daschle," PBS.org, February 11, 2002. Online at: http://www.pbs.org/newshour/bb/congress/jan-june02/daschle_2-11.html.

24 Rep. Dennis Kucinich, "A Prayer for America." Online at: http://www.commondreams.org/views02/0226-09.htm.

25 Edgar B. Anderson, "Leftists Rally against Bush in Los Angeles," FrontPageMag.com, February 22, 2002. Online at: http://www.frontpagemag.com/Articles/ReadArticle.asp?ID=3150.

26 Ibid.

27 R. W. Apple Jr., "A Military Quagmire Remembered: Afghanistan as Vietnam," *New York Times*, October 31, 2001. Online at: http://www.wellesley.edu/Polisci/wj/Vietnam/apple-afghan.html.

28 Bill Sammon, *Fighting Back: The War on Terrorism––from inside the Bush White House* (Washington, D.C.: Regnery, 2003), p. 351.

29 "Daschle Stands by War Comments," CNN, March 1, 2002. Online at: http://archives.cnn.com/2002/ALLPOLITICS/03/01/daschle.war.on.terrorism/index.html.

30 "Online NewsHour: Political Wrap Background," PBS.org, March 1, 2002, http://www.pbs.org/newshour/bb/political_wrap/jan-june02/wrap_3-1a.html.

31 Quoted in Sammon, *Fighting Back*, pp. 353–54.

32 Juliet Eilperin, "Democrat Implies Sept. 11 Administration Plot," *Washington Post*, April 12, 2002, p. A16. Online at: http://www.washingtonpost.com/ac2/wp-dyn?pagename=article&contentId=A34565-2002Apr11. See also Michelle Malkin, *Unhinged: Exposing Liberals Gone Wild* (Washington, D.C.: Regnery, 2005), p. 35.

33 Several outlets excerpted her April 12, 2002, press release. Appropriately, at this time, the full press statement is available online only at the website of *The Final Call*, the newspaper of the Rev. Louis Farrakhan's Nation of Islam. Michael T. Klare, "McKinney Presses for Probe of Bush Admin. Links to 9/11 Attacks," *The Final*

Call, April 30, 2002. Online at: http://www.finalcall.com/perspectives/mckinney04-30-2002.htm.

34   "Cynthia McKinney and the 'What Bush Knew' Debate," *The Nation*, May 19, 2002. Online at: http://www.thenation.com/blogs/thebeat?pid=62.

35   Sammon, *Fighting Back*, p. 360.

36   "Gephardt Holds Press Conference Regarding '9/11 Blame Game,'" CNN, May 16, 2002. Online at: http://transcripts.cnn.com/TRANSCRIPTS/0205/16/se.02.html.

37   "U.S. Senator Thomas Daschle: News Conference on 9-11 Admissions by the White House," May 16, 2002. Online at: http://www.truthout.org/docs_02/05.17AA.Daschle.Bush.NU.htm.

38   Anthony York, "The Best Defense Is a Good Offense," Salon.com, May 18, 2002. Online at: http://dir.salon.com/story/politics/feature/2002/05/18/white_house/index.html.

39   Although both the House and the Senate were investigating the pre-9/11 intelligence, calls circulated for the appointment of a new investigative body. Ultimately, this became the 9/11 Commission, whose report concluded: "the threats received [by Bush] contained few specifics regarding time, place, method, or target. . . . *We cannot say for certain whether these reports, as dramatic as they were, related to the 9/11 attacks.*" (Emphasis added.) *The 9/11 Commission Report*, chapter 8. Online at: http://www.9-11commission.gov/report/911Report_Ch8.htm.

3   *Why America Went to War*

1   Al Gore, *The Assault on Reason* (New York: Penguin, 2007), p. 104.

2   Ibid., p. 103.

3   Ibid.

4   http://bostonreview.net/BR31.1/stateofthenation.pdf

5   Ibid.

6   William Shawcross, *Allies: The U.S., Britain, Europe, and the War in Iraq* (New York: Public Affairs, 2004), p. 149.

7   Hans Blix, *Disarming Iraq* (New York: Pantheon, 2004), p. 89.

8   Shawcross, *Allies*, p. 131.

9   Frank Rich, *The Greatest Story Ever Sold: The Decline and Fall of Truth from 9/11 to Katrina* (New York: Penguin, 2006), p. 3.

10   Michael Isikoff and David Corn, *Hubris: The Inside Story of Spin, Scandal, and the Selling of the Iraq War* (New York: Crown, 2006), pp. 158, 163.

11   Shawcross, *Allies*, p. 148. Villepin's actual words were "*quelles que soient les circonstances.*"

12   Rich, *Greatest Story*, p. 70.

13   Ibid.

14   David Kay, *Statement on the Interim Progress Report on the Activities of the Iraq Survey Group*, October 2, 2003. Online at: http://www.globalsecurity.org/wmd/library/report/2004/isg-final-report/.

15   Ibid.

16   Question ID: USGallup.042841, RK08A.

17   Gore, *Assault*, p. 104.

18   Ibid., pp. 107 et seq.

19   Ibid., p. 110. This is the gravamen of Gore's entire argument about the decision to go to war.

20   http://www.cbsnews.com/stories/2003/03/17/iraq/printable544377.shtml.

21 Prime Minister Tony Blair, March 18, 2003, speech to the House of Commons, http://politics.guardian.co.uk/iraq/story/0,,916790,00.html. This is the source for all the quotations in the balance of this section.

22 Gore, *Assault*, p. 38.

23 Frank Rich, "Never Forget What?" *New York Times*, September 14, 2002.

24 Gore, *Assault*, p. 1.

25 http://www.whitehouse.gov/nsc/nss.html. (Emphasis added.)

26 http://www.whitehouse.gov/news/releases/2002/10/20021002-2.html.

27 "Kennedy's 'Texas' Remark Stirs GOP Reaction," CNN, September 18, 2003. Online at: http://www.cnn.com/2003/ALLPOLITICS/09/18/kennedy.iraq.

28 http://www.whitehouse.gov/news/releases/2003/01/20030128-19.html.

29 Gore, *Assault*, p. 39.

30 Gore, "Our Larger Tasks," February 12, 2002. Online at: http://www.cfr.org/publication/4343/commentary_on_the_war_against_terror.html.

31 Blair, speech to the House of Commons, http://politics.guardian.co.uk/iraq/story/0,,916790,00.html.

32 E.g., Sen. Barbara Boxer called Iraq "a war of choice, not necessity," in her July 6, 2005, speech to the Commonwealth Club, "Iraq: Credibility, Responsibility, and Action." Online at: http://www.truthout.org/docs_2005/071005A.shtml. Former President Jimmy Carter declared on NBC's *Today* show on September 30, 2004: "The war has been unnecessary." *Today* transcript of Carter segment: "Jimmy Carter: 'The War Has Been Unnecessary.'" Online at: http://www.commondreams.org/headlines04/0930-02.htm.

33 Gore, *Assault*, p. 38.

34 Bush, "State of the Union," 2002, http://www.whitehouse.gov/news/releases/2002/01/20020129-11.html.

35 Stephen F. Hayes, *The Connection: How al-Qaeda's Collaboration with Saddam Hussein Has Endangered America* (New York: HarperCollins, 2004), pp. 11–12, 50, 54.

36 President George W. Bush, "Statement by the President in Address to the Nation," September 11, 2001, http://www.whitehouse.gov/news/releases/2001/09/20010920-8.html.

37 Hayes, *The Connection*, p. 22.

38 Tenet, *Center of the Storm*, p. 352. Tenet's admissions are particularly striking, as they are intended to *counter* alleged overreaching by administration officials and others.

39 Quoted in Richard Miniter, *Disinformation: Twenty-Two Media Myths That Undermine the War on Terror* (Washington, D.C.: Regnery, 2005), p. 111.

40 "Online NewsHour: The 9/11 Plot," PBS.org, June 16, 2004. Online at: http://www.pbs.org/newshour/bb/terrorism/jan-june04/911_06-16.html.

41 Terrorist Abu Zubaydah, quoted in Hayes, *The Connection*, p. 15.

42 Tenet, *Center of the Storm*, pp. 350–354.

43 Speech text online at: http://www.whitehouse.gov/news/releases/2002/06/20020601-3.html.

44 Eric Schmitt, "U.S. Plan for Iraq Is Said to Include Attack on 3 Sides," *New York Times*, July 5, 2002. Online at: http://www.commondreams.org/headlines02/0705-04.htm.

45 Ivo H. Daalder and James M. Lindsay, "No Presidential War," *Washington Post*, July 31, 2002, p. A19. Online at: http://www.brookings.edu/views/op-ed/daalder/20020731.htm.

46 President George W. Bush, "President's Remarks at the United Nations General

Assembly," September 12, 2002. Online at: http://www.whitehouse.gov/news/releases/2002/09/20020912-1.html.

47 Monte Reel and Manny Fernandez, "100,000 Rally, March against War in Iraq," *Washington Post*, October 27, 2002, p. A1. Online at: http://www.washingtonpost.com/ac2/wp-dyn/A24432-2002Oct26?language=printer.

48 The study counts every protest *in the world*, and, of course, most protesters participated in more than one demonstration. Dominique Reynié of the Institut d'Études Politiques in Paris. Online at: http://dominiquereynie.typepad.com/my_weblog/files/demonstrations_against_war_in_iraq.pdf. See also http://www.socialistworker.co.uk/article.php?article_id=6067.

49 Gore, "Iraq and the War on Terrorism," http://www.commonwealthclub.org/archive/02/02-09gore-speech.html.

50 Jimmy Carter, "The Troubling New Face of America," *Washington Post*, September 5, 2002, p. A31. Online at: http://www.washingtonpost.com/ac2/wp-dyn?pagename=article&node=&contentId=A38441-2002Sep4.

51 Sammon, *Misunderestimated*, p. 89.

52 Associated Press, "Officials Double Saddam's Oil-for-Food Theft," Fox News, November 15, 2004. Online at: http://www.foxnews.com/story/0,2933,138617,00.html.

53 Stephen F. Hayes, "The Baghdad Democrats," *The Weekly Standard*, October 14, 2002. Online at: http://www.weeklystandard.com/Content/Public/Articles/000/000/001/737zcgnk.asp?pg=2. See also Sammon, *Misunderestimated*, pp. 84–88.

54 Hayes, "Baghdad Democrats."

55 David Freddoso, "McDermott Won't Retract Baghdad Attack on Bush," *Human Events*, October 7, 2002. Online at: http://findarticles.com/p/articles/mi_qa3827/is_200210/ai_n9140422.

56 Bill Clinton, "Labour Party Conference 2002," William J. Clinton Foundation, October 2, 2002. Online at: http://www.clintonfoundation.org/100202-sp-cf-gn-gha-moz-rwa-irq-irl-gbr-sp-wjc-addresses-labour-party-conference.htm.

57 Ted Barrett, "Lawmaker under Fire for Saying Jews Support Iraq War," CNN. Online at: http://www.cnn.com/2003/ALLPOLITICS/03/11/moran.jews.

58 Gareth Porter, "Israel Urged U.S. to Attack Iran—Not Iraq," *Asia Times*. Online at: http://www.atimes.com/atimes/Middle_East/IH30Ak04.html.

59 "Congressional Record Weekly Update," October 7–11, 2002.

60 Ibid.

61 Quoted in "Best of the Web Today," OpinionJournal, March 14, 2007. Online at: http://www.opinionjournal.com/best/?id=110009785.

62 Sen. Russ Feingold, "Statement of U.S. Senator Russ Feingold on Opposing the Resolution Authorizing the Use of Force against Iraq," October 9, 2002. Online at: http://www.senate.gov/~feingold/speeches/02/10/2002A10531.html.

63 Rep. Pete Stark, "'The Bottom Line Is I Don't Trust the President and His Advisors,'" Salon.com, October 10, 2002. Online at: http://dir.salon.com/story/politics/feature/2002/10/10/stark/index.html.

64 "Jimmy Carter Wins Nobel Peace Prize," BBC News, October 11, 2002. Online at: http://news.bbc.co.uk/2/hi/europe/2319289.stm.

65 "Online NewsHour: Background: Nobel Peace Prize," PBS.org, October 11, 2002. Online at: http://www.pbs.org/newshour/bb/international/july-dec02/bkgdnobel_10-11.html.

66 Jimmy Carter, "Nobel Lecture," December 10, 2002. Online at: http://nobelprize.org/nobel_prizes/peace/laureates/2002/carter-lecture.html.

4   The Democrats' War Against the War

1   Sen. Robert Byrd, "The Arrogance of Power," March 13, 2003. Online at: http://byrd.senate.gov/speeches/byrd_speeches_2003march/byrd_speeches_2003march_list/byrd_speeches_2003march_list_4.html.
2   *American Morning with Paula Zahn*, CNN, March 18, 2003. Online at: http://edition.cnn.com/TRANSCRIPTS/0303/18/ltm.15.html. The union was AFSCME—the American Federation of State, County, and Municipal Employees.
3   "Poll: Vast Majority Believes Iraq Mission Not Accomplished," CNN, May 1, 2006. Online at: http://www.cnn.com/2006/POLITICS/05/01/iraq.poll/index.html.
4   "Saddam Hussein Is Losing Grip on Northern Cities in Iraq," *Inside Politics*, CNN, April 10, 2003. Online at: http://transcripts.cnn.com/TRANSCRIPTS/0304/10/ip.00.html.
5   Tom Curry, "Peace Groups Open Baghdad Office," MSNBC, July 21, 2003. Online at: http://web.archive.org/web/20031210170546/http://msnbc.com/news/941541.asp?osl=-23&cp1=1.
6   David Aaronovitch, "Lost from the Baghdad Museum: Truth," *Guardian* (UK), June 10, 2003. Online at: http://www.guardian.co.uk/Iraq/Story/0,2763,974193,00.html.
7   Jason Burke, "Priceless Treasures Saved from Looters of Baghdad Museum," *Guardian* (UK), June 8, 2003. Online at: http://arts.guardian.co.uk/news/story/0,,973714,00.html.
8   "Iraq Watch: The Global Implications," March 30, 2004. Online at: http://www.house.gov/inslee/issues/iraq/images/iraq_watch_pdf/iraq_watch_3.30.04.pdf.
9   Ibid.
10 Nicholas Kristof, "Missing in Action: Truth," *New York Times*, May 6, 2003, p. A31.
11 Plame listed her home address and CIA front on her contribution to Gore, blowing the cover of everyone she worked with in the process. It should be noted that Wilson, a registered Democrat, also made donations to a handful of Republicans. Critics have pointed out that these were people in a position to get him a job.
12 Judy Keen and Toni Locy, "White House Expects Calls for Its Records," *USA Today*, October 1, 2003. Online at: http://www.usatoday.com/news/washington/2003-10-01-leak-usat_x.htm.
13 "The envoy's debunking of the forgery was passed around the administration and seemed to be accepted—except that President Bush and the State Department kept citing it anyway." Ibid.
14 John B. Judis and Spencer Ackerman, " The Selling of the Iraq War: The First Casualty," *The New Republic*, June 30, 2003. Online at: http://www.globalpolicy.org/security/issues/iraq/unmovic/2003/0630selling.htm.
15 http://www.politicsoftruth.com/bio.html
16 Susan Schmidt, "Plame's Input Is Cited on Niger Mission," *Washington Post*, July 10, 2004, p. A9.
17 The full report can be downloaded at: http://www.butlerreview.org.uk/report. Also quoted in Podhoretz, *World War IV*.
18 Schmidt, "Plame's Input."
19 Walter Pincus, "CIA Did Not Share Doubt on Iraq Data," *Washington Post*, June 12, 2003, p. A1.
20 Bonnie Azab Powell, "Representative Ellen Tauscher says she 'will not sit idly by and be duped' by Bush administration again," UC Berkeley News, July 2, 2003. Online at: http://www.berkeley.edu/news/media/releases/2003/07/02_tauscher.shtml.

21   Al Gore, "Remarks to MoveOn.org," MoveOn.org, August 7, 2003. Online at: http://www.moveon.org/gore-speech.html.

22   Leon D'Souza, "Levin: Bush War Motives All Suspect," *Port Huron (Michigan) Times Herald*, August 7, 2003. Quoted in Hayes, *Cheney*, p. 419.

23   Ibid.

24   Hayes, *Cheney*, p. 418.

25   "Kennedy's 'Texas' Remark Stirs GOP Reaction," CNN, September 18, 2003. Online at: http://www.cnn.com/2003/ALLPOLITICS/09/18/kennedy.iraq.

26   See below, p. 73 (in this MS).

27   Hayes, *Cheney*, p. 420.

28   Rep. Louise Slaughter, "Statement," Senate.gov, July 22, 2005. Online at: http://democrats.senate.gov/dpc/hearings/hearing23/slaughter.pdf.

29   Deep Throat Returns, "The 'No Oil Bidness Left Behind' Act," Hackworth.com, October 25, 2002. Online at: http://www.hackworth.com/dto18.html. See also Edwin Black's excellent overview, "The Pentagon Insider Who Spread Rumors That Sounded Anti-Semitic," History News Network, September 27, 2004. Online at: http://hnn.us/articles/7582.html.

30   Deep Throat Returns, "Crimes of Omission," Hackworth.com, December 26, 2002. Online at: http://www.hackworth.com/dto34.html.

31   Steinberg sent this interview out via e-mail as a "Memorandum for the Files" to his disturbingly extensive list of contacts. See Black, "Pentagon Insider."

32   Scarborough, *Sabotage*, pp. 41–2.

33   Ibid.

34   Malkin, *Unhinged*, pp. 32–33.

35   David Horowitz and Richard Poe, *The Shadow Party* (Nashville: NelsonCurrent, 2006).

36   "Bush 'Betrayed Us,'" CNN, February 9, 2004. Online at: http://www.cnn.com/2004/ALLPOLITICS/02/09/gore.bush.ap/index.html.

37   Patricia Wilson, "Kerry on Iraq: 'Wrong War, Wrong Place, Wrong Time,'" Reuters, September 6, 2004. Online at: http://www.commondreams.org/headlines04/0906-02.htm.

38   Each of the articles is linked in the post "*New York Times* Streak of Page One Stories on Abu Ghraib Ends at 32 Days!" FreeRepublic, June 2, 2004. Online at: http://www.freerepublic.com/focus/f-news/1145998/posts.

39   "Senate Condemns Iraqi Prisoner Abuse," Fox News, May 11, 2004. Online at: http://www.foxnews.com/story/0,2933,119546,00.html.

40   "Remarks by Al Gore," MoveOn.org., May 26, 2004. Online at: http://pol.moveon.org/goreremarks052604.html.

41   Ibid.

42   "Gore Gone Crazy," PowerLineBlog.com, May 26, 2004. Online at: http://www.powerlineblog.com/archives/006781.php.

43   Quoted in "A Rumsfeld Vindication," *Wall Street Journal*, August 26, 2004. Online at: http://www.opinionjournal.com/editorial/feature.html?id=110005528.

44   Agence France Presse, "Kerry Renews Call for Rumsfeld to Resign over Abu Ghraib Abuses." Online at: http://findarticles.com/p/articles/mi_kmafp/is_200408/ai_n6856082.

45   Michael Moore, "Heads Up . . . from Michael Moore," MichaelMoore.com, April 14, 2004. Online at: http://www.michaelmoore.com/words/message/index.php?messageDate=2004-04-14.

46   Associated Press, "Democrats Screen 'Fahrenheit 9/11' in D.C.," *USA Today*, June

24, 2004. Online at: http://www.usatoday.com/news/washington/2004-06-23-fahr-enheit-dc-premiere_x.htm.

47   Daschle later disputed that this hug occurred. Charles Hurt, "Daschle Cools on Plaudits for '9/11,'" *Washington Times*, July 10, 2004. Online at: http://web.archive.org/web/20050222193120/http://www.washtimes.com/national/20040709-110742-8538r.htm.

48   Osama bin Laden, "Full Transcript of Bin Laden's Speech," Al Jazeera, November 2, 2004. Online at: http://english.aljazeera.net/English/archive/archive?ArchiveId=7403.

49   On *Larry King Live*, CNN, October 29, 2004. Quoted in Malkin, *Unhinged*, p. 42.

50   "MoveOn to Democratic Party: 'We Bought It, We Own It,'" CNN, December 10, 2004. Online at: http://web.archive.org/web/20041230201414/http://www.cnn.com/2004/ALLPOLITICS/12/09/democrats.critics.ap/index.html.

51   "Purported al-Zarqawi Tape Vows to Fight Election," MSNBC, January 24, 2005. Online at: http://www.msnbc.msn.com/id/6855496.

52   Sen. Edward M. Kennedy, "Address Delivered at the Johns Hopkins School of Advanced International Studies," GlobalSecurity.org, January 27, 2005. Online at: http://www.globalsecurity.org/wmd/library/news/iraq/2005/01/050127-emk.htm.

53   Hayes, *Cheney*, p. 472.

54   *Meet the Press*, NBC, January 30, 2005. Online at: http://www.msnbc.msn.com/id/6886726.

55   Patrick Cockburn, "Voters Clap and Cheer as Sunni Turnout Is Higher than Expected," *Independent* (UK), January 31, 2005. Archived on the International Occupation Watch website: http://web.archive.org/web/20050210213322/http://www.occupationwatch.org/article.php?id=9034.

56   *Meet the Press*, January 30, 2005.

57   Farah Stockman, "Bush Calls Vote 'Resounding Success' for Democracy," *Boston Globe*, January 31, 2005. Online at: http://www.boston.com/news/world/middleeast/articles/2005/01/31/bush_calls_vote_resounding_success_for_democracy.

58   Ibid.

59   Ibid.

60   Associated Press, "Reid Calls for Iraq Exit Strategy," Fox News, January 31, 2005. Online at: http://www.foxnews.com/story/0,2933,145859,00.html.

61   Commission on the Intelligence Capabilities of the United States Regarding Weapons of Mass Destruction. Online at: http://www.wmd.gov/report/report.html.

62   http://www.motherjones.com/news/qa/2005/03/ratner.html.

63   Neil Lewis, "In Rising Numbers, Lawyers Head for Guantanamo Bay," *New York Times*, May 30, 2005. Online at: http://www.nytimes.com/2005/05/30/politics/30detain.html?ex=1187928000&en=633167460a8c78c1&ei=5070.

64   Stewart passed messages from Sheikh Omar Abdel Rahman to his terrorist followers in Egypt. http://www.frontpagemag.com/Articles/Read.aspx?GUID={22921890-5532-47F9-8BE5-7B8FAC47184D}.

65   http://www.nytimes.com/2005/05/30/politics/30detain.html?ex=1187928000&en=633167460a8c78c1&ei=5070; cited at http://antiprotester.blogspot.com/2005/06/michael-ratner-and-ccr-fighting.html.

66   http://www.npr.org/templates/story/story.php?storyId=12344597. Authorities named only five, but they state that at least thirty have returned to the battlefield following release.

67   "Transcripts: Live From . . ." CNN, June 13, 2005. Online at: http://archives.cnn.com/TRANSCRIPTS/0506/13/lol.04.html.

68 This was gained from firsthand observation by Lt. Col. Gordon Cucullu. "Mothering Terrorists at Gitmo," FrontPageMag.com, August 5, 2005. Online at: http://www.frontpagemag.com/Articles/Read.aspx?GUID=0F5B6BE5-72D6-4A10-A0A1-264DA597F561.

69 Michael Melia, "A Growing Threat at Guantanamo? Detainees Fatten Up," ABC News, October 3, 2006. Online at: http://www.abcnews.go.com/International/story?id=2521953&page=1.

70 "Harry Potter Popular with Guantanamo Detainees; Report," ABC News, August 8, 2005. Online at: http://www.abc.net.au/news/newsitems/200508/s1432952.htm.

71 Andrew Selsky, "Guantanamo Inmates Turn to Library Books," ABC News, September 26, 2006. Online at: http://abcnews.go.com/International/wireStory?id=2485063.

72 Associated Press, "Red Cross Complains to U.S. on Guantanamo," MSNBC, November 30, 2004. Online at: http://www.msnbc.msn.com/id/6618051.

73 Richard Norton-Taylor, "Guantanamo Is Gulag of Our Time, Says Amnesty," *Guardian* (UK), May 26, 2005. Online at: http://www.guardian.co.uk/usa/story/0,12271,1492349,00.html.

74 Human Rights Watch, "Getting Away with Torture? Command Responsibility for the U.S. Abuse of Detainees." See the relevant section at: http://www.hrw.org/reports/2005/us0405/4.htm#_Toc101408092.

75 "Administration Appalled by Durbin Remarks," Fox News, June 16, 2005. Online at: http://www.foxnews.com/story/0,2933,159748,00.html.

76 See, e.g., "Rights Group Slams Guantanamo Trials," Al Jazeera, August 23, 2004. Online at: http://english.aljazeera.net/English/archive/archive?ArchiveId=5947. "ICRC Highlights Guantanamo Torture," December 3, 2004. Online at: http://english.aljazeera.net/English/archive/archive?ArchiveId=7958. "HRW: U.S. Defies Law on Detainees," October 12, 2004. Online at: http://english.aljazeera.net/English/archive/archive?ArchiveId=7049.

77 " 'Sex-Up' Tactics at Gitmo?" WCBSTV.com, May 1, 2005. Online at: http://wcbstv.com/topstories/.Sex.Up.2.252360.html.

78 Simon Freeman, "Guantanamo chief cleared over prisoner abuse," London Times Online, July 14, 2005. Online at: http://www.timesonline.co.uk/tol/news/world/us_and_americas/article543914.ece. The full Schmidt-Furlow report can be read at http://www.defenselink.mil/news/Jul2005/d20050714report.pdf.

79 Brian Ross and Richard Esposito, "CIA's Harsh Interrogation Techniques Described," ABC News, November 18, 2005. Online at: http://abcnews.go.com/WNT/Investigation/story?id=1322866.

80 Hayes, *Cheney*, pp. 480–82.

81 "Clinton Urges Guantanamo Closure," BBC News. Online at: http://news.bbc.co.uk/2/hi/americas/4110388.stm..

82 "Biden Says Prison at Guantanamo Bay Should Be Closed," *Washington Post*, June 6, 2005, p. A2. Online at: http://www.washingtonpost.com/wp-dyn/content/article/2005/06/05/AR2005060501043.html. Associated Press, "Carter Urges Closing of Guantanamo Prison," *Washington Post*, June 8, 2005, p. A2. Online at: http://www.washingtonpost.com/wp-dyn/content/article/2005/06/07/AR2005060701631.html.

83 "Murtha/Pelosi Blueprint for Defeat," *Washington Times*, July 30, 2007. Online at: http://www.washingtontimes.com/apps/pbcs.dll/article?AID=/20070730/EDITORIAL/107300002.

84 David B. Rivkin Jr. and Lee A. Casey, "The Gitmo Distraction," *Wall Street Journal*, July 9, 2007.

85 Matt Welch, "The Politics of Dead Children," *Reason*, March 2002. Online at: http://www.reason.com/news/show/28346.html.

86   The report appeared on May 12, 1996.

87   Welch, "Dead Children."

88   Associated Press, "Officials Double Saddam's Oil-for-Food Theft," Fox News, November 15, 2004. Online at: http://www.foxnews.com/story/0,2933,138617,00.html.

89   Les Roberts, Riyadh Lafta, Richard Garfield, Jamal Khudhairi, and Gilbert Burnham, "Mortality before and after the 2003 Invasion of Iraq: Cluster Sample Survey," *The Lancet*, October 29, 2004. Archived online by the radical publication *Z* magazine at: http://www.zmag.org/lancet.pdf. See also Roberts's interview with the Socialist Worker Online, "Counting the Dead in Iraq," April 23, 2005. Online at: http://www.socialistworker.co.uk/article.php4?article_id=6271.

90   Socialist Worker Online, "Counting the Dead."

91   http://reports.iraqbodycount.org/a_dossier_of_civilian_casualties_2003-2005.pdf. Cf. also http://www.frontpagemag.com/Articles/Read.aspx?GUID=1B5492CA-1B09-430B-ABB5-5C0D3F16E77A.

92   Gilbert Burnham, Riyadh Lafta, Shannon Doocy, and Les Roberts, "Mortality after the 2003 Invasion of Iraq: A Cross-Sectional Cluster Sample Survey," *The Lancet*, October 11, 2006. Online at: http://www.thelancet.com/webfiles/images/journals/lancet/s0140673606694919.pdf.

93   "An Interview with Les Roberts," That's My Congress! January 25, 2006. Online at: http://www.thatsmycongress.com/lesroberts.html.

94   Osama bin Laden tape transcript of September 6, 2007. Online at: http://www.politico.com/pdf/PPM43_osamabinladen_tapetranscript_090607.pd

95   *Hamit Dardagan, John Sloboda, and Josh Dougherty,* "Reality Checks: Some Responses to the Latest *Lancet* Estimates," Iraq Body Count, October 16, 2006. Online at: http://www.iraqbodycount.org/analysis/beyond/reality-checks.

96   See http://iraqbodycount.org.

97   Bob Woodward, *State of Denial: Bush at War, Part III* (New York: Simon & Schuster, 2006), p. 359.

98   Leslie Fulbright, "Conflict in Iraq," *San Francisco Chronicle*, December 27, 2004. Online at: http://sfgate.com/cgi-bin/article.cgi?f=/c/a/2004/12/27/BAG3LAHDM61. DTL. "Staff, Board, and Advisors," Middle East Children's Alliance. Online at: http://www.mecaforpeace.org/section.php?id=29.

99   Agence France Presse, "Relatives of U.S. Servicemen Killed in Iraq to Hold Vigil on Jordan Border," CommonDreams.org, December 31, 2004. Online at: http://www.commondreams.org/headlines04/1231-06.htm.

100 Bill Varble, "Author to Share His Story of Activism," *(Medford, Oregon) Mail Tribune*, March 17, 2007. Online at: http://archive.mailtribune.com/archive/2007/0317/local/stories/farrell-bv.htm.

101 Joe Piasecki, "Fernando Suarez del Solar," *Los Angeles City Beat*, December 23, 2004. Online at: http://www.lacitybeat.com/article.php?id=1482&IssueNum=81

102 Maureen Dowd, "Why No Tea and Sympathy?" *New York Times*, August 10, 2005. Online at: http://www.nytimes.com/2005/08/10/opinion/10dowd.html?ex=12813264 00&en=3bcb17b6396946de&ei=5088&partner=rssnyt&emc=rss.

103 Dataguy, "Framing Cindy Sheehan—We Are Making Errors," DailyKos.com, August 13, 2005. Online at: http://www.dailykos.com/story/2005/8/13/9565/81042.

104 This can be downloaded at: http://www.codepinkalert.org/article.php?id=451.

105 Cindy Sheehan relates that Casey's exact words were, "Where my chief goes, I go." Duncan Campbell, "'I Feel I'm Carrying the World on My Shoulders,'" *Guardian* (UK), December 9, 2005. Online at: http://www.commondreams.org/headlines05/1209-10.htm.

106 Jane Shahi, "Cindy Sheehan Unplugged," FrontPageMag.com, August 19, 2005. Online at: http://www.frontpagemag.com/Articles/Read.aspx?GUID={70D0F40C-259D-4D82-89D9-B379B7A89C18}. This is a transcript of a rally at San Francisco State University on April 27, 2005, to honor convicted defender of terrorists Lynne Stewart. Sheehan praised Stewart as "my human Atticus Finch," a reference to the lawyer in *To Kill a Mockingbird*—who was in fact human—who defended a black man against charges of rape. See also Cliff Kincaid, "Those Antiwar 'Media Events,'" Accuracy in Media, September 21, 2005. Online at: http://www.aim.org/media_monitor/A4011_0_2_0_C. "Cindy Sheehan's Speech to the VFP Convention 2005," Veterans for Peace, August 8, 2005. Online at: http://web.archive.org/web/20050812234406/http://www.veteransforpeace.org/convention05/sheehan_transcript.htm. "Sheehan Plays 'Hardball' with Matthews," MSNBC, August 16, 2005. Online at: http://www.msnbc.msn.com/id/8972147.

107 Cathy Young, "The Cindy Sheehan You Don't Know," *Boston Globe*, August 22, 2005. Online at: http://www.boston.com/news/globe/editorial_opinion/oped/articles/2005/08/22/the_cindy_sheehan_you_dont_know. Sheehan changed her story numerous times about the e-mail, but she claimed someone at *Nightline* changed its text. She also claimed the original e-mail was mysteriously deleted from her computer. See Blake Wilson, Sidebar to "Cindy Sheehan's Moral Blackmail," Slate. com, August 19, 2005. Online at: http://www.slate.com/id/2124788/sidebar/2124791.

108 Sheryl Gay Solberg and Anne Kornblut, "State of the Union: The Scene," *New York Times*, February 1, 2006. Online at: http://select.nytimes.com/gst/abstract.html?res=FA0D13FD345B0C728CDDAB0894DE404482. Ben Johnson, "Shouting Down the President," FrontPageMag.com, February 1, 2006. Online at: http://www.frontpagemag.com/Articles/Read.aspx?GUID={3AC3F400-FE1D-41ED-8D26-38F636AE551D}.

109 Hayes, *Cheney*, p. 477.

110 John F. Burns and Dexter Filkins, "Iraqi Officials Count Ballots Following Saturday's Vote," *New York Times*, October 16, 2005. Online at: http://www.nytimes.com/2005/10/16/international/middleeast/16cnd-iraq.html?pagewanted=3&ei=5070&en=d8d909dfobobe7a6&ex=1186804800.

111 "Iraq," Australian Government Department of Foreign Affairs and Trade. Online at: . http://www.dfat.gov.au/geo/iraq/iraq_brief.html.

112 Formerly online at: http://kennedy.senate.gov/~kennedy/statements/05/10/2005A13816. html. Currently neither available nor archived online.

113 "English Translation of Ayman al-Zawahiri's Letter to Abu Musab al-Zarqawi," *The Weekly Standard*, October 12, 2005. Online at: http://www.weeklystandard.com/Content/Public/Articles/000/000/006/203gpuul.asp.

114 Ibid.

115 "Rep. Waters Creates New 'Out-of-Iraq Congressional Caucus,'" Progressive Democrats of America, June 16, 2005. Online at: http://www.commondreams.org/news2005/0616-32.htm.

116 http://www.blackfive.net/main/2006/06/the_zarqawi_ope.html.

117 *Meet the Press*, NBC, June 11, 2006. Online at: http://www.msnbc.msn.com/id/13296235/page/2.

118 Howard Fineman, "Iraq Debate Reaches a Turning Point," *Newsweek*, November 28, 2005. Online at: http://www.msnbc.msn.com/id/10118733/site/newsweek/print/1/displaymode/1098/.

119 Ted Barrett, "'Unwinnable' Comment Draws GOP Fire," CNN, May 10, 2004. Online at: http://www.cnn.com/2004/ALLPOLITICS/05/06/murtha.iraq/index.html.

Michael Barone, "John Murtha's Call for Withdrawal," *U.S. News & World Report*, November 21, 2005. Online at: http://www.usnews.com/blogs/barone/2005/11/21/john-murthas-call-for-withdrawal.html?s_cid=rss:barone:john-murthas-call-for-withdrawal. Murtha also had said, "We cannot prevail in this war."

120 *Meet the Press*, NBC, June 11, 2006. Online at: http://www.msnbc.msn.com/id/13296235/page/2.

121 Fineman, "Turning Point."

122 "Rep. John Murtha Urged Somalia Pullout in '93," NewsMax.com, November 21, 2005. Online at: http://www.newsmax.com/archives/ic/2005/11/21/100353.shtml.

123 Noel Sheppard, "Reconstructing Murtha III: It's Somalia Déjà Vu," American Thinker, November 23, 2005. Online at: http://www.americanthinker.com/2005/11/reconstructing_murtha_iii_its.html.

124 *Meet the Press*, June 11, 2006. Online at: http://www.msnbc.msn.com/id/13296235.

125 Jonathan Weisman and Lois Romano, "Democrats Pick Hoyer over Murtha," *Washington Post*, November 17, 2006, p. A1. Online at: http://www.washingtonpost.com/wp-dyn/content/article/2006/11/16/AR2006111600514.html.

126 "Transcript of Special Prosecutor Fitzgerald's Press Conference," *Washington Post*, October 28, 2005. Online at: http://www.washingtonpost.com/wp-dyn/content/article/2005/10/28/AR2005102801340.html.

127 Sharon Kehnemui Liss, "Senate Dems Force Rare Closed Session," Fox News, November 3, 2005. Online at: http://www.foxnews.com/story/0,2933,174187,00.html.

128 Charles Babington and Dafna Linzer, "GOP Angered by Closed Senate Session," *Washington Post*, November 2, 2005, p. A1. Online at: http://www.washingtonpost.com/wp-dyn/content/article/2005/11/01/AR2005110101037.html.

129 Babington and Linzer, "GOP Angered". Online at: http://www.washingtonpost.com/wp-dyn/content/article/2005/11/01/AR2005110101037_2.html.

130 Quoted in Hayes, *Cheney*, pp. 384–87. Among the six Democrats who read the report before voting on the Authorization for the Use of Military Force resolution were John Edwards and Joseph Biden. "Records: Senators Who OK'd War Didn't Read Key Report," CNN, May 29, 2007. Online at: http://www.cnn.com/2007/POLITICS/05/28/clinton.iraq/index.html.

131 Michael A. Fletcher, "Testimony Adds New Element to Probe of CIA Leak," *Washington Post*, April 7, 2006, p. A9. Online at: http://www.washingtonpost.com/wp-dyn/content/article/2006/04/06/AR2006040602062.html.

132 Ibid.

133 Ibid.

134 Pete Yost, "Ex-Cheney Aide Says Bush Authorized Leak," *The Scotsman*, April 7, 2006. Online at: http://news.scotsman.com/international.cfm?id=532982006.

135 Richard Keil, "Bush OK'd Leak of Iraq Info: Court Filing," *Chicago Sun-Times*, April 7, 2006. Online at: http://findarticles.com/p/articles/mi_qn4155/is_20060407/ai_n16191852.

136 Rep. John Conyers, "What Did the President and Vice President Know and When Did They Know It?" Huffington Post, October 28, 2005. Online at: http://www.huffingtonpost.com/john-conyers/what-did-the-president-an_b_9692.html.

137 Dana Priest, "CIA Holds Terror Suspects in Secret Prisons," *Washington Post*, November 2, 2005, p. A1. Online at: http://www.washingtonpost.com/wp-dyn/content/article/2005/11/01/AR2005110101644_pf.html.

138 "'Al-Qaeda' Claims Jordan Attacks," BBC, November 10, 2005. Online at: http://news.bbc.co.uk/1/hi/world/middle_east/4423714.stm.

139 Scarborough, *Sabotage*, pp. 126–27.

140 Rep. Edward Markey, "Markey Blasts Extraordinary Rendition," July 7, 2006. Online at: http://markey.house.gov/index.php?option=com_content&task=view&id=1791&I temid=55.

141 H.R. 952, introduced by Rep. Edward Markey, D-MA. For more, see http://thomas. loc.gov/cgi-bin/bdquery/z?d109:h.r.00952.

142 Sen. Robert Menendez, "Menendez: 'President Bush Should Take Notes' from CIA," April 21, 2006. Online at: http://menendez.senate.gov/newsroom/record. cfm?id=254633.

143 Mark Mazzetti and Borzou Daragahi, "U.S. Military Covertly Pays to Run Stories in Iraqi Press," *Los Angeles Times*, November 30, 2005. Online at: http://www.commondreams.org/headlines05/1130-07.htm.

144 Associated Press, "Pentagon Quizzed on Iraq Propaganda Program," MSNBC, December 2, 2005. Online at: http://www.msnbc.msn.com/id/10272171.

145 Michael C. C. Adams, *The Best War Ever: America and World War II* (Baltimore: Johns Hopkins University Press, 1994), p. 9.

146 John F. Burns, "The Struggle for Iraq: The Sunni Vote," *New York Times*, December 16, 2005, p. A1. Online at: http://select.nytimes.com/gst/abstract.html?res=F00C11F F3D540C758DDDAB0994DD404482.

147 Ellen Knickmeyer and Jonathan Finer, "Iraqi Vote Draws Big Turnout of Sunnis," *Washington Post*, December 16, 2005, p. A1. Online at: http://www.washingtonpost. com/wp-dyn/content/article/2005/12/15/AR2005121500228_2.html?sub=AR.

148 "Iraqis Flock to Polls in Historic Elections," *The (Lebanon) Daily Star*, December 16, 2005. Online at: http://www.dailystar.com.lb/article.asp?edition_id=10&categ_ id=2&article_id=20810.

149 Robert Kagan and William Kristol, "Happy Days!" *The Weekly Standard*, December 26, 2005. Archived at the Carnegie Endowment for International Peace website: http://www.carnegieendowment.org/publications/index.cfm?fa=view&id=17834&pr og=zgp&proj=zusr.

150 Dexter Filkins, "Iraqis, Including Sunnis, Vote in Large Numbers on Calm Day," *New York Times*, December 16, 2005, p. A1. Online at: http://select.nytimes.com/ gst/abstract.html?res=F40E11FF3D540C758DDDAB0994DD404482.

151 *The Daily Texan*, December 15, 2005

152 Kristen Lombardi, "Full Text: Hillary Clinton Talks Iraq," *The Village Voice*, November 30, 2005. Online at: http://www.villagevoice.com/news/0549,lombardi,70569,2. html.

153 Crystal Patterson, "Kennedy Responds to Bush as the Iraqi Elections Approach," TedKennedy.com. Online at: http://www.tedkennedy.com/journal/361/kennedy-responds-to-bush-as-the-iraqi-elections-approach.

154 Rep. Louise Slaughter, "Rules Committee Republicans Unanimously Vote-out Hunter Resolution to Immediately Withdrawal Troops from Iraq," November 18, 2005. Online at: http://www.louise.house.gov/index.php?option=com_content&tas k=view&id=341&Itemid=106.

155 "House GOP Leaders Pass Bill Rejecting Calls for Pullout from Iraq," Fox News, December 16, 2005. Online at: http://www.foxnews.com/story/0,2933,178883,00. html.

156 James Risen and Eric Lichtblau, "Bush Lets U.S. Spy on Callers without Courts," *New York Times*, December 16, 2005, p. A1. Online at: http://www.nytimes. com/2005/12/16/politics/16program.html?_r=1&oref=slogin.

157 Rick Klein, "GOP Suffers Blow as Senate Blocks Patriot Act Extension," *Boston Globe*, December 17, 2005. Online at: http://www.boston.com/news/nation/washing-

ton/articles/2005/12/17/gop_suffers_blow_as_senate_blocks_patriot_act_extension/.
158 Susan Jones, "Has Bush Committed an 'Impeachable Offense,' Senator Asks,"
     CNS News, December 20, 2005. Online at: http://www.cnsnews.com/ViewPolitics.
     asp?Page=\Politics\archive\200512\POL20051220a.html.
159 Rep. Jim McDermott, "The Big Chill in Washington, D.C.," May 9, 2006. Online
     at: http://www.house.gov/mcdermott/sp060510.shtml.
160 "Congress Demands NSA Spying Answers," CBS News, May 11, 2006. Online at:
     http://www.cbsnews.com/stories/2006/05/11/politics/main1609261.shtml.
161 Sen. Robert C. Byrd, "Finding the Truth on Domestic Spying; Standing for the Bill
     of Rights," March 2, 2006. Online at: http://byrd.senate.gov/speeches/2006_march/
     wiretap_commission.html.
162 Al Gore, "'We the People' Must Save Our Constitution," CommonDreams.org,
     January 16, 2006. Online at: http://www.commondreams.org/cgi-bin/print.cgi?file=/
     views06/0116-34.htm.
163 "Transcript of 60 Minutes on Echelon," CBS, February 27, 2000. Archived online
     at: http://cryptome.org/echelon-60min.htm.
164 Gore, "'We the People.'"
165 "Report: 108 Died in U.S. Custody: Prisoners Died While Being Held in Iraq,
     Afghanistan," CBS News, March 16, 2005. Online at: http://www.cbsnews.com/
     stories/2005/03/16/terror/main680658.shtml.
166 Associated Press, "Prisoner Deaths in U.S. Custody," San Francisco Chronicle, March
     16, 2005. Archived at: http://web.archive.org/web/20050317033435/http://www.sfgate.
     com/cgi-bin/article.cgi?f=/n/a/2005/03/16/national/w113007S95.DTL.
167 "Press Briefing by Tony Snow," WhiteHouse.gov, June 23, 2006. Online at: http://
     www.whitehouse.gov/news/releases/2006/06/20060623-4.html.
168 "Political Headlines: New York Times Reports Financial Surveillance Program," Fox
     Special Report, Fox News, June 26, 2006. Archived at the Center for National Policy:
     http://www.cnponline.org/index.php?tg=articles&idx=More&topics=86&article=15
169 Rep. Maxine Waters, "H. Res. 895, Supporting Intelligence and Law Enforcement
     Programs to Track Terrorists and Terrorist Finances," June 29, 2006. Online at:
     http://www.house.gov/list/speech/ca35_waters/FS060629_HRes895.html.
170 Jim Abrams, "House Blasts Media over Terrorist Finance Tracking Stories," Associ-
     ated Press story archived on FindArticles.com, June 30, 2006. Online at: http://www.
     findarticles.com/p/articles/mi_qn4188/is_20060630/ai_n16517742.
171 Jim Miklaszewski and Mike Viquera, "Lawmaker: Marines Killed Iraqis 'in Cold
     Blood,'" NBC News, May 17, 2006. Online at: http://www.msnbc.msn.com/
     id/12838343.
172 "U.S. Troops Killed Iraqis 'In Cold Blood,'" Al Jazeera, May 21, 2006. Online at:
     http://english.aljazeera.net/English/archive/archive?ArchiveId=22898.
173 Mark Walker, "Accused Haditha Marine Says He Acted Properly in Shootings,"
     North County Times, June 14, 2007. Online at: http://nctimes.com/articles/2007/06/14/
     news/top_stories/1_01_12_00a.txt.
174 Mark Walker, "Hearing Officer Challenges Haditha Prosecution," North County
     Times, June 15, 2007. Online at: http://nctimes.com/articles/2007/06/16/news/top_
     stories/1_01_090_12_00.txt.
175 "Charges Dropped against 2 Marines in Haditha Case," Reuters, August 9, 2007. On-
     line at: http://www.reuters.com/article/domesticNews/idUSN0921973920070809.
176 "Statements from Lt. Gen. James Mattis," SignOnSanDiego.com, August 9, 2007.
     Online at: http://www.signonsandiego.com/news/military/20070809-1224-haditha_
     statements.html.

177 The case against the fourth Marine is still pending.

178 Anton LaGuardia, "Arrests Reveal Zarqawi Network in Europe," *Telegraph* (London), December 22, 2005. Online at: http://www.telegraph.co.uk/news/main.jhtml?xml=/news/2005/12/22/wterr22.xml&sSheet=/news/2005/12/22/ixworld.html.

179 Sen. John Kerry, "Statement by John Kerry on the Death of Abu Musab al-Zarqawi," June 8, 2006. Online at: http://kerry.senate.gov/cfm/record.cfm?id=256690.

180 "Video: Hillary!'s [sic] Take Back America Speech," HotAir.com, June 14, 2006. Online at: http://hotair.com/archives/2006/06/14/hillarys-take-back-america-speech.

181 His experience consisted of serving two terms as a selectman for Greenwich, CT.

182 "Hillary Clinton Strategist Joined Ned Lamont Team," NewsMax.com, August 25, 2006. Online at: http://www.newsmax.com/archives/ic/2006/8/25/163815.shtml.

183 Steven Stalinsky, "Arab and Muslim Jihad Fighters in Iraq," Middle East Media Research Institute. Online at: http://www.memri.org/bin/articles.cgi?Area=sr&ID=SR1903.

184 Eric Davis, "Iraqi Sunni Clergy Enter the Fray," *Religion in the News*, Winter 2005, vol. 7, no. 3. Online at: http://www.trincoll.edu/depts/csrpl/RINVol7No3/IraqiSunnisJoinFray.htm.

185 Saleh al-Mutlaq, "Our Problem with America," *Asharq Alawsat*, May 18, 2006. Online at: http://www.asharqalawsat.com/english/news.asp?section=2&id=4991.

186 "Code Pink Alert," Code Pink, August 22, 2006. Online at: http://www.codepink-alert.org/article.php?id=1178.

187 Jeeni Criscenzo, "Listening to the Iraqis with Open Ears and Heart," Daily Kos, August 6, 2006. Online at: http://www.dailykos.com/story/2006/8/6/174940/7106.

188 Ibid.

189 "Endorsements," Jeeni Criscenzo for U.S. Congress—49th District. Online at: http://web.archive.org/web/20070209231956/http://www.jeeniforcongress.com/Endorsements.asp.

190 "Transcript: Tennessee Senate Candidate Harold Ford on 'FNS,'" *Fox News Sunday*, Fox News. Appearance: October 29, 2006; transcript dated October 30, 2006. Online at: http://www.foxnews.com/story/0,2933,226104,00.html?sPage=fnc.politics/youdecide2006.

191 Mark Mellman, "The Shape of Democratic Victory," *The Hill*, November 29, 2006. Online at: http://thehill.com/mark-mellman/the-shape-of-democratic-victory-2006-11-29.html.

192 Associated Press, "Murtha Says Army Is Broken," Military.com. Online at: http://www.military.com/NewsContent/0,13319,81810,00.html.

193 Tom Raum, "Cheney: Quick Iraq Pullout 'Illusion,'" *Rutland (Vermont) Herald*, November 22, 2005. Online at: http://www.rutlandherald.com/apps/pbcs.dll/article?AID=/20051122/NEWS/511220333/1024/NEWS04.

194 Matt Bai, "Can Bloggers Get Real?" *New York Times*, May 28, 2007. Online at: http://www.nytimes.com/2006/05/28/magazine/28wwln_lede.html?ex=1306468800&en=462a4046cd0170c6&ei=5088.

195 Markos Moulitsas Zúniga, "Every Death Should Be on the Front Page," comment in response to "Corpses on the Cover," Daily Kos, April 1, 2004. Online at: http://www.dailykos.com/story/2004/4/1/144156/3224. Quoted in Malkin, *Unhinged*, p. 84.

196 "Dean: U.S. Can't Win Iraq War," CNN, December 6, 2005. Online at: http://www.cnn.com/2005/POLITICS/12/06/dean.iraq.1935.

197 "Fox News/Opinion Dynamics Poll," December 15, 2005. Online at: http://www.foxnews.com/projects/pdf/poll_121505.pdf.

198 Ibid.

199 John Besnahan, "House Democrats' New Strategy: Force Slow End to War," The Po-
     litico, February 13, 2007. Online at: http://www.politico.com/news/stories/0207/2751.
     html.

200 Robert D. Novak, "Murtha in Command," *Washington Post*, February 19, 2007, p.
     A19.

201 Shailagh Murray, "Reid Backs Iraq War-Funds Cutoff," *Washington Post*, April 3,
     2007, p. A4.

202 Ben Johnson's interview with Rep. Howard Berman, D-CA, March 16, 2007.
     See also Ben Johnson, , "One Responsible Antiwar Democrat," FrontPageMag.
     com, March 22, 2007. Online at: http://www.frontpagemag.com/Articles/Read.
     aspx?GUID={F19F9CC7-9006-4339-8234-CC2796BEF2C1}.

203 Robert D. Novak, "New Moderate Democrats Mostly Bow to Leadership," *Hu-
     man Events*, April 18, 2007. Online at: http://www.humanevents.com/article.
     php?id=20297.

204 "Bush Vetoes Iraq War Spending Bill," Fox News, May 1, 2007. Online at: http://
     www.foxnews.com/story/0,2933,269393,00.html.

205 "Pelosi Calls Bush to Complain of Cheney's Comments on Democrats' Iraq
     Strategy," Fox News, February 22, 2007. Online at: http://www.foxnews.com/sto-
     ry/0,2933,253604,00.html.

206 Ibid.

207 "Fact Sheet: The New Way Forward in Iraq," WhiteHouse.gov, January 10, 2007.
     Online at: http://www.whitehouse.gov/news/releases/2007/01/20070110-3.html.

208 Peter Baker, "General Is Front Man for Bush's Iraq Plan," *Washington Post*, Febru-
     ary 7, 2007, p. A1. Online at: http://www.washingtonpost.com/wp-dyn/content/ar-
     ticle/2007/02/06/AR2007020601918.html.

209 Frederick W. Kagan and Kimberly Kagan, "The New Strategy in Iraq," *The Weekly
     Standard*, July 9, 2007, vol. 12, issue 40. Online at: http://www.weeklystandard.
     com/Content/Public/Articles/000/000/013/818pmqsq.asp.

210 Alister Bull, "U.S. Says Iraq Troop Surge Complete," Reuters, June 15, 2007. Online
     at: http://www.alertnet.org/thenews/newsdesk/BUL522174.htm.

211 Tom Curry, "McCain, Clinton Clash over Troop Morale," MSNBC, January 24,
     2007. Online at: http://www.msnbc.msn.com/id/16773074.

212 Sen. Carl Levin, "Opening Statement of Senator Carl Levin at the Senate Armed
     Services Committee Hearing to Consider the Nomination of Lt. Gen. David Pe-
     traeus to be General and Commander, Multi-National Forces–Iraq," January 23,
     2007. Online at: http://levin.senate.gov/newsroom/release.cfm?id=267820.

213 Reid attempted to defend his statement that the war is "lost" by noting that Gen.
     Petraeus had said the solution was not strictly military. Yet, when asked if he be-
     lieved Gen. Petraeus when he reported the surge is working, Reid replied, "No, I
     don't believe him." "Transcripts: *The Situation Room*," CNN, April 23, 2007. Online
     at: http://transcripts.cnn.com/TRANSCRIPTS/0704/23/sitroom.02.html.

214 Ned Parker, "Generals Say 'Surge' Plan Has Saved Lives," *Times* (London), March
     16, 2007. Online at: http://www.timesonline.co.uk/tol/news/world/iraq/article1522563.
     ece.

215 Ibid. See also Sudarsan Raghavan, "For U.S., Sadr, Wary Cooperation," *Washington
     Post*, March 16, 2007, p. A1. Online at: http://www.washingtonpost.com/wp-dyn/
     content/article/2007/03/15/AR2007031502447.html.

216 Raghavan, "For U.S., Sadr."

217 "'War in Iraq Lost': U.S. Democrat Leader," Breitbart.com, April 19, 2007. Online at:
     http://www.breitbart.com/article.php?id=070419174958.d2ni8f1d&show_article=1.

218 "Reid: Someone Tell Bush the War in Iraq Is Lost," Fox News, April 19, 2007. Online at: http://www.foxnews.com/story/0,2933,267181,00.html.

219 "Pelosi and Reid Call on President to Listen to the Will of the American People on Iraq," The Gavel (Speaker Pelosi's official blog). Online at: http://www.speaker. gov/blog/?p=483.

220 Jim Michaels, "Major Attacks Decline in Iraq," *USA Today*, August 12, 2007. Online at: http://www.usatoday.com/news/world/iraq/2007-08-12-lede13_N.htm.

221 Jim Michaels, "25,000 Turn against Insurgency, Military Says," *USA Today*, .August 5, 2007. Online at: http://www.usatoday.com/news/world/2007-08-05-tribes_N.htm.

222 Michael E. O'Hanlon and Kenneth M. Pollack, "A War We Just Might Win," *New York Times*, July 30, 2007. Online at: http://www.nytimes.com/2007/07/30/ opinion/30pollack.html?_r=2&oref=slogin&oref=slogin.

223 Brad Shannon, "Baird Sees Need for Longer U.S. Role in Iraq," *The Olympian*, August 17, 2007. Online at: http://www.theolympian.com/news/story/192500.html.

224 http://www.politico.com/static/PPM41_moveon.html.

225 Although the Left likes to accuse its opponents of McCarthyism, Joe McCarthy became most infamous for browbeating a uniformed general on live television during the Army-McCarthy hearings—tactics the Left now repeated.

226 Gen. David H. Petraeus, "Report to Congress on the Situation in Iraq," September 10–11, 2007. Online at: http://www.politico.com/pdf/PPM43_general_petraeus_tes-timony_10_september2007.pdf.

227 "The Crypt," Politico.com, September 11, 2007. Online at: http://www.politico. com/blogs/thecrypt/0907/Clinton_Believing_Petraeus_and_Crocker_requires_will-ing_suspension_of_disbelief.html.

228 "U.S. General's Plan Means 10 More Years of War: Democrats," Yahoo.com, Sep-tember 12, 2007. Online at: http://news.yahoo.com/s/afp/20070912/pl_afp/usiraqpo litics6thleadwrap_070912123438.

229 Thomas E. Ricks, "Reid Faults Petraeus as Not 'In Touch,'" *Washington Post*, June 15, 2007, p. A10. Online at: http://www.washingtonpost.com/wp-dyn/content/ar-ticle/2007/06/14/AR2007061402093.html.

230 Matthew Jaffe, "Dems Bash Upcoming Petraeus Report," ABC News, September 8, 2007. Online at: http://abcnews.go.com/Politics/story?id=3575785&page=1.

231 Ibid.

Conclusion

1 http://www.whitehouse.gov/news/releases/2001/09/20010920-8.html.

2 http://sfgate.com/cgi-bin/article.cgi?file=/c/a/2006/12/10/BAGJGMSTAQ1. DTL&type=printable.

3 As summarized in Zawahiri's letter to Zarqawi, quoted on p. 71 in our MS above.

4 http://www.whitehouse.gov/news/releases/2006/09/20060905-7.html. The bin Laden message was published on jihadist websites on December 28, 2004.

5 The commander was Brig. Gen. Kevin Bergner. "Iran Training Iraqi Insurgent Groups, General Says," U.S. State Department. Online at: http://usinfo.state.gov/ xarchives/display.html?p=washfile-english&y=2007&m=July&x=20070703102256dm slahrelleko.3060114.

6 James Glanz, "U.S. Says Arms Link Iranians to Iraqi Shiites," *New York Times*, February 12, 2007. Online at: http://select.nytimes.com/gst/abstract.html?res=F108 1FFC345B0C718DDDAB0894DF404482. Michael R. Gordon, "Deadliest Bomb in Iraq Is Made by Iran, U.S. Says," *New York Times*, February 10, 2007. Online at:

http://www.nytimes.com/2007/02/10/world/middleeast/10weapons.html.

7   Michael Howard, "Mahdi Army Commanders Withdraw to Iran to Lie Low during Security Crackdown," *Guardian* (UK), February 15, 2007. Online at: http://www.guardian.co.uk/Iraq/Story/0,,2013441,00.html.

8   Javad Zarif, "How Not to Inflame Iraq," *New York Times*, February 8, 2007. Online at: http://www.nytimes.com/2007/02/08/opinion/08zarif.html?ex=1328590800&en=1dbb8e0f82d1dc11&ei=5088&partner=rssnyt=rss.

9   Kim Murphy, "Iran seen as key to untangling Iraq," *Los Angeles Times*, February 13, 2007. Full text posted at: http://regimechangeiniran.com/2007/02/iran-seen-as-key-to-untangling.

10 Powell, "Representative Ellen Tauscher," http://www.berkeley.edu/news/media/releases/2003/07/02_tauscher.shtml.

11 http://www.atimes.com/atimes/Middle_East/GJ28Ak03.html.

12 Todd S. Purdum, "Inside Bush's Bunker," *Vanity Fair*, October 2007.

13 From his dissent on *Terminiello v. Chicago*, 1949. Quoted in Henry Abraham, "Mr. Justice Robert H. Jackson (1892–1954): An Attempt to Place Him into Some Historical Perspective," a lecture delivered at the Robert H. Jackson Center of Jamestown, New York, on March 18, 2003. Online at: http://www.roberthjackson.org/Man/theman2-6-15.

14 Calvin Woodward, "Bush Tells Biographer: 'I Do Tears,'" Associated Press, September 4, 2007. Online at: http://www.charlotte.com/nation/story/263361.html.

15 Hayes, *Cheney*, p. 427.

16 Rep. Nancy Pelosi, "Democratic Leaders Send Letter to Bush on Securing the Peace in Iraq," July 28, 2003. Online at: http://www.house.gov/pelosi/press/releases/July03/prDemsIraqLettertoBush072803.html.

17 See Jo Johnson, "No French or German Turn on Iraq," *Financial Times*, September 26, 2004. Online at: http://www.ft.com/cms/s/36048bf8-0ff7-11d9-ba62-00000e2511c8.html.

18 Nile Gardiner, "America Isn't Alone in the War on Terror," Heritage Foundation, October 21, 2004. Online at: http://www.heritage.org/Press/Commentary/ed102104b.cfm.

19 William Branigin and Howard Schneider, "Dodd Introduces Bill to Cap U.S. Troops in Iraq," January 17, 2007, *Washington Post*. Online at: http://www.washingtonpost.com/wp-dyn/content/article/2007/01/17/AR2007011700976.html.

20 Barry Schweid, "Ex-Advisers Offer Revised Iraq Plans," *Washington Post*, February 1, 2007. Online at: http://www.washingtonpost.com/wp-dyn/content/article/2007/02/01/AR2007020101309.html.

21 "VFW Urges Reid to Stop Defeatist Rhetoric," Veterans of Foreign Wars, April 10, 2007. Online at: http://www.vfw.org/index.cfm?fa=problnews.newsDtl&did=3978.

22 Diana West, "Killed by the Rules," *Washington Times*, August 17, 2007. Online at: http://washingtontimes.com/article/20070817/EDITORIAL04/108170016/1013/EDITORIAL.

23 Cited in Podhoretz, *World War IV*, p. 12.

24 http://www.cnn.com/2004/ALLPOLITICS/10/10/bush.kerry.terror/index.html.

25 The bill was introduced by Sen. Jim Webb, D-VA. For more information, see Elana Schor, "Dems Divided over Webb's Proposal Requiring Approval for Attacking Iran," *The Hill*, April 17, 2007. Online at: http://thehill.com/leading-the-news/dems-divided-over-webbs-proposal-requiring-approval-for-attacking-iran-2007-04-17.html.

26 Associated Press, "Lieberman Favors Iran Military Strike," *USA Today*, June 10, 2007. Online at: http://www.usatoday.com/news/washington/2007-06-10-us-iran_N.htm.

Index

Abbas, Abu, 85
ABC, 35, 53, 145
Abercrombie, Neil, 96, 101
Abu Ghraib prison scandal, 106–8, 109, 113, 159
Achille Lauro hijacking, 85
Afghanistan, 57, 58, 59, 79; bin Laden, Osama in, 38; Iran and, 22; Islamic jihad and, 3, 15; Operation Enduring Freedom and, 56; September 11 and, 5; Soviet invasion of, 26, 30, 88–89; Taliban in, 83; as threat, 5; War on Terror and, 6, 16, 17
African embassy bombings (1998), 38, 86
Ahmadinejad, Mahmoud, 22–23, 156
Aideed, Mohammed Farah, 16, 34–35
Akkad, Moustapha, 132
Albright, Madeleine, 105, 119
Al Jazeera, 116
Alpirez, Julio Roberto, 43
al-Qaeda, 7, 34, 45, 50,

79, 85; African Embassy bombings (1998) and, 38; Iraq and, 86, 130; Islamic jihad and, 3; Jordan and, 132; September 11 and, 45–46, 153; War on Terror and, 15, 16, 56
Amnesty International, 116
Andropov, Yuri, 8
Annan, Kofi, 76, 120
Ansar al-Islam, 86
anthrax, 58
anti-Americanism, 8–9, 24
anti-Semitism, 124
appeasement, 22, 23, 25–27, 31
Apple, R.W., Jr., 58–59
Arafat, Yasser, 48, 122
Armed Forces of National Liberation (FALN), 46
Armitage, Richard, 102, 128
Arnett, Peter, 37
Arraf, Jane, 90
The Art of War (Sun Tzu), ix
Aspin, Les, 35, 39
The Assault on Reason (Gore), 63–64, 81

Association for Muslim Studies, 142
Atta, Mohammad, 48
Authorization for the Use of Military Force against Iraq resolution, 82
Awahiri, Ayman al-, 125
Aziz, Tariq, 90

Baghdad Museum, 96
Baird, Brian, 148–49
Bartlett, Dan, 156–57
Begala, Paul, 54
Beirut, Lebanon, 37
Benjamin, Medea, 95, 121–24
Berge, Gunnar, 93
Berger, Sandy, 35, 37, 39, 40–41
Berlin discotheque bombing (1986), 30
Berman, Howard, 145
Biden, Joseph, 117
bin Laden, Osama, ix, 45, 105, 127; in Afghanistan, 38; Clinton, Bill and, 36–37, 48; "The

bin Laden, Osama (cont.)
Declaration of War" of,
36–37; fatwas of, 110,
121; Hussein, Saddam
and, 73; indictment of,
86; Iraq and, 86; Iraq
War and, 154; Islamic
jihad and, 17; Islamic
Revolution in Iran
and, 21; Khobar Towers
bombing (1996) and, 36;
Moore, Michael and,
110; mujahideen and,
26–27; September 11
and, 4, 40, 60; Somalia,
U.S. withdrawal from
and, 35; Vietmalia Syn-
drome and, 39; WMDs
and, 39
biological weapons, 3,
71, 74, 77, 78, 83. See
also weapons of mass
destruction (WMDs)
Black Panther Party, 55
Blair, Tony, 66, 68, 69,
75–78, 83–84
Blame America First,
25, 30
Blix, Hans, 66, 69
Bonior, David, 90
Borge, Tomás, 43
Bosnia, 84
Boston Globe, 54
Boxer, Barbara, 109, 136, 143
Breaux, John, 52
Britain, 5, 7, 68
Brucella, 71
Brzezinski, Zbigniew, 28
Bullock, Bob, 51
Burns, John, 134
Bush, George H.W., 31,
34, 92
Bush, George W.: Amer-
ican public, selling of
Iraq War to and, 73–75;
Axis of Evil and, 57–58,
77; bipartisanship and,
52–54, 56; conservatism
of, 52; Constitution,

U.S. and, 4; Democratic
attacks on, 4–17, 55–60,
160–63; economic poli-
cies of, 56–57; education
and, 52; Election 2000
and, 49, 51–52; foreign
policy and, 52; intel-
ligence manipulation
and, 5, 7–8, 97–104, 113,
128–29, 130–31; Iraq
War, rationale for and,
63–64, 67; Islamic jihad
and, 17; Jesus Christ
and, 13; pre-emption
and, 57, 88, 92; Sep-
tember 11, response to
of, 53–55, 153; Sheehan,
Cindy and, 122–24;
State of the Union ad-
dress (2002) of, 57, 85,
101; State of the Union
address (2003) of, 7;
State of the Union ad-
dress (2006) of, 124; tax
cuts and, 52; terrorism,
response to of, 49–50;
as Texas governor, 51;
War on Terror and,
15–16, 17, 86–87
Bush Doctrine, 83–86, 88
The Butler Report, 99
Byrd, Robert, 53, 59, 81,
92, 94, 137

California, University of,
Berkeley, 100
Cambodia, 9, 24–25
Cambone, Stephen, 108
Carter, Jimmy, 89; ap-
peasement and, 22, 23,
26, 27, 31; CIA and,
28; Cold War and, 30;
Communism and, 26;
defense spending and,
33, 42; Guantanamo
Bay detainee abuse and,
117; human rights and,
22, 27, 29; intelligence

agencies, hamstringing
of and, 25, 28; Iran and,
23, 27–29; Iran hostage
crisis (1979) and, 22,
29, 30; Moore, Michael
and, 55–56, 109–10; No-
bel Peace Prize of, 93;
Persian Gulf War and,
31; policy failures of, 30;
Soviet Union and, 26,
30, 33
The Case for Impeachment
(Lindorff and Olshan-
sky), 67
Castro, Fidel, 55, 114
Center for Constitutional
Rights, 67, 113, 114
Center for Economic and
Social Rights, 119
Central Intelligence
Agency (CIA), 40;
airline safety and, 36;
bin Laden, Osama and,
39; Carter, Jimmy and,
28; Clinton, Bill and,
43–44, 47–48; Cold War
and, 44, 48; Democratic
Party crippling of, 43;
detainee rights and, 138;
intelligence manipula-
tion and, 104, 113; Left
assault on, 48; Water-
gate and, 28; Wilson
affair and, 99
Chance, Clifford, 114
Chávez, Hugo, 22
chemical weapons, 3, 74,
77, 83. See also weap-
ons of mass destruction
(WMDs)
Cheney, Dick, 102, 128;
intelligence manipula-
tion and, 104, 113; Iraq
War, criticism of and,
157–58; Iraq War, fund-
ing for and, 145–46;
Wilson affair and, 98
China: Iraq War and, 68,
95; Islamic jihad and,

3; U.S. nuclear secrets, theft of and, 42, 48, 52
Chomsky, Noam, 120
CIA. See Central Intelligence Agency
Civil War, U.S., 4, 10, 84
Clarke, Richard, 40
Cleland, Max, 143
Clinton, Bill: appeasement and, 31; bin Laden, Osama and, 39–41, 48, 86; campaign-ffinance scandals and, 52; defense spending and, 42; Guantanamo Bay detainee abuse and, 117; Hussein, Saddam and, 37–38, 40, 46; intelligence agencies, purging of and, 42–45, 47–48; Iraq, regime change in and, 5, 10–11, 79; Iraq, U.S. withdrawal from and, 141; Iraq Liberation Act (1998) and, 10–11, 46; Islamic jihad and, 33, 48–49; military and, 33, 42; national security and, 37, 47; nation-building and, 34; pardoning of terrorists by, 46–47, 52; scandals and, 38, 40, 46, 52; security failures of, 52–53, 60; September 11 and, 51; surge force and, 148; terrorism, response to of, 16, 34–39, 48; U.S. nuclear secrets, theft of and, 42, 48, 52; World Trade Center bombing (1993) and, 16, 33–34
Clinton, Hillary Rodham, 66; Clinton, Bill foreign policy and, 35; Clinton, Bill scandals and, 46; Iraq, U.S. withdrawal from

and, 135, 142; Iraq War authorization and, 5; political ambitions of, 46; September 11 and, 54, 60
Coalition of the Willing, 158
Code Pink, 95, 121, 122, 123, 141, 142–43
Cold, 122
Cold War, 8, 39, 42, 47, 58; bipartisanship and, 14; Carter, Jimmy and, 30; CIA and, 44, 48; Clinton, Bill and, 40; containment and, 10; Reagan, Ronald and, 30; Soviet Union and, 10, 33; United States and, 10
Cole, USS bombing (2000), 38
Communism, 23, 25, 26, 101
conservatism: of Bush, George W., 52; compassionate, 52; neo-, 74, 103, 104, 124
Constitution, U.S., 4, 58, 137, 161, 164
containment, 10
Conyers, John, 67, 126, 131
Cooper, Cynthia L., 67
Corn, David, 67
Council on Foreign Relations, 30, 57
Covington & Burling, 114
Criscenzo, Jeeni, 143
Cronkite, Walter, 110, 134

The Daily Kos, 123, 142, 144
Daschle, Tom, 54, 56, 58, 59, 95, 109
Dean, Howard, 13, 97, 105, 111, 123, 131, 143, 144
DeConcini, Dennis, 44
Deep Throat, 103
de la Vega, Elizabeth, 67
Dellums, Ron, 55

democracy: dissent and, 11; in Iraq, 111–13; spread of, 64
Democratic National Committee (DNC), 7, 97, 105, 111
Democratic Party, Democrats: antiwar movement and, 23–25; Bush, George W., attacks on by, 4–17; Bush, George W. economic policies and, 56–57; CIA and, 43; Gore, Al and, 88; Hussein, Saddam as threat and, 82–83; intelligence agencies, purging of and, 28, 45; Iraq, U.S. withdrawal from and, 135–36; Iraq Liberation Act (1998) and, 11; Iraq War, authorization of and, 79, 82; Iraq War rationale and, 64, 84; leaking of classiffied information and, 131–39; "netroots" in, 105, 142; radicalized, 104–6; Vietnam War and, 23–25; War on Terror and, 17. See also Left
Deutsch, John, 44, 45, 47
de Villepin, Dominique, 68
Diaz, Nidia, 122
District of Columbia, 24
DNC. See Democratic National Committee
Dobrynin, Anatoly, 30
Dodd, Christopher, 30
domestic wiretapping program, 136–37
Dorsey & Whitney, 114
Dowd, Maureen, 122–23
Draper, Robert, 157
Durbin, Dick, 116, 128–29, 131, 151
Dymally, Mervyn, 30

"An Easter Sermon"
    (Wright), 13
Echelon program, 137–38
Edwards, John, 7–8, 13,
    17, 66, 105
Egypt, 3, 31
Election 2000, 49, 51–52
El Salvador, 26, 30
Energy Department,
    U.S., 41
Erwa, Elfatih, 39
Evans, Jodie, 123
Evans, Linda, 47
Executive Intelligence
    Review (EIR), 103

FAA. See Federal Avia-
    tion Administration
Fahrenheit 9-11, 55, 109, 159
Falk, Richard, 29
FALN. See Armed
    Forces of National
    Liberation
Farrell, Mike, 122
fascism, 15, 101, 162
Fazio, Vic, 30
Fedayeen, 96
Federal Aviation Admin-
    istration (FAA), 36
Federal Bureau of Inves-
    tigation (FBI): airline
    safety and, 36; Cole,
    USS bombing (2000)
    and, 38; Left assault
    on, 48
Feingold, Russ, 92, 145
Feith, Douglas J., 104,
    108
Filner, Bob, 143
Fineman, Howard, 126
Fisk, Robert, 36
Fitzgerald, Patrick, 86, 128
Fleischer, Ari, 60
"The Foes of Our Own
    Household" (Roos-
    evelt), ix
Ford, Gerald, 44
Ford, Harold, Jr., 143

France, 5, 68, 95
Frank, Barney, 53
Frank amendment (1987), 53
Freeh, Louis, 38, 42
Frost, Martin, 91
Frum, David, 56
Furlow, John, 116

Gandhi, Mahatma, 29
Garver, Christopher, 147
Gaza Strip, 17, 22
George Bush versus the
    Constitution (ed.
    Miller), 67
Gephardt, Richard, 53,
    56, 60, 90
Germany, 14, 68, 84
Golden Mosque bombing
    (2006), 148
Gonzalez, Elian, 46
Goodspeed, Daniel, 122
Gore, Al, 55, 81; Abu
    Ghraib prison scan-
    dal and, 107–8; airline
    safety and, 36; Axis
    of Evil and, 57; Bush,
    George W., attacks on
    by, 105–6; Democratic
    Party and, 88; Election
    2000 and, 49, 51–52;
    Iraq, regime change
    in and, 79, 105–6; Iraq
    War, support for of,
    88, 101; Iraq War as
    distraction from War
    on Terror and, 79; Iraq
    War rationale and,
    63–64, 73, 83, 84–85;
    "Reinventing Govern-
    ment" effort of, 42;
    September 11, response
    to of, 84–85; terrorism
    and, 84–85; terrorist
    surveillance program
    and, 137–38; Wilson,
    Joseph and, 98
Gorelick, Jamie, 44
Graham, Bob, 101

The Greatest Story Ever
    Sold (Rich), 66–67, 68
Guantanamo Bay detain-
    ees, 113–18

Hadley, Steve, 123
Hagin, Joe, 123
Halliburton, 103, 110
Hamas, 3, 85, 114, 162
Harkin, Tom, 109
Hastert, Dennis, 56
Hayden, Tom, 58
Hayworth, J.D., 143
Hezbollah, 3, 22, 85, 91,
    155, 162
HILLPAC, 142
Hitler, Adolf, 72–73
Holbrooke, Richard, 35
Holocaust, 120
Holtzman, Elizabeth, 67
Homeland Security De-
    partment, U.S., 114
Hossaini, Mohammad
    Ali, 155
House Judiciary Com-
    mittee, 67
House Permanent Select
    Committee on Intel-
    ligence, 43
House Telecommunica-
    tions and Internet
    Subcommittee, 137
Hoyer, Stenyh, 145
Hubris (Corn and
    Isikoff), 67
Huffington Post, 103
human rights: Carter,
    Jimmy and, 22, 27, 29;
    Guantanamo Bay de-
    tainees and, 89, 113–18;
    Iran and, 27
Human Rights Watch, 116
Humphrey, Hubert, 10
Hussein, Qusay, 75, 93, 94
Hussein, Saddam, 5; bin
    Laden, Osama and,
    73; capture of, 104–5;
    Clinton, Bill and,

37–38, 40, 46; inter-
national law and, 66;
Kuwait, annexation of
and, 31; Niger uranium
case and, 97–100, 101;
nuclear weapons and, 7,
77; as threat, 7, 82–83;
UN economic sanctions
and, 119; UN Secu-
rity Council Resolu-
tion 1441 and, 65–69;
WMDs and, 63, 69–72,
73–79, 82
Hussein, Uday, 75, 93, 94

Immigration and Nation-
ality Act, 53
*The Impeachment of George
W. Bush* (Holtzman and
Cooper), 67
Independent Panel to
Review Department
of Defense Detention
Operations, 108
Indochina, 24
International ANSWER,
87
International Occupation
Watch, 112
Iran, 96; Ahmadinejad,
Mahmoud and, 22–23,
156; as America's enemy,
155–56; Axis of Evil
and, 57; Carter, Jimmy
and, 23, 27–29; hu-
man rights and, 22, 27;
Iran-Iraq War and, 77;
Iraq, U.S. withdrawal
from and, 154; Islamic
jihad and, 3, 15; Islamic
Revolution in, 21, 26,
27, 28–29; nuclear
weapons and, 22, 42,
74; Radical Islam and,
154–56; as state sponsor
of terrorism, 22, 23
Iran hostage crisis (1979),
22, 29, 30

Iran-Iraq War, 77
Iraq: al-Qaeda and, 86,
130; Axis of Evil and,
57, 77; bin Laden,
Osama and, 86; Clin-
ton, Bill and, 5, 10–11,
40, 46; constitution in,
124–25; democracy in,
111–13; Islamic jihad
and, 16; Niger uranium
case and, 97–100, 101;
nuclear weapons and,
70–72; regime change
in, 5, 10–11; September
11 and, 85–86; as state
sponsor of terrorism,
85–86; UN economic
sanctions against,
119–20; U.S. with-
drawal from, 124–27,
135, 140–44, 154; War on
Terror and, 17. *See also*
Iraq War
Iraq Body Count project,
120–21
Iraqi Intelligence Service, 71
Iraq Liberation Act
(1998), 10–11, 46
Iraq National Dialogue
Front, 142
Iraq Occupation Watch,
95, 121
Iraq Satellite Channel, 90
Iraq Survey Group (ISG), 70
Iraq War: Abu Ghraib
prison scandal and,
106–8, 109, 113, 159;
anti-American pro-
paganda and, 109–11;
antiwar movement and,
54, 87–88; authoriza-
tion for, 5, 7, 11, 79, 82,
87; bipartisanship and,
56; Blame America
First and, 100–102;
collateral damage and,
118–22; cost of, 11, 79,
95; criticism of, 156–59;
Democratic attacks on,

87–93, 160–63; detainee
abuse and, 113–18; as
distraction from War
on Terror, 6, 79–80,
88; as "George Bush's
war", 5; intelligence
manipulation and, 5,
63, 97–104, 113, 128–29,
130–31; legitimacy of, 7,
12; media, anti-war and,
106–8; military surge
and, 157; morality of,
5, 6, 153, 160; Niger uranium case and, 69–70,
97, 127–29; as "quag-
mire", 5; surge force
and, 146–48; Treason-
gate and, 127–29; UN
Security Council Reso-
lution 1441 and, 65–69;
Vietnam War vs., 8–10;
as war of choice, 5,
84; WMDs and, 5, 63,
65–69, 129–31. *See also*
Iraq; Iraq War rationale
Iraq War rationale:
American public, sell-
ing of decision to and,
72–79; Bush Doctrine
and, 83–86, 88; pro-
grams versus stockpiles
and, 69–72, 78–79, 82;
UN resolutions and,
65–69, 77–78, 82, 87,
94–95
Islamic jihad: allies of,
3; American economy
and, 4; American
response to, 14–15; bin
Laden, Osama and, 17;
Bush, George W. and,
17; caliphate, restoration
of and, 21; Clinton, Bill
and, 33, 48–49; goal of,
4; Iraq and, 16; nature
of, 3, 15, 85; political
fronts of, 4; Radical
Islam and, 3; supporters
of, 3–4; United States

Islamic jihad (cont.)
  and, 17; War on Terror
  and, 15, 162; WMDs
  and, 3; World Trade
  Center bombing (1993)
  and, 16, 34
Islamic Revolution, 21,
  26, 27, 28–29
Islamofascism, 17, 153,
  155, 165
Israel, 22, 91, 104, 124, 125

Jackson, Jesse, 49
Jackson, Robert H., 157
Japan, 72–73
Jensen, Robert, 119, 120
jihad. See Islamic jihad
Johnson, Lyndon B., 10, 127
Jordan, 5, 76, 96, 132
Justice Department, U.S.,
  38, 46

Kay, David, 70–72
Kennedy, Edward, 82;
  Abu Ghraib prison
  scandal and, 107; Cold
  War and, 30; democra-
  cy in Iraq and, 111, 112;
  intelligence manipula-
  tion and, 103, 104; Iran
  and, 27–28; Iraq, U.S.
  withdrawal from and,
  125; Iraq War and, 92,
  101–2; leaking of clas-
  sified information and,
  133–34; No Child Left
  Behind Act (2001) and,
  52; Persian Gulf War
  and, 31; Soviet Union
  and, 30; Wilson, Joseph
  and, 98
Kennedy, John F., 10, 24,
  30, 49
Kenya embassy bombing
  (1998), 38, 86
Kerry, John, 66, 105; Abu
  Ghraib prison scan-

dal and, 108; Berlin
  discotheque bombing
  (1986) and, 30; intelli-
  gence agencies, purging
  of and, 44; intelligence
  manipulation and, 131;
  Iraq War, authorization
  of and, 82; Iraq War,
  criticism of and, 158;
  Iraq War, opposition
  to and, 13, 106; Persian
  Gulf War and, 31;
  Wilson, Joseph and, 98;
  Zarqawi, Abu Musab
  al-, death of and, 141
Khobar Towers bombing
  (1996), 36, 38, 43, 45
Khomeini, Ayatollah, 21,
  28–29, 155
Kim Jong Il, 22
King, Peter, 139
Kirkpatrick, Jeane, 25
Kosovo Liberation Army
  (KLA), 46
Kristof, Nicholas, 97
Kubaysi, Sheikh Ahmad
  al-, 142
Kucinich, Dennis, 58, 126
Kunstler, William, 114
Kurpius, Gary, 159
Kuwait, 31
Kwiatkowski, Karen, 103–4

Labour Party (Britain), 68
Lake, Anthony, 24–25
LaRouche, 103
Leahy, Pat, 43
Lebanon, 3, 17, 22, 127
Lee, Barbara, 54–55, 126
Left: anti-American-
  ism and, 24; antiwar
  campaign of, 12–13;
  antiwar movement
  and, 23–25; Democratic
  Party and, 12; intel-
  ligence agencies, assault
  on by, 48; Islamic jihad
  and, 3; Reagan, Ronald

and, 26; Wilson affair
  and, 96–100. See also
  Democratic Party,
  Democrats
Lehrer, Jim, 58
Levin, Carl, 101, 148, 150
Lewinsky, Monica, 40, 46
LewRockwell.com, 103
Libby, Scooter, 128, 131
Libya, 15, 30, 42
Lieberman, Joseph, 142,
  148, 162–63
Lincoln, Abraham, 84
Lincoln Group, 133
Lindorff, Dave, 67
Lone Survivor (Luttrell), 159
Los Angeles Times, 133, 138
Lott, Trent, 56

McAuliffe, Terry, 109
McCain, John, 117
McCarthy, Mary, 132, 133
McClellan, Scott, 59
McDermott, Jim, 90–91,
  105, 136
McGovern, George, 9–10,
  23–24, 25, 27
McKinney, Cynthia, 59
Mahdi Army, 148, 155
Malaysia, 35
Markey, Edward, 133, 137
Massachusetts Institute of
  Technology (MIT), 64
Mattis, James, 141
media: Abu Ghraib pris-
  on scandal and, 106–8;
  Iraq War, criticism of
  and, 161; leaking of
  classified information
  and, 131–39
Meehan, Martin, 54, 112–13
Meet the Press, 112, 127
Mendoza, Glenn and
  Patricia, 45
Menendez, Bob, 133
Middle East Children's
  Alliance, 122
Mikulski, Barbara, 98

Miller, Anita, 67
Miller, John, 35
Miller, Judith, 161
Miller, Zell, 52
Mineta, Norman, 52
Mitchell, Harry, 143
Mogadishu, Somalia, 16, 34, 37, 127
Mohammed, Khalid Sheikh, 117
Mondale, Walter, 28
Moore, Michael, 55–56, 109–10
Moran, James, 91, 126
Morris, Dick, 39
Moussaoui, Zaccarias, 44
MoveOn.org, 101, 105, 110–11, 142, 149, 151, 159
Moynihan, Daniel Patrick, 27
mujahideen, 26–27, 142
Murtha, Jack, 126–27, 139–40, 144; Iraq War, funding for and, 145–46
Muskie, Edmund, 29
Mutlaq, Saleh al-, 142

Nadler, Jerrold, 47
The Nation, 98
National Intelligence Estimate, 5, 129, 164
National Lawyers Guild, 114
national security: Clinton, Bill and, 37, 47; leaking of classiffied information and, 131–39
National Security Agency (NSA), 136
Nazism, 14, 15, 101, 162
neoconservatism, neoconservatives, 74, 103, 104, 124
"netroots", 105, 142
New Republic, 98
Newsweek, 45, 126
New Testament, 13
New York Times, 6, 7, 13, 43, 56, 58, 66, 87, 97,

102, 106–7, 115, 122, 131, 134, 136, 138, 139, 148, 149, 156, 161
Nicaragua, 26, 30, 43
Nidal, Abu, 85
Niger uranium case, 14, 69–70, 97, 127–29
Nixon, Richard, 9, 28, 49
No Child Left Behind Act (2001), 52
Northern Alliance, 45
North Korea, 3, 22, 42, 57, 72
North Korean Workers World Party, 87
Novak, Robert, 102, 128
nuclear weapons, 3, 83; Hussein, Saddam and, 7, 77; Iran and, 22; Iraq and, 70–72; United States and, 42; U.S. nuclear secrets, theft of and, 42. See also weapons of mass destruction (WMDs)

Obama, Barack, 66, 92
Office of Facts and Figures, 134
Offfice of War Information, 134
O'Leary, Hazel, 41
Olshansky, Barbara, 67
O'Neill, Tip, 30, 127
"Openness Initiative", 42
Operation Anaconda, 59
Operation Bojinka, 36
Operation Desert Storm, 85
Operation Enduring Freedom, 56, 130
Operation Iraqi Freedom. See Iraq War
Operation USA, 122
Ortega, Daniel, 43
Ottoman Empire, 21
Out-of-Iraq Congressional Caucus, 126

Pacepa, Ion Mihai, 8–9
Pakistan, 3, 35, 38, 45
Palestinian Islamic Jihad, 162
Pariser, Eli, 110
Patriot Act, 89, 114, 136
Patten, Wendy, 116
Patterson, Buzz, 37
Pearl Harbor, 72–73, 124, 153
Pelosi, Nancy, 91, 95, 126; intelligence manipulation and, 130; Iraq, U.S. withdrawal from and, 135, 136, 154; Iraq War, cost of and, 11; Iraq War, criticism of and, 158; Iraq War, funding for and, 145–48; Iraq War vs. War on Terror and, 6
Persian Gulf War, 31, 37, 65
Petraeus, David H., 146–48, 149–51, 159
Philippines, 23
Pittsburgh Post-Gazette, 127
Plame, Valerie, 43, 99–100, 102–3, 127–29, 131, 161
The Politics of Truth (Wilson), 99
Pol Pot, 116
polygamy, 29
Popular Islamic Conference (1990), 85
Posner, Gerald, 53
Powell, Colin, 68, 69
"A Prayer for America" speech, 58
Priest, Dana, 132
propaganda, anti-American, 109–11
Puerto Rico, 46
Purdum, Todd, 156

Qaddafi, Mohammar, 30
Qahtani, Mohammed al-, 117
Qom, Iran, 28

Radical Islam: Iran and, 154–56; jihad and, 3, 17
Rahman, Omar Abdel, 114
Rangel, Charles, 98, 126
Rasul v. Bush, 114
Ratner, Michael, 113–14
Reagan, Ronald, 26, 40; Berlin discotheque bombing (1986) and, 30; bin Laden, Osama and, 26–27; Cold War and, 30; "Evil Empire" speech of, 58; immigration and, 53; Lebanon and, 127; Soviet Union and, 30–31; U.S. foreign policy and, 30–31
Red Cross, 108, 116
Reich, Robert, 58
Reid, Harry, 113, 128–29, 136, 144, 145, 147–48, 150–51, 159
Republican Party, Republicans: big government and, 52; border control and, 143; Iraq, U.S. withdrawal from and, 135–36; Iraq Liberation Act (1998) and, 11; Iraq War and, 9, 79; Nixon, Richard and, 9; Vietnam War and, 23
Rice, Condoleezza, 108
Rich, Frank, 66–67, 68–70, 79–80
Richardson, Bill, 45
Ridenour, Ron, 98
Robb, Chuck, 113
Roberts, Les, 120–21
Roosevelt, Franklin D., 72–73
Roosevelt, Theodore, ix
Rosenberg, Susan, 47
Rove, Karl, 92, 110
Ruben, Justine, 110
Rumsfeld, Donald, 108, 117
Russert, Tim, 127
Russia, 78; Iraqi WMDs and, 5; Iraq War and,

68, 95; Islamic jihad and, 3; World War II and, 72–73. See also Soviet Union

Sadr, Muqtada al-, 142, 148, 155
Said, Edward, 120
Saudi Arabia, 15, 45; Islamic jihad and, 3; Khobar Towers bombing (1996) in, 36, 38, 45; Persian Gulf War and, 31
Saving Private Ryan, 92
Schakowsky, Jan, 123, 126
Scheuer, Michael, 39
Schlesinger, James, 108
Schmidt, Randall, 116
Schumer, Chuck, 131
Scowcroft, Brent, 158–59
Senate Armed Services Committee, 86, 101, 116
Senate Democratic Policy Committee, 98
Senate Intelligence Committee, 99, 101, 104
September 11, 36; Afghanistan and, 5; bin Laden, Osama and, 4, 40, 60; Iraq and, 85–86; Islamic jihad and, 85; response to, 51–60, 153; "warnings" about, 59–60
9-11 Commission, 36, 40
Serrano, José, 46
Sevareid, Eric, 134
Sharratt, Justin, 141
Sheehan, Casey, 122–24
Sheehan, Cindy, 122–24
Shinseki, Eric, 11–12, 158–59
Sick, Gary, 28
Silberman, Laurence, 113
Silberman-Robb Commission, 113
Sistani, Ali al-, 107

Slaughter, Louise, 103, 135
Snow, Tony, 139
Solzhenitsyn, Alexander, 116
Somalia, 3, 16, 17, 34–35, 37, 39, 127
Soros, George, 14, 15, 16, 17, 26, 105
South Korea, 26
South Vietnam, 24, 25
Soviet Union: Afghanistan, invasion of by, 26, 30, 88–89; Carter, Jimmy and, 26, 33; Cold War and, 10, 33; as "evil empire", 30; Reagan, Ronald and, 30–31; United States, discrediting by, 8–9. See also Russia
Spain, 68
Stahl, Lesley, 119
Stark, Pete, 92
State of War: The Secret History of the CIA and the Bush Administration (Risen), 136
Steinbeck, John, 134
Steinberg, Jeffrey, 103
Stewart, Lynne, 114
Suarez del Solar, Fernando, 122
Sudan, 15, 38, 39
Sun Tzu, ix
Supreme Court, U.S., detainee rights and, 114
Syria, 3, 15, 31, 74, 78, 96

Taheri, Amir, 162
Taliban, 16, 38, 59, 83
Tanzania embassy bombing (1998), 38, 86
Tauscher, Ellen, 100, 155
tax cuts, 52
Tenet, George, 40–41, 48, 52, 86, 101, 108, 129
Terrorist Finance Tracking Program, 139

terrorist surveillance program, 137–38
Tester, Jon, 143
Thompson, Mike, 90
Thurmond, Strom, 138
Torricelli, Robert, 43–44
Torture Outsourcing Prevention Act, 133
totalitarianism, 162
Treasury Department, U.S., 139
Trippi, Joe, 123
Truman, Harry S., 10
Turabi, Hassan al-, 86
Turkey, 3
Turner, Stansffield, 28

United Arab Emirates (UAE), 40
United for Peace and Justice, 95
United Nations (UN): international law, enforcement of and, 87, 93; international law and, 64; Iraq, economic sanctions against and, 119–20; Oil for Food program of, 90, 119–20; Somalia and, 34
UN Security Council, 31, 93
UN Security Council Resolution 1441, 65–69, 77–78, 93
United States: Cold War and, 10; foreign policy in, 9; as "Great Satan", 22, 28, 35, 116, 156; Islamic jihad and, 3, 4, 17; Islam vs., ix; jihad and economy of, 4; nuclear weapons and, 42; Soviet campaign to discredit, 8–9
U.S. v. Bush (de la Vega), 67

Vance, Cyrus, 29
Venezuela, 3, 22
Vermont, 12
Vietmalia Syndrome, 35, 39
Vietnam Syndrome, 25, 27, 31
Vietnam War, 8–9, 37, 56, 125, 127; antiwar movement and, 23–25, 39; campaign against, 8–10; Democrats and, 23–25; Iraq War vs., 8–10; Republican Party and, 23; War on Terror and, 59

Wall Street Journal, 17, 118, 138
Ware, Paul, 139
War on Terror: Afghanistan and, 6, 16, 17; al-Qaeda and, 15, 16; bipartisanship and, 52–53, 57–58; border control and, 143; Bush, George W. and, 15–16, 17, 86–87; Democratic criticism of, 17; Democrats and, 17; ideology of, 15; Iraq and, 17; Iraq War as distraction from, 6, 79–80, 88; Islamic jihad and, 162; jihad and, 15; nature of, 86–87; Vietnam War and, 59. See also Afghanistan; Iraq War
Washington, D.C., 24
Washington Post, 24, 43, 87, 89, 97, 99, 102, 132, 161
Washington Times, 115, 117
Watergate, 24, 25, 28, 40, 43, 44
Waters, Maxine, 58, 126, 139, 143
Watson, Diane, 58
Waxman, Henry, 100
weapons of mass destruction (WMDs): bin

Laden, Osama and, 39; British intelligence on Iraqi, 7; Clinton, Bill and, 48; Hussein, Saddam and, 63, 69–72, 73–79, 82; Iraq War and, 5, 63, 129–31; Iraq War rationale and, 65–72; jihad and, 3; programs versus stockpiles and, 69–72
Weather Underground, 47
Webb, Jim, 143
White, Mary Jo, 44
Wilkerson, Lawrence, 91
Wilmer, Cutler, Pickering, Hale & Dorr, 114
Wilson, Joseph, 97–100, 101, 103, 127–29
Wolfowitz, Paul, 108
Wolfson, Howard, 142
Woodward, Bob, 121
Woolsey, James, 44
Woolsey, Lynn, 112, 124, 126
World Trade Center bombing (1993), 15, 16, 33–34, 85, 114
World War I, 84
World War II, 5, 14, 72–73, 89, 157
Wright, Robert, 13, 15, 16
Wyden, Ron, 91

Yasin, Abdul Rahman, 16, 34, 85
Young, Andrew, 29
Yousef, Ramzi, 33–34, 36

Zarif, Javad, 155
Zarqawi, Abu Musab al-, 86, 107, 111, 112, 125, 127, 141
Zinn, Howard, 120
Zionism, 22, 156
Zúñiga, Markos Moulitsas, 144

A NOTE ON THE AUTHORS

DAVID HOROWITZ, the author of *Left Illusions* and numerous other books, is a celebrated political convert from radicalism. From the Cold War to the War on Terror, he has won fame for relentlessly unmasking the enemies of American freedom. He is president of the David Horowitz Freedom Center in Los Angeles.

BEN JOHNSON is managing editor of FrontPage Magazine.

This book was designed and set into type

by Mitchell S. Muncy,

with cover design by Stephen J. Ott,

and printed and bound

by Bang Printing,

Brainerd, Minnesota.

The text face is Adobe Caslon,

designed by Carol Twombly,

based on faces cut by William Caslon, London, in the 1730s,

and issued in digital form by Adobe Systems,

Mountain View, California, in 1989.

The paper is acid-free and is of archival quality.

54